Human Life, Action and Ethics

ST ANDREWS STUDIES IN PHILOSOPHY AND PUBLIC AFFAIRS

Founding and General Editor:
John Haldane
University of St Andrews

Volume 1:
Values, Education and the Human World
edited by John Haldane

Volume 2:
Philosophy and its Public Role
edited by William Aiken and John Haldane

Volume 3:
Relativism and the Foundations of Liberalism
by Graham Long

Volume 4:
Human Life, Action and Ethics:
Essays by G.E.M. Anscombe
edited by Mary Geach and Luke Gormally

Volume 5:
The Institution of Intellectual Values:
Realism and Idealism in Higher Education
by Gordon Graham

Human Life, Action and Ethics

Essays by G.E.M. Anscombe

Edited by
Mary Geach and Luke Gormally

St Andrews
Studies in
Philosophy and
Public Affairs

IMPRINT ACADEMIC

Published in the UK by Imprint Academic
PO Box 200, Exeter EX5 5YX, UK

Published in the USA by Imprint Academic
Philosophy Documentation Center
PO Box 7147, Charlottesville, VA 22906-7147, USA

ISBN 1 84540 013 5

A CIP catalogue record for this book is available from the
British Library and US Library of Congress

Cover Photographs:
St Salvator's Quadrangle, St Andrews by Peter Adamson
from the University of St Andrews collection.
Portrait of G.E.M. Anscombe by Mary Gustafson.

For

Peter Geach

in his ninetieth year

Contents

Preface   *Luke Gormally* ix
Introduction   *Mary Geach* xiii

Human Life

1 Analytical Philosophy and the Spirituality of Man 3
2 Has Mankind One Soul:
   An Angel Distributed Through Many Bodies? 17
3 Human Essence 27
4 Were You a Zygote? 39
5 Embryos and Final Causes 45
6 Knowledge and Reverence for Human Life 59
7 The Dignity of the Human Being 67

Action and Practical Reason

8 Chisholm on Action 77
9 The Causation of Action 89
10 Practical Inference 109
11 Practical Truth 149

Ethics

12 Does Oxford Moral Philosophy Corrupt Youth? 161
13 Modern Moral Philosophy 169
14 Good and Bad Human Action 195
15 Action, Intention and 'Double Effect' 207
16 The Controversy over a New Morality 227
17 Must One Obey One's Conscience? 237
18 Glanville Williams' The Sanctity of Life and
   the Criminal Law: A Review 243
19 Who is Wronged? Philippa Foot on Double Effect 249
20 Prolegomenon to a Pursuit of the Definition of Murder:
   The Illegal and the Unlawful 253
21 Murder and the Morality of Euthanasia 261
22 Commentary on John Harris' 'Ethical Problems in the
   Management of Severely Handicapped Children' 279
23 Sins of Omission?
   The Non-Treatment of Controls in Clinical Trials 285

Index 292

Preface

Three volumes of *Collected Papers* by Elizabeth Anscombe were published in 1981.[1] Those volumes brought together a selection of papers previously published between 1947 and 1979, together with a small number of previously unpublished papers. The present volume is the first of what, it is hoped, will be a number of volumes bringing together a selection of hitherto uncollected published papers along with some unpublished ones.[2] *Human Life, Action and Ethics* collects eighteen previously published papers, together with five that have not hitherto appeared in English; two of those have appeared in Spanish.

The work of collecting and preparing the papers for the present volume has been based on information gathered in the course of cataloguing Professor Anscombe's papers filed in her study at her home in Cambridge. It should be emphasised that the task of cataloguing, for which my principal duties have left few opportunities, is far from complete. Moreover, since Professor Anscombe was not a very systematic collector of her own papers, it is possible there may be some deposited elsewhere of which she did not keep copies. So there may be other papers of hers in existence which would have qualified for inclusion in this volume.

---

[1] *The Collected Philosophical Papers of G.E.M.Anscombe*. Volume 1: *From Parmenides to Wittgenstein*; Volume 2: *Metaphysics and the Philosophy of Mind*; Volume 3: *Ethics, Religion and Politics* (Oxford: Basil Blackwell, 1981).

[2] The contents of a prospective volume on *Religion, Belief and Practice* have already been identified though not yet prepared for publication.

The main focus of *Human Life, Action and Ethics* is on Professor Anscombe's writings in moral philosophy. The first part of the volume contains a number of papers with some relevance to her understanding of the proper valuation of human life, a topic of fundamental importance to her work in moral philosophy. The second part contains two papers on the causation of human action, and papers on practical inference and practical truth. The third part collects twelve papers, ranging from more general topics in moral philosophy to particular substantive ethical issues. We have included in this section the famous and influential 1958 paper on 'Modern Moral Philosophy' which has already appeared in a previous volume of the *Collected Papers*[3] and which has been anthologised in a number of volumes. It is included here for the benefit of readers new to Professor Anscombe's work in moral philosophy; a reading of it will serve to throw light on a number of other items in the volume.

One point should be noted about the presentation of the papers in this volume. Numbered footnotes are Professor Anscombe's own, though in some cases what are merely bibliographical data have been amplified by me. Footnotes indicated by an asterisk (*) are by me. For the most part they provide information about the original occasion of a text where I have been able to establish this; details about the original publication of previously published texts; and acknowledgements to copyright owners in the case of papers over which Professor Anscombe did not retain the copyright. Very occasionally I have provided a footnote indicating alterations to previously published versions of the text where these seem to me to be authorised by alterations and corrections made in Professor Anscombe's hand to offprints or typescripts on file. In a very few places I have inserted an obviously missing word; these insertions are indicated by square brackets.

---

[3]   In Volume 3: *Ethics, Religion and Politics*, pp. 26-42.

It remains to acknowledge debts incurred in the editing of these papers. I am very grateful to the two institutions to which I belong — The Linacre Centre for Healthcare Ethics, in London, and Ave Maria School of Law, in Ann Arbor, Michigan — for allowing me to find time to work on this project. Without their moral and material support it would have been impossible. Gratitude is owing to Professor John Haldane for suggesting inclusion of this volume in the series he is editing and thereby ensuring its appearance at a much earlier date than had previously seemed likely. I am grateful to him for also providing generous support in the initial stages of compiling the volume. I would like to thank Jose Maria Torralba of the University of Navarre at Pamplona, who is doing research on Professor Anscombe's work, for providing me with copies of the texts of lectures she gave at his university in the 1970s and 1980s.

The greatest debt of gratitude is owing to Professor Peter Geach not only for providing ready access to Elizabeth Anscombe's papers but also for providing generous and convivial hospitality on the occasions on which I was working on them. In the latter connection I owe thanks also to More Geach.

Finally, it has been a pleasure and a privilege to work with my wife in editing this collection of her mother's papers. We are at one in dedicating this volume to her father as a token of filial affection in his ninetieth year.

Luke Gormally

Introduction

'Philosophy', said my mother, 'is thinking about the most difficult and ultimate questions'. She defined her subject in this way for the university prospectus when she was a professor at Cambridge, in the chair which had been occupied by her teacher, Wittgenstein. Some people might want to qualify the word 'thinking' as it occurs in this definition, but Anscombe did not go in for a special, different kind of thinking: as her daughter, coming home from school, I learned from the way she met my own philosophical problems (problems arising not from philosophy lessons mostly, but from conversation and from the school curriculum) that philosophy was, as I put it to myself, 'just thinking' — merely thinking about certain topics.

So to read Anscombe you need no key, except when she is discussing some text in detail: then it helps to have the book itself. However, you do have to pay close attention. Her style was dense and unrepetitive, and it is hard to know sometimes whether it would be more clarificatory to go on to the next sentence, or to return to the previous one. She does not carry the reader along, as some authors do (Newman is an example). Yet some people prefer her sort of writing, like the confection *panforte*, all fruit and nuts and no dough, very chewy and tough.

Not all the essays here are equally difficult, however. She did vary her style according to audience. One work here was a radio talk. She was given the title 'Does Oxford Moral Philosophy

Corrupt Youth?' (Someone had implied it did.) She replied no; this philosophy made no difference to the young; it only taught them to go along with the ways of society and to accept its standards. But she made it plain that she was radically opposed to those standards, to its rules, both as expressed and as carried out.

It was for this radical opposition, no doubt, that the BBC had chosen her to address the question about corrupting youth. Anscombe had recently got into the international press for opposing the degree which Oxford University gave to ex-President Harry Truman. He was notorious for having ordered the bombings of Hiroshima and Nagasaki. She had risen in the ancient house of Congregation, asked permission to speak in English, and given a speech in which she compared Oxford's proposed action to that of honouring Hitler or Nero or Ghengiz Khan. However, Congregation granted the degree; men came to vote, urged on to do so by the news that 'the women' were going to make trouble in Congregation. Only four people said *'non placet'*.

This episode made her give the course of lectures which became the book *Intention*. If people were capable of excusing Truman by saying he had only signed his name on a piece of paper, it was clear that there were some things which she understood and they did not. A more sophisticated version of this was produced later by Nowell-Smith in *The Listener* — he pointed out that Truman's action had many descriptions, and wanted to know for which of those it should be judged. No one now would ask this question except rhetorically; *Intention* changed the consciousness of Anglo-Saxon philosophy, making everyone aware that actions are *intended* under descriptions, and that they are at least to be judged under those. Here, in this collection, the Anscombe of *Intention* is to be found in the essay on Chisholm, a work of philosophical psychology with no ethics in it.

I think it was while she was giving the course on 'Intention' that she heard my father say about some medicine 'I'm a big man, and I need a big dose, so I'll take … You know', he added, 'my father really used to reason like that'. Anscombe was at the time wondering about practical syllogisms, and was arrested by the word 'reason'. So *that* was what practical reasoning was! It was a chain of reasoning ending 'So I'll'.

Her interest in practical reasoning is continued in the essay on von Wright on 'Practical Inference' here reproduced, in which she brings it out that 'I believe *p*' is not usually the conclusion of an argument: belief in the conclusion of an argument is as much an additional step, not logically implied by the premisses, as is action in the light of an argument. Anscombe does not beat any drums or sound any trumpets in pointing out this vital fact; Moore had long ago pointed out that '*p* but I do not believe that *p*' is a self-contradiction of non-logical kind, but it is an example of Anscombe's genius for making unexpected connections that she compares belief to action in this way, directing our attention to a fact which should be noted by anyone who regards as unanswerably correct the opinion of Hume that rationality only belongs to beliefs, and not to actions or the passions that impel them. (Of course, since an assertion is an action, Moore's paradox already shows that an action can be self-contradictory, even when it does not consist in the assertion of logically contradictory propositions.)

Hume's reflections on ethics have greatly influenced our culture. I have seen a sentence in French beginning 'Vous avez bien fait de …' translated into an English one beginning 'I'm glad you were able to …'. I doubt if the translator had a philosophical axe to grind: he was simply trying to make a piece of dialogue sound natural, and it seemed more natural to him in an English speaker that he should express his pleasure at a good action than that he should tell the agent that he had done well.

'Doing well' is the topic of the essay on 'Practical Truth'. She had been thinking about this subject when she was visiting a friend, a farmer's wife who was a near neighbour on the Welsh border. Both women had a daughter with them, and one, my sister, was describing her activities outside abortion clinics, trying to prevent mothers from having their children killed. 'That was well done,' said the farmer's daughter. Doing well! Again my mother found an Aristotelian example in everyday life.

My mother regarded all abortion as evil, as she did all killing of the innocent (see the paper on 'Murder and the Morality of Euthanasia'), and was not as ready as some Catholic moralists to accept the idea that it is permissible to remove a pregnant tube. This emerges in the review of Glanville Williams which was turned down by the law journal that commissioned it. Williams was one of the grey eminences of the English Establishment, that part concerned to 'up-date' the law, so that it might express the rulers' disrespect for human life, for the family, and for decent standards of justice. Bodies like the Law Commission work out in detail the laws which government puts to Parliament, and the principles on which these bodies work are the principles of men like Williams. Sometimes Parliament runs ahead of the Law Commission: the flavour of their beliefs can be tasted in the comment of one former Law Commissioner on a private member's Bill, which became the Forfeiture Act, giving the courts discretion to allow those guilty of unlawful killing to inherit the goods of their victims. Stephen Cretney speaks of the sponsors having to make an exception of murder 'notwithstanding the fact that there may well be murder cases — some instances of so-called mercy killing, for example — in which the forfeiture rule might operate harshly and unjustly'.[1] Sometimes public outcry prevents 'updating' of laws; the Criminal Law Revision Committee,[2]

---

[1]   Stephen Cretney, *Law, Law Reform and the Family* (Oxford: Clarendon Press, 1998), p. 83.

[2]   The work of the Criminal Law Revision Committee (established 1959, inactive since 1986, though not formally disbanded) has in effect been inherited by the Law Commission (established 1965); see, for example, the statement of indebtedness of the latter to the work of the former in The Law Commission, *Offences Against the Person and General Principles* (Law Com No 218; 1993), #1.5

of which Williams was a member, proposed at one time that the laws about evidence be changed. Anscombe, with an American lawyer called Joe Feldman, wrote a heavily satirical piece (not included here) suggesting a few more radical changes.[3]

I remember at that time she told me about a thing Wittgenstein had said: that when people enunciated some instance of the law of non-contradiction, they were generally 'pulling a fast one' — performing some piece of dialectical sleight-of-hand. The Lord Chancellor came on the radio shortly after, discussing the proposed changes in the law of evidence. 'Either you trust the jury', he said, 'or you don't'. We laughed heartily.

Anscombe came to write 'Modern Moral Philosophy' when Philippa Foot, who ordinarily taught ethics in Somerville,[4] asked her to do it while she (Foot) was away in America. My mother settled down to read the standard modern ethicists and was appalled. The thing these people had in common, which had made Truman drop the bomb and the dons defend him, was a belief which Anscombe labelled 'consequentialism'. I believe she invented the term; it has come to mean much the same as 'act-utilitarianism', but without the view that the good is to be equated with pleasure and evil with pain. As Anscombe first explained it, however, consequentialism is the view that there is no kind of act so bad but it might on occasion be justified by its consequences, or by the likely consequences of not performing it. One might hold this without thinking that right action is always that which produces the best consequences. A virtue ethicist might be a consequentialist. It needs to be discussed: Could a virtuous man be a consequentialist in the sense explained by

---

(referring to the Fourteenth Report of The Criminal Law Revision Committee, *Offences against the Person*, 1980).

[3]   G.E.M. Anscombe and J. Feldman, 'On the Nature of Justice in a Trial'. *Analysis* 35/2 (1972): 33–36.

[4]   Anscombe and Foot where at the time jointly responsible for teaching the philosophy syllabus at Somerville.

Anscombe? Or: are there kinds of act which are always inconsistent with virtue?

Anscombe's study of action and intention was an important part of her opposition to consequentialism. To hold that some actions are out of the question, we need to distinguish between the intended and the known or foreseen. The Williams review and the essay on 'double effect' apply her action theory to ethical topics. Both essays show her disagreeing with the usual opinion of Catholic moralists. She expresses an opinion about the case of ectopic pregnancy which instantiates her view that the corruption of Catholic teaching was in the abuse of the double effect doctrine. She had not, I think, looked at the actual arguments and her view was influenced by an account of an ectopic pregnancy coming successfully to term, which surely could not have been in the fallopian tube. Her view was later modified by a description of the crisis that occurs in ectopic pregnancy if it is not diagnosed before the tube starts to rupture.

Her views on the early embryo would also be widely reprobated by people with whom she would be in sympathy about many important matters; by other faithful Catholics, that is: but this is a question which the Church leaves open. In her unpublished paper on 'The Early Embryo: Theoretical Doubts and Practical Certainties' (not reproduced here) she says that 'the proposal to procure an abortion is a proposal to kill either a growing baby, or, if it should be so early that there can be some doubt … whether it is reasonable to call it *a* human, it is a proposal to kill a living individual whole whose life is — all going well — to be the life of one or lives of more than one human being'. She casts doubt on the 'rigid' definition of murder as the (wilful and unjust) killing of a human being and says 'even if it were certain that, for example, a week-old conceptus is not a human being, the act of killing what is in the earliest stages of human life has evidently the same sort of malice as killing it later on when it is unquestionably a human, or more than one.'

For her, the question 'Is this a human being?' asked of a human *in utero* is like the question 'Is this a cat?' asked about a cat *in utero*. But if the early embryo is not (because of its capacity to split) to count as a member of the species, there is a question what the malice consists in, when we kill a human embryo which we are sure is not yet a man. The answer, I think, may be found in her essay on 'The Dignity of the Human Being', where she argues that neither vengeful killing nor capital punishment is an offence against human dignity, because to kill someone on the ground that he deserved it is to recognise him as a rational being, answerable for his actions. Some killing, however, treats a human being's death as a convenience. Abortion is this kind of killing; it treats a baby as disposable material. Supposing its noble *telos* to confer upon it the dignity of humanity, an early embryo's killing would show a similar malice, as Anscombe says.

These doubts about the early embryo show that Anscombe's interest in human life as a topic was not only motivated by an interest in ethics. Her interest in the human soul predates the involvement in ethics which was brought on by the Truman episode and by her disgusted reading of Hume, Butler, Sidgwick, *et al.* The rather tentative papers in the first part of this book can be seen as a return on her part to an old love. When I said that my chosen research topic would be the soul, she told me that this was what she had named as her interest, I think when she put in for her research fellowship. These papers display her really radical anti-Cartesianism, shown not only in her readiness to divide up the material and immaterial along Aristotelian lines, but in her view that it needs arguing for if it *must* be the case that the seed of one species of plant has something different about it from the seed of another — apart from being of that species. The reply we might reasonably make to this very radical remark is that, after all, they have found out that inherited differences, whether of species or of individual peculiarities, are always mapped in the DNA, so whether there is a reason independent of discovery for thinking that different kinds of seeds must be different in their internal arrangements, well, it just is so. However, I do think that an argument to show that it must be so — that even if we did not know about DNA, we would know that there must be something like that to be looked for — would be valuable, if it could be made. It could bring out something important about the relation of matter and form.

Another question about her philosophy arises from her view that the word 'moral', the concept of 'moral obligation' as used by unbelievers, should be dropped if possible. People have in fact followed her advice by trying to discuss virtues, like Aristotle. But her paper on whether a mistaken conscience binds is not expressed in terms of virtues, and it is hard to see how it could be. The question of whether a mistaken conscience binds could translate like this: If a man supposes an action to be contrary to a virtue, does he reduce that virtue in himself by performing the action, perhaps under the influence of another virtue which requires the action in question? (What is in question might be an omission rather than an action.) Huck Finn's virtue of friendship requires that he do a thing which he regards as stealing. Does 'stealing' Jim make him unjust?

Her work on practical inference represents a way of moving by means of Aristotle's philosophy towards some substitute for the concept of moral obligation which she, of course, felt free to use here as she did believe in the divine law. She sees that there is no way of criticizing actions whose ends are objectively good ones otherwise than as inimical to other good ends, so that if an action is apt for one good end, it is only criticizable as bad if there is a last end which governs all. So the people who do not believe in a divine law, but do believe in such an end, might express the question of whether a mistaken conscience binds by asking whether the act of a man who does what he mistakenly conceives as inconsistent with this ultimate good, is on this account inconsistent with his ultimate good, even when not doing the act would in itself be inconsistent with that good.

But in pointing people along the road of virtue ethics, without getting them to ponder the question of the architectonic end, perhaps she only gave them another way of being consequentialist. I hope that this book may do something to fill the gap, if only by showing that it is there.

The difference between a philosopher, as we in the West understand that word, and a sage who is giving of his wisdom, is in this: that the way to show respect for a sage is to accept his teaching, but the way to respect the philosopher is to argue. There is plenty here to argue with. My mother loved it; she was always ready for a bout.

Mary Geach

HUMAN LIFE

Analytical Philosophy and the Spirituality of Man

It is often and not wrongly said that 'analytical philosophy' comprises methods rather than doctrines. However, there is at any rate one philosophical position which is extremely common — though not peculiar to nor universal — among analytical philosophers: so common that it is often assumed without argument. That is: the rejection of the idea of immaterial substance.

I will first make some historical remarks. In modern and indeed, I think, in medieval times 'immaterial substance' has been equated with 'mind', 'spirit', 'intelligence' or 'intellect', and 'soul' — at least 'rational soul'. So much so, that it may seem difficult to imagine not making the equation. But remember that Plato's Ideas were immaterial substances. At least, he called them 'ousiai', beings — the only really real beings — and that word 'ousia' is the word that came to be translated 'substance' as it was used by Aristotle. Remember, too, that the great mathematical philosopher Frege held numbers to be objective immaterial enti-

* Text of a lecture given under this title at the University of Navarre, Pamplona, in 1979. It was published under the title 'On the notion of immaterial substance' in Mary Louise O'Hara (ed) *Substance and Things: Aristotle's Doctrine of Physical Substance in Recent Essays* (Washington, DC: University Press of America, 1982), pp. 252–262. The present text reproduces handwritten corrections and changes Professor Anscombe made to the previously printed text.

ties, though he used not the word 'substances' but rather 'objects' for them.

We might say, however, that neither Platonic forms, nor numbers as understood by Frege, are what we would mean by 'substance'. The crucial point is this: substances act. And Frege himself says that numbers, though they are real objects, are not *actual* — 'wirklich', which is clearly connected with being 'wirksam', that is with being active, having effects. As for Plato, the natural and original conception of the Forms is that they are not active: 'becoming shares in the power of being acted on and acting, but neither of these accords at all with being';[1] and he was only able to suggest how Forms might be acted upon by saying that to know something, to be acquainted with it, is to act on it! We need not pursue this. Generally speaking, Platonic Forms are not supposed to act. The only immaterial substances ever proposed in this sense, connoting agency, are spirits, minds, intelligences, all of these terms being taken to be equivalent — see any old fashioned rational psychology in the scholastic tradition. Or indeed any modern writing that broaches the idea of immaterial substance at all.

Matter stands in various contrasts: matter and form; or again: concrete (i.e. material) entitities versus abstract ones (such as classes) — but in the domain of *substance* the contrast is: matter and spirit.

Nevertheless, I can't help thinking that the Platonic substance, the Idea or Form, is of importance in the tradition whereby intellect came to be thought of as immaterial substance. For that which could grasp those immaterial beings, the Forms, had itself to be immaterial: the soul, Plato said, is *akin to* the Forms.

This reminds us of an old and well known argument for the immaterial nature of the mind. Thought and understanding are immaterial because no act of a bodily part *is* thought or understanding. Thought is not the activity of any bodily organ. Since it is itself immaterial, it must be the act of an immaterial part. But why is it said that thought is not the act of any bodily part? This dictum would actually be rejected by quite a lot of modern analytic philosophers, who suppose thought to be brain-events. Was it supposed to have been *observed* that thought was not the act of a bodily part? Surely not! For you could not even describe observing this, *nor yet* observing thought being the act of a bodily part. Just what would you observe in either case? Here I must refer to a fact that is known, though not well known enough. The divide between matter and mind was drawn differently by the ancients and medievals from the way it is drawn in modern times. So far as I know, the source of the new way of drawing the line is Descartes, and the *locus classicus* for the change is the Second Meditation. Early in that meditation he thinks of nutrition, motion and perception as attributes of soul. This ought to puzzle a modern. Sensation, yes that can intelligibly be called mental and so ascribed to soul. But nutrition? and locomotion? Descartes is referring here to his Aristotelian heritage: nutrition and locomotion are characteristic of living things, no less than is sensation; hence they are considered to be activities of soul, nutrition of vegetative and locomotion of animal soul. That does not make them any the less activities of body: they are activities of bodies *qua* ensouled. Thus they are also material activities, and they obviously cannot occur without bodies to occur in. Two pages later Descartes has detached sensation from the body altogether by using his method of doubt: he doubts whether he has a body, but cannot doubt that he hears, sees, etc., or rather *seems* to do so — and this, he now says, is what having sensations really is!

A huge trick has been successfully performed. Nutrition and locomotion are now purely material, mechanical; sensation, on the other hand, does not after all essentially require the body; the acts of soul, of immaterial substance, are all those psychological states and events given expression in an *indubitable* first person present indicative: 'I feel pain', 'I see', 'I hear', 'I have images', 'I will', 'I hope', 'I reflect'. They are all sub-species of 'cogito', 'I think'. All these are supposed to be immune to the dissolving powers of Cartesian doubt. And *now* the divide between mind and matter is the divide between what is expressed by such a first person present indicative of a 'psychological verb' and what is not to be so expressed. But the attribute of immateriality, the character of being an immaterial substance, is carried over into the new conception of soul. A medieval philosopher would have been surprised to hear that sensation and mental images were supposed to be *immaterial*. Their attribution to the soul, I believe, did not in the least carry that implication until Descartes struck his axe blow along that line.

Nowadays the belief in an immaterial mind is exclusively associated with Cartesian dualism. And there seem to philosophers to be three options: to hold to Cartesian dualism of some sort, as some analytic philosophers do; or to believe in the identity of all mental states and happenings with brain-states and brain-events; or to adopt behaviourism: that is, the doctrine that all mental states or events are to be explained reductively as human behaviour.

For the moment I want to call attention to this one point: that the idea of the immaterial nature of the soul is now dissociated from its original sources, and associated exclusively with a conception of what is expressed by a first person present indicative psychological verb in serious assertoric use. One may have good reason to reject immaterial substance so conceived, and then take it for granted that with that rejection the whole question of the immateriality of the soul is settled. If so, one may believe that any metaphysics of the spirituality of man's nature has also been discredited.

> Edel sei der Mensch, hilfreich und gut.
> Den das allein unterscheidet ihn von allen Wesen

wrote Goethe, thus giving expression to the idea that there is no metaphysically determined human dignity possessed by the good and the bad alike. We might formulate a question like this: Is spirituality a qualification like wisdom or virtue, to which a man may attain, or does it belong to his substance?

In describing the options that seem to the present day analytic philosopher to be open for consideration, I have left out Wittgenstein. Most people who do not try to follow him closely classify him as a behaviourist; thus he does not seem to them to offer a different possibility. It is true that his so-called 'behaviourism' is allowed to be of a rather special kind, and called 'logical behaviourism', because it appears to be connected with questions about how words like 'pain' get and manifest their meaning; but still it is supposed to be *a* form of behaviourism, and therefore of denial of the 'inner'.

Wittgenstein and those who attempt to follow him closely deny that he is a behaviourist. To others the matter perhaps seems to be obscured by a sort of evasiveness: a failure to come out in the open and plump for any one of what seem to be all the alternatives. Does Wittgenstein, do Wittgensteinians, believe that mental events are material events? No. Do they believe they are events taking place in a immaterial substance? Certainly not. Then, if not behaviourism, what do they believe?

I will quote the passage in which Wittgenstein seems most evidently to attack the concept of spirit. It is at *Philosophical Investigations* Part I, no. 35. He has introduced the idea of pointing to the shape of an object as opposed to pointing to its colour. For when we grasp an ostensive definition — an explanation of a word by pointing to its object — we have to know what is being pointed to: whether to the shape of some object, to the kind of stuff it is made of, its colour, or whatever else may be in question. I quote:

> To repeat: in certain cases, especially when one points 'to the shape' or 'to the number', there are characteristic experiences and ways of pointing — characteristic because they recur often (not always) when shape or number are 'meant'. But do you also know of an experience characteristic of pointing to a piece *as a*

> *piece in a game*? All the same, one can say: 'I mean that this *piece* is
> called the 'king', not this particular bit of wood I am pointing at.

The answer to the question asked in this passage is clearly No. So
there does not *have* to be a *particular* experience characteristic of
an act of pointing to this, not that, character or aspect of a thing.
When there is a characteristic experience, say associated with
'meaning the shape', it doesn't happen in all cases in which I
'mean the shape'. And even if there was an experience which did
happen in all such cases, it would still depend on the circumstances — that is, on what happened before and after the pointing
— whether we would say that the pointing was a case of pointing
to the shape, not the colour. (*Ibid.*)

That is to say, it is not such an experience that *identifies* an act as
an act of pointing, say, to the colour. We look for some single
thing that this phrase refers to, some happening that it always
relates to, and we don't find it.

And then Wittgenstein says:

> And we do here what we do in a host of similar cases: because we
> can't give any *one* bodily action which we call pointing to the
> shape (as opposed, for example, to the colour), we say that a *spiri-
> tual* activity corresponds to these words.
>
>   Where our language suggests a body and there is none: there,
> we should like to say, is a *spirit*.[2]

This looks like a general attack on the idea of spirit. It applies,
however, only to cases where 'our language suggests a body', e.g.
some bodily action, as does the phrase 'to point to' and none is
really what is in question.

It applies, for example, to the language of the imagination; of
'hearing a tune running in one's head', of 'seeing such and such
before one' — as if the imagination were another medium. Our
language 'suggests a body and there is none'. Since Descartes we
have been inclined to speak of spirit or mind, or soul here. But

---

[2]   *Philosophical Investigations* I, 36

this spirit or mind is as it were a sort of stuff, as it were immaterial matter, a refined ethereal medium in which things go on.

It is highly characteristic of this sort of philosophy of mind that it *assimilates* all that is mental to perception, sensation. Among the empiricists that is quite explicit. Locke and Hume speak, on the one hand, of 'outer sense' and 'impressions' (Locke uses the word 'ideas' equivalently) of sensation, and, on the other, of 'inner sense' and 'impressions' of reflection. The objects of inner sense are broadly classified as themselves perceivings or willings; which are thus supposed to be given us as objects of a kind of perception. One who still wished to talk in the Cartesian fashion of the thinking substance would then conceive this substance as a kind of stuff in which inner sense perceives these events to take place. This stuff of the mind, so conceived, is very justly characterisable as it were as 'immaterial matter'. And it is such a conception that we have when, as Wittgenstein puts it, 'our language suggests body and there is none', so that we want to speak of *spirit*.

No such conception is present to start with, when we remark about *thinking* that it is not a material activity. Any material-sounding description of thinking, such as 'laying hold of', 'grasping', 'reviewing', strikes us as metaphor. By contrast it is no *metaphor* to speak of 'seeing the scene before me', 'hearing the very tone of his voice' when one vividly remembers. It is a secondary use of verbs of sense, and such a use is the *primary* expression of having images.

Talk of thinking, on the other hand, is neither metaphorical nor a matter of secondary use of words. When I tell you my thought, you are to understand the words I use as having *whatever meaning they would have in context anyway.* And so the observation that thought is an immaterial activity is not based on the idea of a quasi-corporeal performance which is not yet corporeal. Thought is not quasi-corporeal either.

But when we have the argument: 'Thinking is not the activity of any bodily part; therefore it is the activity of an immaterial part' — then don't we get the 'language that suggests a body'?

The argument assumes that thinking is the activity of a part — as it were of an organ, and then calls it 'immaterial'.

But why should we not say, with several modern philosophers, it is the activity of the man, the human being whose thinking it is? If we say this it will perhaps be asked: '*Where* does the man perform this activity?' But here, once again, language is 'suggesting a body'. Not, of course, that there is no body; but *there is no body in the role being suggested for one*.

This point of course held also for the case of 'pointing to the colour as opposed to the shape'. The role was that of an *act* of pointing so differentiated as to determine its object. The physical act doesn't do that, and so we look for an act as it were of mental pointing which does. Similarly there is no locatedness of thought *as* there is locatedness of the processes of a machine in the parts of a machine. And so we looked for a non-dimensive locatedness in a mental medium, and fancied that we found it through our consciousness of thought. But that only means: by reflecting on the occurrence of thoughts — perhaps reflecting that this very reflecting is such an occurrence. As I have said, it was wrongly assimilated to, say, 'consciousness of sound'. A sound occurs in a soundspace, phenomenologically speaking. This is brought home to us by stereophonic headphones. Thought doesn't occur in a thought-space.

Even in that form of meditative reflection, thought is much more unlike sensation and also much more unlike physical action than is suggested by this idea of *consciousness of the activity of an immaterial part*.

Let us go back to pointing. Wittgenstein contrasted pointing to the shape (as opposed to the colour) with pointing to the chair (as opposed to the table). But that a physical act is an act of pointing *at all* is not a physical characterisation of it. Suppose you find a bit of straight stick. It is in a certain position and therefore pointing in a certain direction. Or rather, it is pointing in two directions, and in itself it is not pointing as a man points at all. The force of Wittgenstein's contrast was not to say: pointing to a physical object is a physical act, pointing to a colour (say) is something else. He could have said: pointing to this colour as opposed to that one is to be *contrasted with* pointing to the colour as opposed to the shape. Given that someone is pointing to physical objects, the act of pointing to one is physically differentiated from the act of pointing to the other. For the direction is different. Similarly for pointing to two different colours. But a difference of this kind, even if it occurred, would not identify the object of pointing as colour rather than kind of stuff. It would not do so any more than some characteristic experience would. 'It would depend on what happened before and after the pointing, whether we would say that the pointing was a case of pointing to the shape, not the colour.' (*Loc. cit.*)

Upon *what*, that happened before and after the pointing? One thing that is requisite is that the person pointing should possess the concept 'colour'; the only guarantee of this would be that he spoke a language in which that concept was represented. Given that prerequisite, the situation needs to be one in which something is, or is to be, accomplished by pointing to the colour — that someone will match something, or will try to, for example; or that someone learns a colour word, being held to apply it correctly when he had not known it before.

What we have, then, is not a single event which somehow has the character of being an act of *pointing to the colour* no matter what the context in which it occurs, but a number of events which hang together so as to constitute the physical act of pointing as a pointing to the colour. We started out from the fact that no bodily action *as such* could manage to be this act of pointing to the colour. And we were deflected from looking for a single mental act which should accompany or inform the bodily act and make it be what in itself it could not be. If we accepted Wittgenstein's criticism, we rejected any such conception as really being a fantasy of an immaterial sort of act, like a bodily one except in being immaterial. That conception of *mind* or *spirit* and their activity made them, Wittgenstein said, much too like the body and its acts. The difference was in fact far greater than we supposed if we adopted such a picture.

And now there are two paths which we might take. One is as it were reductive. I will explain this by considering the facts about two familiar *verbs*: 'to pay' and 'to win'. The quasi-reductive account of thinking proceeds by making an analogy between the use of the verb 'think' and the uses of such verbs as 'pay' and 'win'.

One always pays a sum of money by performing some act — e.g. handing over coins. Clearly, the act which counts as an act of paying must be embedded in the practice of a community, and must occur in a situation which exemplifies that practice. Without those surroundings it will not be an act of paying. There is a difference between paying and winning. It does hold of winning too that it involves a practice, the whole practice of a game or competition in which someone wins. But *here* there is no such thing as an act, a proceeding, of winning. 'Winning' is not the name of a proceeding, even though it may be assigned to a particular moment at which one performed some winning act or made a winning move. Think of a winning jump in a competition. That jump comes to have been the winning jump because no other competitor equalled it, and so we could say that with that jump this competitor won; nevertheless, winning itself is not an action which one carries out as paying a sum of money is.

A quasi-reductive treatment of thinking would claim that the verb 'to think' should be explicable in the same general style. Sometimes a thought, in the sense of what is thought, is expressed by a person's material activities: by writing or speaking, for example, or again by gesture or other behaviour. One can even see someone thinking something: 'This pencil's blunt. Oh well, it'll do.' One sees a behaviour. If the person gives his thought in words afterwords, he may be using words to give the meaning of his behaviour, just as one can use words to give the meaning of other words. The behaviour can be called having that thought *just as much as* coming out with a sentence can. When there is a sentence spoken, or such another piece of behaviour, the thought in question need not be an accompanying event or process — in fact when thoughts accompany sentences, they are usually *other* thoughts.

Often there is a material activity or various perhaps scattered bits of material activity, to which one might refer in saying that someone had certain thoughts. The statement is an interpretation of this activity, one which can be quite certain. In saying this, we describe the operation of the concept 'thinking' in such a report. This was roughly the path taken by Gilbert Ryle in his last years, when he devoted a great deal of thought to the topic of thinking.

Naturally, the account which I am calling 'quasi-reductive' required that there be some material activity with reference to which we speak of thinking. And so Ryle was left with a special problem, which he called the problem of 'Le Penseur', after Rodin's statue, where there isn't any activity which is done thinkingly, but only thinking. For this Ryle had to construct a quite different theory.

When someone points to the colour (as opposed to the shape) there is a material happening with a meaning. There are vast numbers of material happenings with meanings in this sense. And meanings are sometimes referred to points of time when only the scantiest material happenings were relevant or even when there were no material happenings for them to be the meanings of. There is such a reference of a meaning to a time whenever one says: 'At that moment I had the thought . . . ' And on consideration, it does not seem to matter whether there was a very small material happening, or none. In either case there is a great contrast with a full-blown case of the 'visible thought' like the following: someone is e.g. doing a jig-saw puzzle, and one wants to say he just had the thought 'Perhaps it'll fit in *this* place, but the other way round'. The player has been trying the piece in a certain position; then his glance shifts, he gives a slight start, turns the piece round, and tries to fit it ... Contrast with this the case where there is a mere narrowing of the eyes, or a slight smile, but the person himself reports that at that moment he was struck by a certain thought about the binomial theorem. Now should we fasten on to relevant material events occurring at the time of a thought as of enormous importance in explicating the concept of thinking? Only if we do can these scanty phenomena seem to make much difference.

This is so whether we take 'winning' or 'paying' as our model. If we think of thinking on the analogy of *paying*, there must be an act which is the act of thinking such and such, even though it would not be that in different surroundings. But there may be no such act. If we take 'winning' as our model, we are better off, for we don't have to call anything an act *of* thinking. Since it is even possible to win by default of the other competitors so that there isn't even a winning move, this model may seem satisfactory in the case where there is no act at the time of the thought. Nevertheless, in pursuing this line one is hopelessly stuck with the cases of thinking which have nothing to do with one's surroundings or with any activities in which one is currently engaged.

The reductive or quasi-reductive programme has these difficulties. What is the other path? Well, we can describe the multifarious use of the verb 'to think', and this will include assignments by speakers of various thoughts to particular times regardless of there being any events round about those times, the totality of which materially carry the thinking.

In fact the difference between *no* material event and some slight flicker or twitch is unimportant. Nor, even, is *this* point especially connected with the role of material events as conceived since Descartes. Some have thought that the occurrence of a mental image or images was essential to thought; but it may be that one can find nothing even of that sort. Nor even as it were the experience of a slight click in the mind, which occurs at the moment which one says was the moment of a certain thought.

That is to say: the whole enterprise is a mistake, of finding some other events which are to carry a thought at a particular moment. A dualist may say at this point: 'Right! So you see there is the immaterial event, which proves the immaterial substance or medium in which this immaterial event takes place.'

To this we may reply: '*Just* on this sort of occasion, when the other events are few or none? Surely the immaterial nature of thought is there, even when there is a full-blown material occurrence to identify as the occurrence of a thought.' I mean, for example, when there is pursuit of ends by intelligent handling of things in the light of scientific knowledge or thorough practical acquaintance. Or when there is the manipulation of signs in rapid calculation on paper. And in these cases there is no reason to believe that this immateriality of thought involves the occurrence of an immaterial event in an immaterial medium.

That is to say, the pre-Cartesian, indeed originally Platonic conception is right. To quote a remark I once heard from Jerome Lejeune: 'They say I do not find the soul at the end of my scalpel. Do I find mathematics at the end of my scalpel?'

The immateriality of the soul consists at bottom in the fact that you cannot specify a material character or configuration which is equivalent to truth.

This thought is more like a chapter heading for many thoughts, the fruits of many investigations, than a conclusion of one. But it is already implicit in the consideration that the physical act of pointing, considered purely as a material event, is not even an act of pointing — it is just the fact that a finger, say, has a certain line. Nevertheless, pointing might be a phenomenon of purely animal life.

We say that we cannot find a bodily act of pointing which in respect of its physical difference has to be an act of pointing to the shape as opposed to the colour. (There might of course easily be a *convention* here.) That is to say, in the sense in which pointing to *this* colour as opposed to that one must be pointing in a different direction. For the colours must lie in different places.

Now if that is so we can say that man *qua* body can't be described as pointing to the colour rather than the shape. For his act of pointing to the colour is certainly a bodily act; but it is not *qua* bodily act that it is determined as pointing to the colour. This does not mean that we have to postulate a different, *another* act of pointing by a *different sort* of substance, an immaterial one — that path to the concept of 'spirit' which Wittgenstein implicitly criticises. But we can say that this bodily act is an act of man *qua* spirit.

What does it do for us to say this? Is it an explanation? I mean, an explanatory hypothesis? No. It might indeed in certain circumstances help to explain the concept of spirit.

2

Has Mankind One Soul – An Angel Distributed Through Many Bodies?

If the human soul is a subsistent immaterial thinking thing, then must it not be like an angel? For angels are also subsistent immaterial thinking things. Now all angels are specifically different from one another. It is spatiality with its spread-out-ness that makes it possible to have many things all of one kind, like a sheet of postage stamps all the same. But if something has no dimensive quantity to it, if its essence does not involve any matter but it is a pure form, then there can only be one of it — just as Plato called his forms monads: there could only be one form of each kind of thing.

So if the human soul is a subsistent immaterial thinking thing, how can there be more than one of it? We shall see further reason to find this possibility difficult later on. To give you an advance hint: the difficulty rises from the nature of intellect and its objects and the intellectual nature of the human soul.

There is no such thing as an intrinsically evil being. The devils are not such, but are fallen angels who rebelled against God and with their leader Lucifer, the top angel and greatest of all created

* The Casassa Lecture, Loyola Marymount University, Los Angeles, March 21, 1985. Published for Loyola Marymount University by Marquette University Press, Milwaukee 1985. Reprinted by permission of Loyola Marymount University.

beings, were thrust out of heaven. The philosopher-theologian Origen thought that they were punished by being immersed in matter, so that we humans are those angels enveloped in bodies. I might frame a different fantasy: with the rebellious host thrown out of heaven, there were empty places to be filled. How could they be filled? Perhaps a whole crop of new angels could be created. But no: one hero among the good angels offered himself, saying: disperse me through matter; make a being that is material and that has animal life, but distribute me among the many members of this species, and continue this until a sufficient number of these mixed creatures have climbed into heaven to take the places of the fallen ones.

Now if the human soul is indeed a subsistent immaterial thinking thing, and so is like an angel, why should it not in fact be an angel — just one — which has been distributed through many bodies?

I will try to tell you.

There is a primary principle of the life of any kind of material living thing. I mean: a primary principle of dandelion life in a dandelion, of lion life in a lion. This primary principle I call its soul. There are also non-primary principles such as the brain of an animal or the structure of a cell.

We see that there is a primary principle from the fact of cell differentiation to form the different material parts or organs of a many-celled creature and from e.g., the fission of an amoeba which gives two amoebas. The result is dependent on the kind, for the division of a cell or its place in a cluster could not account for differentiations, nor mere fission for the production of two new creatures endowed with the powers of nutrition, growth and further reproduction.

There might be no telling the seeds of two kinds of plant apart, except by knowing which plants they came from. We have a strong inclination to think things can't be so 'in principle'. It's just that sometimes we don't know a test that will reveal a difference.

Except, of course, the test of growing new plants from our two seeds. But that will not give us a way of telling which other seeds in our batches will produce this plant and which the other, and we feel there must be a way of telling this without knowing where the seeds come from, even if we can't find it. Now whether there always is such a way 'in principle' I don't know. If it is built into our concepts of causality that there is, maybe we should change them. If we ought not to change them, this needs to be shown.

Still, let's *assume* that 'there always is a difference', as there is a difference anyone can see between caraway seeds and poppy seeds. Does that mean that if you could make something exactly like a given seed, and it and the natural seed of the plant couldn't be told apart, then such a plant would come from it? You found a difference between the natural seed and the seed of any other plant. This satisfies your conviction that 'there must be a difference'. So you have replicated it. Why, because that conviction was satisfied, must the manufactured seed yield what comes from its natural model? There is another conviction which now appears. Namely, that the properties which are discoverable without knowing where the seed comes from or what it will produce are important, not just for telling what seed it is, but for explaining its growth into the plant. And the explanation must be total, in the sense that having it we now understand how this plant is produced. Being able to tell this seed from any other kind doesn't *eo ipso* give us any such understanding. It means that we can know the kind a seed is, as anyone can know an acorn or the winged pairs of seeds of the sycamore tree. Knowing the kind, you know from what it came and what, if anything, it will naturally grow into. Knowledge of the kind determines that further knowledge so long as in knowing the kind you know that it is a seed and the seed of such a tree. This is because the kind determines what plant this seed will become if it grows. The notion of the kind includes that of a determinative principle or form according to which the life develops and proceeds. Thus the single-celled creature splits into two structural replicas of itself, and the many-celled plants and animals have cell differentiation and organization of many differentiated tissues into a whole of a certain pattern. Knowledge of the pattern proper to the kind is implicit in the doctor's and geneticist's concept of a 'syndrome'. You don't call it a syndrome that a baby learns to stand up and walk, holds its head up, looks about it and goes towards objects which it then clutches. A syndrome is a set of phenomena that are not according to the pattern proper to the kind but are damaging to it.

With these considerations I justify the idea of a primary principle of the life of a living creature of a particular kind. I don't mean a general principle of life, but a particular primary principle of horse life, say, or strawberry life or human life. The primary principle of life, or the form, I call the soul of the living plant or animal. It may sound odd, because unusual, to speak of the soul of a daffodil. But a daffodil plant is certainly not inanimate, and so must have such a primary principle, its determinative form, as the principle of its being a living daffodil.

I would not restrict the notion of form to living things. Here there is a contrast which is relevant. If you divide up a piece of gold into several parts, each is still gold, but if you divide a horse into several parts your horse is no more and the parts aren't horses. It may be said: 'But an amoeba divides into two amoebas!' Yes, but it must divide in a particular way (which it does under its own steam). I presume that not just any dissection of an amoeba will produce parts that are amoebas. With plants we get closer, though not very close, to mere stuff. You often get new plants by division, though it usually matters what you separate off. Nevertheless you don't kill either part of a suitable plant by taking cuttings, though a cutting is not yet the plant but the form of the plant's life is there in sufficient strength to develop it into a complete plant of its kind. But again, you couldn't usually do this with just a leaf.

These considerations make me fairly friendly to Quine's idea that water — all the water in the world — is one scattered object, and similarly for other kinds of stuff. There may be reasons against this. But at first sight it is not so grotesque as it would be to speak of the set of all cats as a cat — the Cat of all cats, there being just one Cat-life which is scattered through many parts. There is a plaque set in a wall in a street at the University of Chicago declaring that where it was (below it or behind it, I don't know) Man first split the atom. And if I remember right, the first man to step on the moon said to the world something like that he was taking a big step for Man.

I don't think much of these thoughts. But there is a rather stronger reason to take them seriously than first appears. This is found in the peculiar character of the human soul. This soul is not merely the life of the animal body whose form it is; it is intellectual.

For the other animals, their souls are the primary principles of all their vital operations and processes, as also of their sensations, appetites, movements, estimates and imaginations.

All of these things are corporeal. This is as obvious for sensation, which requires organs, as it is for vital processes and movements. But it is also true of imagination as we are justified in ascribing it to non-human animals. In the human case it hangs together with sensation in various complicated ways, but we only know of this from the characteristic language of imagination and from various human activities involving imagination. With the other animals we would rightly ascribe imagination where there is behaviour in response to sensory objects which we understand as responses to the apprehension of danger or the prospect of pleasure. The first we have sometimes when a horse shies, the second when a dog leaps about enthusiastically as his lead is produced, or brings it to his master. 'He hopes to be taken for a walk', we say. But the walk is not present in actuality like a bone he can see. Being moved by an object of sense that is not present is having imagination. Sense and imagination offer objects of desire and fear: desire and fear prompt action; such action is itself a vital activity and so one of the operations of the animal soul.

In these ways the animal soul, no less than the vegetative, is the primary principle of a life that is all corporeal. This is more obvious in the case of the vegetative soul whose vital functions are principally nutrition, growth and reproduction. Sensation we sometimes ascribe to plants; imagination not at all. I don't know if anyone ascribes sensation to sunflowers. But standing in ranks they uniformly turn their faces to the sun, not to where the sun will be before it is there. So they do not manifest imagination.

The vegetative functions are performed in animal life too. But, except for growth, they are transposed to a new key. And similarly the remaining vegetative functions and the animal activities and powers are transposed in the life of man. For here there is again something new: the intellective principle is the differentia of the human soul.

This is manifest in various ways. The one we are most likely to be conscious of in philosophy nowadays is language, its syntax, its application and aptnesses in circumstances, the logical multifariousness of its bits, and the connection of one sentence with others in a whole context of sentences. 'Why aren't you in bed?' I ask a child about three years old, and get an answer 'I haven't had my bath yet'. Think of the request which, the story has it, brought death to Archimedes: 'Don't disturb my circles'. He was speaking of circles drawn in the sand where he sat. But:

> If two circles intersect, they divide one another into two parts.
>
> Well then, I'll buy three pounds of butter.
>
> No; for, since non-Euclidean geometry is Euclidean in the infinitesimal, the Euclidean keeps a corresponding pre-eminence.

For it is the noise that babes hear at birth and that old men hear as they die in their beds, and it is the noise of our households all our long lives long.

This country is an island.

You won't be able to, because producing long word-salads is difficult unless you suffer from a rare mental illness, whose victims often rattle them off with apparent ease.

I'm afraid that leopards are disappearing.

Here I have produced a number of disparate sentences, which exhibit very various logical structures and logically different uses of words. Hearing or seeing sentences is hearing particular sounds or seeing particular marks. Understanding them involves understanding forms which are general and non-material. 'My bath' is formally different from 'my circles' and formally the same as 'my exam'. 'Leopards disappearing' is grammatically more akin to 'rare illness' than to 'leopards running'. 'Non-Euclidean geometry' is a different sort of subject from 'Two circles' or 'producing long word-salads'. In 'I'm afraid that leopards are becoming rare' is 'I'm afraid' an expression of an emotion of fear?

The generality and immateriality of what is grasped by the understanding comes out if we reflect on the identification of morphemes and morphemic clusters. To make the point in a simple case, the first 'ing' in the words 'singing', 'swinging', 'springing' is not a morpheme and the second 'ing' is one. The understanding of sentences involves an implicit grasp of the role which marks a morpheme; and this is something general. Nor need the general thing that is involved be any bit of print or any sound occurring in a range of examples like the participial ending. The form of a relational expression may not involve any such thing, but be recognizable in 'father of A', 'brother of B', 'bigger than C', 'distant from D'. We have a generality which is not repetition of some one sound or mark: it is formal and not material. The generality and non-materiality of its objects are characteristic of intellectual work or operation. Intellect contrasts in this with both sense and imagination. That this is so for things sensed is obvious enough. It is not so obvious for things imagined. You and I may be both imagining a cockroach without either of us imagining a particular cockroach. So the image does not have to be particular! But this is wrong: an image has to be particular in the way a given drawing is particular, even if a drawing of a cockroach is not a drawing of a particular cockroach. In these remarks 'a particular cockroach' means 'some actual cockroach'. But the fact that an image or a drawing may not be of any actual cockroach, though it is of a cockroach, does not show that it may be of a general cockroach. (If one could call a drawing a drawing of a general cockroach it would e.g. be a schematic drawing and the generality would reside in its use.)

The question arises, how alike our drawings or images are. But suppose we are thinking of a cockroach, though of no actual cockroach. The question cannot arise how like the cockroach in my thought is to the cockroach in your thought. For they are the same.

It is this result of generality and immateriality that makes something serious of the idea that there is just one human soul for the whole of mankind. The intellect frames or somehow receives general concepts. If these general concepts are to be found in a lot of particular intellects, then they are not general: one could find particular examples of a general concept in all the particular intellects that had it. The general concept would have a particular instantiation in the individual intellect. But that conflicts with what the intellect is supposed to have; it grasps universals, the content of general terms like 'cockroach', 'square root', 'relation'. The difficulty would be avoided if there was one big intellect which was doing the thinking whenever any thinking of an intellectual sort was going on in separate human beings.

This view has been seriously maintained by Arabic philosophers, in particular by Averroes, who ascribed it to Aristotle.

If one also holds that the intellectual principle in the soul is the differentia of the human being, one would also have to hold that we are all one human being. The difference between Socrates and Alcibiades would merely be the difference between a man with and without a coat on, for example. The Man of all men who would be the set of what we ordinarily call men would have Plato and Alcibiades as his members, all similar members of him, in whom he thought and spoke.

The consequence of the idea of one intellect operating in all men is too absurd to be credited. If so, then the human soul, even in its character of being an intellectual principle, cannot be like an angel distributed through many bodies. If the intellectual character is the differentia of the human animal, then it is the intellectual soul that is the form of this living thing. This means that the thinking and understanding human being *is* individuated like other animals by the spatiality and spread-out-ness of his existence which allows for many individuals with the same form.

What then of the argument that the concepts or ideas in these individual intellects will no more be general than are their images? There must be something wrong with it. We can say straight off that if it were correct, then there could be no multiplicity of intellects at all; the possible multiplicity of angels is not guaranteed by their being specifically different from one another. Each particular specifically distinct one will be incapable of understanding because understanding is of things that are general and not of particulars. The argument would lead to the impossibility of there being more than one intellect at all, *i.e.* the impossibility of any except, say, *my* intellect if I want to take the solipsistic path; or, if I wish rather to be Spinozistic in spirit, any except the divine intellect.

The problem that has to be solved is a genuine one. For the moment, all I can say is that the individuation of intellects and of that by which they think of what they think of cannot after all be an impediment to their understanding of what is general.

3

Human Essence

I guess that any human language has unfortunate features. One in English is that it has no word that quite corresponds to the Latin 'homo', Greek 'ἄνθρωπος', German 'Mensch'. The English word 'man' does indeed often have that meaning, as in 'mankind', 'All men are mortal', 'Man proposes, God disposes', 'Here man first split the atom', 'What a wondrous work of God is man', etc. But it also often connotes the male sex. We have 'master and man', 'man and boy', 'Men are more liable to colour blindness than women', 'I saw a young man running', 'Was it a man or a woman?' And you have to look up the Greek to find out whether the joy of a woman delivered of her child — 'that a man is born into the world' — is joy over the birth of an ἄνθρωπος — a human being — or an ἀνήρ — a male human being. Here — as with the question of Nicodemus to Jesus: 'How can a man be born when old?' — 'man' translates ἄνθρωπος, as indeed one would guess and hope; but our English leaves it a question.

All men not too young and not incapacitated have the blessing of language. They may be incapacitated by brain damage; or again because they are deaf and have not been taught to speak. That a new-born baby is speechless is the same sort of fact as a new-born kitten's being blind. Earthworms are not blind: it does not belong to their nature to be sighted; they have no organ of sight.

---

* Lecture given at the University of Navarre, Pamplona, in 1988. Unpublished in English. Text from manuscript copy.

Here we are encountering the concept of a nature or essence. Consideration shews that, as Wittgenstein observes in the *Philosophische Untersuchungen* (Part I, remark 371) '*Essence* is expressed in grammar'. Consideration of what? Well, for example, of the following absurd sentences: 'Where does this pencil's uncle live?' 'What is the shape of dust?' 'What is a rainbow made of?' 'How many legs has a tree?' 'Where does a chair feel?' 'Do bacteria think?'

In these cases we may be vaguely assuming that there are answers to questions that sin against the grammar of their terms. What do we *call* a chair's feeling something? And so on. We might of course make up meanings.

Somehow it is easier to construct examples of sins against grammar than to describe the grammar. 'To think, a material being must be, not merely an organism, but an animal.' That is a beginning. However, if our question about bacteria was a sin against grammar, then that observation is a grammatical one — it is about the grammar of the verb 'to think'. And so will be the definition: 'man = rational animal'. It has to be understood as unrefuted, for example, by the considerations like that men are often highly irrational; that there is no *not* or *if* in the mind of a young baby, or that some human beings never develop the capacity to use spoken language.

There is a difficulty about such a definition, which Locke felt but did not understand. A mathematical definition is supposed to cover all and only what the defined term covers; as it might be 'plane square'. If you can imagine something covered by your proposed definition which would *not* count as a square, the definition is faulty. Not so with the definition of a man or a flea. The definition of a man suffices if, so far as we know there *are* no animals except men that satisfy it. And so quite generally. Thinking of something geometrical that would not be an X though it were a Y refutes 'Y' as a definition of an X. But *imagining* a rational parrot would not seem to refute the definition 'man = rational animal'.

One would have to *believe* in the rational parrot. If dolphins are rational animals, as some people have believed, *they* would be a refutation of that definition.

If this is right, the definitions of animals, plants and chemical substances might be regarded as forms which certain things fit — and unknown others might fit. But the latter possibility does not make them faulty as definitions *now*. When it comes to mathematical or logical definitions — say Frege's explanation of a concept as a function from objects to truth-values, we should not indeed misquote him as saying: 'concept = function from object(s) to truth-value(s)' but quote him correctly as saying that any concept is a function whose values are truth-values. This would be refuted by producing an undoubted concept which was not such a function. But it can also be taken as restricting what Frege means by 'concept' (*Begriff*). The definition of a man, even though I *take* it as meaning 'man = rational animal' and as implying that any man (human being) is a rational animal, would not be refuted by pointing to an irrational man; nor do we avoid such a pretended refutation by restricting what we mean by 'man'.

Frege's account[1] of numerical functions does not proceed by defining them, but by examples, together with the observation that for a given number as argument a numerical function (with only one argument) always has a numerical value. To my mind the interest of his exposition does not *only* lie in the generality of a numerical function. It lies also in his pointing to the difference between, say '$2 + x^4$' and '$2 + 3^4$'. The former is an expression of a numerical function of which the latter is an example. The latter has a numerical value, the former no determinate one, but is exemplified in as many examples as you like and is an expression of what is common to '$2 + 3^4$', '$2 + 1^4$', '$2 + 5^4$', '$2 + 10^4$', etc. But the difference of meaning between the expression of the numerical

[1]   In *Funktion und Begriff*

function and the expressions of instances of it is not an example of equivocation like 'John gave three rings' (of a door-bell) and 'John gave three rings' (finger rings), nor yet of what linguists call difference of *readings*, like the two readings of 'Flying kites can be dangerous'. The difference between '2 + x' and '2 + 3' is highly significant because the former's point is to signify the form in which the latter is signified: a pattern common to many instances. It thus signifies a function, and with such significations we had made a new step, had achieved something new in arithmetic. Frege of course did not invent functions. He invented a clear way of talking about them which avoids confusing sign ('x + 2') and thing signified, which is the function. Note that the exposition does not give any simple sign for a given function: what is in question is a *pattern*.

We can describe the difference between '3 + 2' and 'x + 2' as follows: 'x + 2' does not signify any particular number, but if you replace the x by a numeral, your expression does signify a particuar number. But isn't it also true that if you replace the 3 in '3 + 2' by another numeral, your new expression will be signifying a particular number? Yes, it is. But '3 + 2' *already* signifies a particular number, since '3' does. Our explanation describes the relevant grammar of the two expressions '3 + 2' and 'x + 2'. In this grammar is expressed the meaning of 'function' when we say that 'x + 2' signifies a function. Generalising the type of explanation we say that the essence *function* is expressed in the word's grammar. But there are different kinds of function. We might call 'x + 2' and 'x + y' functions of the same kind. That would perhaps indicate that the difference does not interest us very much. And we might give a list of simple arithmetical operations O and put in one class all functions of the form xOy, with the proviso that the expression of a function of this class must always contain at least one letter of the alphabet, to mark an argument-place. Our account of the grammar can be adjusted to fit all such functional expressions.

But now suppose we have $x^2 + y^2 = z^2$. Frege adds = to the signs that form functional expressions, but there is a great difference between functions all of whose values are numbers, and functions whose values will be truth and falsehood. So even if we accept what he does, we have ground to distinguish between *numerical* functions and functions from numbers to truth-values. If we learn to speak of the latter, we are learning a *new* bit of grammar, not just adding very similar examples to exemplify the grammar we have already learnt.

We can agree to Wittgenstein's remark (already quoted) that essence is expressed in grammar, when we consider the contrasting but related grammars of '$x + 2$' and '$3 + 2$'. Now Frege's transition to = (and also > and <) as functional signs leads him on to regarding, say, 'x is made of marble' *too* as the expression of a function. Here the function is not limited to being a function from numbers to truth-values, but is quite generally a function from *objects* to truth-values. His account thus explains a *concept* (the signification, we may say, of a predicate) as a function from objects to truth-values.

Here I am not concerned with the strange path of taking = etc. as functional signs, nor yet with Frege's belief that numbers are objects. My concern is the thesis that *essences* are expressed in grammar. This was clear in the case of the essence connected with the general notion *arithmetical function*. However, it is also fairly clear in most cases of familiar concepts of substances and kinds of stuff. Examples: animal, plant, peacock, man, flea, hollyhock, sycamore. Also: acid, wood, metal, milk. I do not mean that we have definitions of all these things, or that it is already decided in our language whether artificial wood — wood that does not come from a tree, but this can't be told by examining or testing it — is really wood. Also 'deeper' definitions of the term 'metal' are found with the progress of natural science — but this doesn't mean that our forefathers did not have the genuine concepts 'metal', 'gold', 'iron'. Archimedes knew what he was being asked to do when the king, as Vitruvius relates, wanted to know whether the goldsmith had made his crown of a mixture of gold and silver (and so stolen some of the gold), though the crown weighed the right amount.

The grammar of terms for natural kinds of stuff is tied up with that of 'a pure sample'. Locke believed the early chemists in Oxford were wasting their time trying to get pure samples. Luckily they took no notice of him. You need 'pure samples' to get knowledge of the properties of the *kind* of stuff you are examining: that gives the grammatical connexion which makes the particular grammar express the essence of the particular kind.

The identity of a lump of stuff is tied up in a vaguish way with the notion of 'nothing added and nothing taken away'. I say 'vaguish' because the loss of a very *little* would seldom count, and whether loss or even replacement of a bit counts against identity depends on our interests.

When we come to plants and animals the idenity of an individual is of a different kind. 'The persistence of a certain pattern in a flow of matter' is how we should explain identity, but the notion of a pattern, as of a shape too, is here special and peculiar. We readily speak of the shape of a horse or of a human being. But we don't say that someone's shape, as we ordinarily mean it, is something that alters when he sits down, for example. Also, the term 'pattern' extends to covering patterns of development over a period of life involving considerable changes, even like those from caterpillar to larva to butterfly.

These observations are contributions to the general grammar of 'piece of stuff' and 'same animal'. The latter phrase has two senses, in one of which two fleas are the same animal, while in the other they are two different ones. This too belongs to the grammar of such terms, and it is not obscure to say that essence — various levels of essence, we may say — gets expressed in grammar.

I have just now been confining myself to substantial terms. The notion of essence is not so confined. We were earlier considering the essence of numerical functions: 'function' as *so* used is certainly not a substatial term. Similarly we might say it belongs to the essence of a square in two dimensions that the square which is twice its area is the square on the diagonal; and either diagonal will do. In the *Meno*, by asking questions Socrates leads a slave to see that the diagonal gives the length of the side of the square double the original one. It is often said that he asks 'leading questions' — but you can ask me any number of 'leading questions' about the Han dynasty in China and I won't be able to answer them if I never knew any thing about it. In response to this objection to Plato I once undertook to demonstrate his point with a nine-year-old girl who, like the slave, had never learned any geometry. I started with a drawing which I called 'a square', and asked Socrates' question: how long will the side be of a square twice as big? To my astonishment and pleasure the child answered *just* as the slave did and we proceeded just as the dialogue did, because she always said the next thing that the slave did. I became convinced that this famous bit of the dialogue was no fiction.

Now, what did she end up knowing? One might say: *if* I drew the squares etc. quite accurately, she ended up knowing that *this* square and *this* one (the first and the second guesses) *weren't* twice the original square, but this *last* one was. But how did she know that? By the way they looked? We certainly weren't doing any measuring. If it was by the way they looked would she have any reason to be sure it would *look the same* another time? 'Well', you might say, 'it would *have* to, if you drew the squares properly.' Would it? Suppose I used different coloured ink and drew a bigger or smaller square to start off with. 'Oh', you will say, 'I didn't mean "same" in *those* ways.' Well, what way of *looking the same* did you mean? 'The same in that the square on the diagonal *was* (and so *looked*) twice the size of the original square.' But how would it look twice the size? You may say: 'By being composed of triangles, each of which is half the original square, and a quarter of the new one.'

If I *don't* draw it so, or at least ask questions which make the other talk of it so, then I am not asking about the geometrical proposition. (For this, accurate drawing does not matter.)

What I am eliciting by my drawing and questions is an *essence* – part at any rate of the essence of a plane square.

Wittgenstein says in the *Remarks on the Foundations of Mathematics* (Part I, Remark 32) that mathematicians produce essences. Now, we can see what he means in the examples of the essences: numerical function and plane square. Functions emerged as a mathematical topic, I believe, in the seventeenth century — remember that I did not say that Frege produced such essences, only that he shewed what they were, and how to avoid confusing sign and thing signified. As for the square of Euclidean geometry, that was an essence produced many centuries before.

I said that not all essences were of objects or substances, and so far I have only mentioned elementary examples of mathematical essences.

In Remark 72 of the same part of Wittgenstein's writing he imagines saying 'This shape consists of these shapes. You have shown me an essential property of this *shape*.' He has been considering, among other things, the composition of a rectangle out of two parallelograms and two triangles:

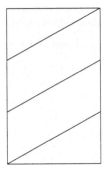

which may astonish or even bewilder someone who first sees it (or, we may say, sees the shapes separated).

Wittgenstein imagines one's saying 'It's as if *God* had put them together like that'. And he says

> so *we are using a simile*. The shape is becoming an ethereal entity which *has* this shape: it's as if it had been put together like this once for all (by whoever put the essential properties into things). For, if the shape becomes a thing composed of parts, then the demiurge of the shape is the one who also made light and darkness, colour and texture, etc. (Imagine someone asking: 'The shape was put together out of these shapes? Who put them together? Was it you?')*

In the previous remark (71) he has said 'Compare Plato's conception of properties as ingredients of a thing.' I therefore think it not inept to translate his 'Werkmeister' in Remark 72 with that Platonic word 'demiurge'.

What lesson can we draw from these examples? It would appear that the notion of the essential constituents of anything except substantial objects (of the various kinds we thought of) is necessarily a simile. And if it is right to say that mathematicians *produce* essences, this reflects the fact that we characteristically use *substantives* like 'function', 'triangle', 'shape' for what they work about. We may say they have *produced grammars* in which esssences are expressed. But it is more important to understand the grammars and their application than to think about essences. The 'essences' produced by mathematicians otherwise look like a sort of illusion.

The claim that one is using a simile means that the thing the simile is a likeness *of* is *not* a simile. This is the coming into existence of various substantial objects, which are made, are generated from others and turn into others when they cease to exist.

---

* Evidently Professor Anscombe was translating anew from the German original in preparing this lecture, for the translation differs from her published translation in Ludwig Wittgenstein, *Remarks on the Foundations of Mathematics*, edited by G.H. von Wright, R. Rhees, G.E.M. Anscombe; translated by G.E.M. Anscombe. (Oxford: Basil Blackwell, 3rd edn. 1978), p. 64.

I now come to my final question. If mathematicians 'produce essences' should we say the same about the rest of the human race? It has languages containing the grammars of many kinds of term. How did the essences expressed in these grammars come into being? Did mankind produce them?

Here we seem to be in the region of 'realism' versus 'idealism'. It is a queer fact about philosophy that it so often seems to hold a gun to our heads and say: 'Come now! Idealist or Realist? Which are you?' Why should one not be partly one, partly the other?

Mankind did not construct, 'produce', the essences corresponding to all our familiar terms, i.e. the grammars in which the essences of objects are expressed in so many human languages. We did not start as *tabulae rasae* and then construct languages, produce grammars of the languages whose sentences then got written upon *us*, the empty tablets. It is human to have language and one who cannot come into possession of it is a human being for whom human development has been impeded.

If you say that mathematicians 'produce essences' and a harmless reasonable account can be given of that — which is a simile — then who or what produced the essences expressed in the grammars of the speech which is so important a part of the life of mankind? The answer cannot be 'mankind' because without language you haven't got mankind — not having human life if there is not human language.

The answer, it seems, must be: whoever or whatever produced mankind. For many people of the present day, this answer will be equivalent to 'Evolution'. But that is only a way of saying 'Well, it happened'. A more rational answer would be 'Intelligence (or intelligences) which made men and other things through the logos of its wisdom.' That logos comprises an infinity of logoi of possible and actual things, and also of *human* inventions.

True objects have essences expressed in the grammars of their names precisely as names of kinds of thing. Among these objects are men with language in which such names occur, along with many other words. These include words that cannot even by simile be said to have grammars in which essences are expressed — such words as 'not', 'perhaps', 'nothing', 'some', 'yet', and the morphemes constructing the forms of moods, tenses and cases; and also many prepositions. All this is constructed by whatever constructed the human mind.

'Why should men not have been created ploughing, sowing and reaping from the first?' This question was once put to me by Wittgenstein, and I could see no objection. But if they were created so 'from the first', they were created also with language with its logical characteristics from the first. Doubtless they developed the many special quirks and peculiarities of their many languages. But nominalisations leading to the construction of illusory essences expressed in their grammar: these are *perhaps* endemic to the whole human race. It is hardly necessary to say I do not know. It is imaginable that the practitioners of linguistics, if learned enough, could find out.

Reverting to my question: what produced the genuine essences expressed in the languages of mankind? This is equivalent to: What produced language-learning man?

Some people think that the possibility of making computers somehow shews that human beings themselves don't have to be made by any intelligence or intelligences. The argument is strange: humans use their intelligence to make computers — so it follows that they themselves don't have to be made by any intelligent being! I suspect that the thought behind the argument is: we human beings make things by pushing bits of matter about. Therefore nature could have made those things, and humans too, by pushing bits of matter about. Accidentally.

This suggestion seems to be answered rightly as follows: the point of the operations of calculating and reasoning lies in their logic. This is not an accidental feature. If scratches on a rock look like $| + | = | \, |$, the arithmetical truth *may* be no part of the explanation of the scratches. (Nor the *mistake* you'd see, if you took the merely vertical strokes as Arabic digits.) But the explanation of most of the marks in a book, for example, *is* that they say something. What produces them is therefore an intelligence — whether the production is direct — as with a pen — or indirect, as with a printing machine or a programmed computer with an input. And so similarly what produces the intelligences that *produce* such things and the rest of language too is also intelligence or intelligences — but of a different kind from the human. (Otherwise we'd have an infinite regress.) The intelligence (or intelligences) must be capable of inventing language even if it is not a language-user as human beings are.

4*

Were You a Zygote?

I

The usual way for new cells to come into being is by division of old cells. So the zygote, which is a — new — single cell formed from two, the sperm and ovum, is an exception. Textbooks of human genetics usually say that this new cell is the beginning of a new human individual. What this indicates is that they suddenly forget about identical twins.

These result from the cleavage of a cell cluster into two cell clusters at some very early stage, which may be within a week of formation of the zygote. In the early 1970s Jérome Lejeune put the outer limit for such cleavage at thirteen days. The multiplication by cell division has not got very far at that stage; not, it seems, as far as thousands, whereas 'The human adult who started life as a single cell has about 10^{14}, or one hundred quadrillion cells'.[1]

All this means that if I ask you 'Were you a zygote?' you might intelligently reply 'No, I was an identical twin'. Then I could say that you and your twin jointly were once a zygote.

A human zygote is alive, and is a human thing, a new beginning of human life, and not a part of any human being. We might

* Text of a lecture given at the Royal Institute of Philosophy, London, in 1984, and subsequently published in A. Phillips Griffiths (ed) *Philosophy and Practice* (Cambridge: Cambridge University Press, 1985), pp. 111–17. Reprinted with the permission of the Director of the Royal Institute of Philosophy, Professor Anthony O'Hear, and of Cambridge University Press.

[1] Levitan and Montague, *Textbook of Human Genetics* (Oxford: Oxford University Press, 1971).

say it is a human *being*: a whole new human entity. But there is an objection because what we mean by *a* human being is a *man* in the sense *a member of the human race*. It is a *Mensch*, if we are talking German, an ἄνθρωπος in Greek, a *homo* in Latin. English suffers from not having a distinct word just for this. I will save myself from having to break into German, Greek or Latin, by adopting the word 'human' as a noun to be used in this sense.

Let me state an argument against the human zygote's being *a* human. Suppose the cell cluster divides and twins result. I'll call the zygote 'A' and the twins 'B' and 'C'. Neither B nor C is identical with A. Therefore *either*:

(1) A, not yet divided, was somehow already two. So A can have been already a pair of humans, B and C. *Or*:

(2) A was just one human, and became two by an extra one growing out of it. *Or*:

(3) A was a single human, which turned into two by splitting, as one amoeba splits and turns into two amoebas. *Or*:

(4) A, though a whole human substantial entity, was not a human yet; nor was it a pair of humans.

So far as I know there is no sufficient evidence for (1). Certainly some ten years ago Professor Lejeune confessed to having no evidence on the point.

> In man we have no data ... In ... [some races of armadillos] the eggs do split every time into four embryos ... always the same number ... So we know looking at the armadillo and the race it belongs to, how many twins are genetically imprinted in the first cell. In that case we know the determination of the number of twins has occurred at the very moment of fecundation. In humans we do not know.

If the opinion that twinning is already imprinted in the first cell *is* true of humans, as it may be, then various problems do not arise. Philosophically, if this were true, we would not have to ask about the odd logical status of the zygote — this human entity which is an individual substance, not part of one, and not *a* human.

(2) also would be acceptable for not raising any such obscure conceptual issues. But once again, there seems not to be evidence.

The third possibility, namely that one human splits into two, I am disposed to reject out of hand. But it needs more discussion. The obvious objection is that in the case of the amoeba there's no doubt we start with one amoeba and it splits into two amoebas. But in the human case it precisely is the question whether what we start off with *is* a human. What account could we give of its becoming two humans? Neither of the two humans that eventually develop can be identified as the same human as the zygote, because they can't *both* be so, as they are different humans from one another. We might indeed say that each *had* been the same human as the zygote was, and so also the same human as the other, though they are not the same human as one another now. But what has become of the human that both of them once were identical with? Has he — or it — simply ceased to exist, as we might say the parent amoeba ceases to exist on splitting?

It is true that present non-identity of B and C does not prove that B and C *were* not identical with A and so with one another. All the same, that does not prove that B and C *may* each have been identical with A. And, whether A is a human entity or an amoeba, there is the obvious objection that before A split into B and C, B and C did not exist.

Should we say that the amoeba, and any cell that divides, does not cease to exist, but continues as two, not one? That the amoeba exists in, or as, any simultaneous set of its descendants? That a single zygote cell which multiplies likewise exists in thousands of millions of its descendants? It is sometimes said: we are all Adam. Is that true in the sense — if there is one — in which the amoeba is all its descendants? No: for the amoeba did not die, but Adam died.

What has multiplied like amoebas is *cells*. We could say to a total collection of cells in the pair of twins: all you cells were once one cell. That would be parallel to the amoebas all having been one amoeba. However, it is because the cells *make up* two humans that we say those *humans* were once one cell. With amoebas, there isn't this intervening term: we start with an amoeba and end with a collection of amoebas. In this way, then, even if the zygote *is* a human, the case of the zygote and the later twin humans is not parallel to that of the amoeba and the later set of amoebas.

Would there be at least this parallel: the amoeba doesn't die, and neither does the human who is a zygote when the zygote multiplies? No! For, assuming that the single human persists through some cell divisions up to the cleavage of cell clusters into two cell clusters which are two separate humans, that human exists in the descendent *cells* up to that cleavage; but the amoeba through division exists in descendent *amoebas*. There will be no parallel ground for saying that the human exists in the 'descendent humans' (as I will call the twins). For the humans are 'descendent' only because they are composed of descendent cells. And in the sense in which the supposed single human persists through a multiplication of cells, it does not persist through the cell cluster's being cloven into two distinct *humans*. It is no more: for nothing but persistence through a multiplication of cells is there to count as its persistence, and that cannot so count, because what it counts as after cleavage is the persistence of two new humans. Yet might we not say a parallel thing about the amoeba and the descendent amoebas? We might; but as an amoeba is one cell, the persistence through cell-division is in the amoeba simply persistence of amoeba-life through division. So the multiplication of cells *is*, formally, the multiplication of amoebas.

II

Let us consider whether I could truly say: I was once a sperm and an ovum. That is, the sperm and the ovum from whose union I came were jointly I. The objection to this is just that the sperm and ovum were not one substance. That is, on a count of individual substances they come out at two until they have formed one cell.

I do not mean that each cell is a substance; most are only parts of substances. That they are so is proved by the fact of cell differentiation which soon begins to happen as they multiply by dividing. Cell differentiation is for the sake of the kind of structured, organized living material whole that gets formed through it. The kind of living thing that gets formed as a result of multiplication and differentiation of cells determines the differentiation and organization of them to the extent that this happens in a normal manner. Everywhere in a textbook of genetics the norms of health and reproduction of undefective specimens of a kind provide the aegis under which the enquirers have worked and the exposition proceeds. Note, for example, the occurrence of the term 'syndrome' in a large work on human genetics. Normally or successfully operating physiques and powers do not constitute 'syndromes'.

If a human zygote is not itself a human, then the way in which the human kind determines its way of developing is not a matter of a species to which it already belongs as a member. It is a matter of one to which belong those individuals whose gametes united to form the zygote, and into a member or members of which it will develop if it develops normally.

If a zygote was the beginning of a new human substance, and I (singly) was that zygote, then wasn't that zygote the beginning of *this* human being? Yes; but if there can be a human substance without its being a human, then either *this* individual human substance did not begin then or at one time *this* individual human substance did indeed exist but wasn't yet a human. So I wasn't yet *a* human? That seems correct. The development from something that was a single human substance only means that I was always *something* human. One can become two, then, but two cannot turn into one such that you could point back to the two and say: that's the existence that was the beginning of the existence of someone.

This needs some qualification; because two lumps of clay become one by being pressed together. The one lump had been two, and its present unity is that of spatial continuity. Two cells, a sperm and an ovum, can also become one. Would it then be true to say the zygote had been two cells? — as, to say the lump of clay had been two lumps?

No; for the latter coming-to-be-one is no substantial change but only one of deletion of boundaries. The same clay continues to exist, however pressed together or separated into lumps. But with fertilization a single — new — organism comes into existence. It has a new genetic make-up. This turns it into the immediate material for development of a member or members of whatever species its parents belong to. The two lives of the sperm and the ovum have ended because they have turned into an individual with a new life, the life carried by the zygote.

Here life = existence. In starting to live, this thing has started to exist. Thus if asked whether the zygote had been the two former cells, one should say: materially, yes; but in form and existence, no. Not in form, because the new living thing is of a new kind from what they were. They weren't organisms only needing nutrition to grow into a certain pattern. And not in existence because the life — its being alive — is not their being alive. But there can occur that cleavage of the multiplied cell cluster which leads to identical twins. Here the division *is* like the division of a lump of clay into two. At this stage the life is divided into two only because the living thing is cloven into two; and hence only inasmuch as it is so cloven. We cannot say yet that we have here two distinct animals. But we can say that we have two materially distinct carriers of the life that started with the formation of the zygote.

Embryos and Final Causes

It is widely believed, especially among Catholics who oppose the procuring of abortion, that the zygote is a human being. It is, as everyone knows, the single cell formed by the union of a sperm and an ovum; each of which is itself a single cell. The famous geneticist, Jérôme Lejeune, is confident that the zygote is not merely human, but a human being — if, I should perhaps add, it is not more than one. At least in the early 1970s he thought that the twoness of twins must already be written into the zygote that was going to develop into identical twins. (See *The Tiniest Humans,* edited by Robert Sassone, who constructed it from interviews with, and other sources by, Jérôme Lejeune and Albert Liley, the 'father of fetology'. Library of Congress No. 77-76811). Lejeune said there was no proof of this fact about identical twinning — monozygotic twinning as people call it now — in the case of human beings, nevertheless he believed it, and there is I think no reason to suppose he has changed his opinion. My most recent source is his long evidence, and his cross examination by counsel, in Maryville, Tennessee, on August 10th, 1989. There he was extremely definite: 'Science has a very simple conception of

* Paper delivered at a Colloquium at the University of Louvain-la-Neuve in May 1990 and published in J. Follon & J. McEvoy (eds) *Finalité et Intentionnalité. Doctrine Thomiste et Perspectives Modernes* (Paris: Librairie Philosophique J. Vrin & Leuven: Éditions Peeters, 1992) pp. 293–303. Reprinted with the permission of Professor The Reverend James McEvoy.

man: as soon as he has been conceived, a man is a man' (p. 47 in a transcript of proceedings in the Circuit Court for Blount County. This transcript of Lejeune's evidence was an excerpt of the whole proceedings, by Peggy M. Giles of Knoxville Court Reporting, Knoxville Tennessee, and substantially corrected — as the original manuscript shewed many mishearings — by Lejeune himself).

I have for long myself had doubts about what is called 'immediate animation' and might more aptly be called 'immediate hominisation'. This Lejeune has long believed in and now he thinks he has scientific proof of it. 'I would say to finish that there is no difficulty to understand that at the very beginning of life, the genetic information and the molecular structure of the egg, the spirit and the matter, the soul and the body must be that tightly intricated because it's a beginning of the new marvel that we call a human' (*Ibid.*, p. 46).

The reason why Lejeune thinks that he now knows what he has long believed, he explains in his evidence as given by the results of genetic researches in the two years before he was giving his evidence in Tennesee.

In this evidence, he gives a swift account of some results of researches in the previous two years. These are three: first, an actual proof of the uniqueness of the early human being. Jeffreys in England invented the possibility of taking a little bit of DNA which he could manufacture a lot of, a bit that is 'specific of some message' in our chromosomes. It is repeated a lot of times in many different chromosomes, and it is probably a regulation system (some indication to do something or not do another thing). You get the DNA, you have it spread in a special medium, you apply the Jeffreys probe, and what you see 'looks exactly like the bar code that you have ... seen in the supermarket'. What you learn is that every individual is different from the next one by its bar code.

The second result was that all this is detectable in one cell, in one nucleus of one individual.

The third was that something known but not understood was now intelligible. It was known that some of the bases of DNA were 'carrying an extra little piece we call a methyl'. What was discovered was that this methylation, different in different samples, would suppress something — so that we have some silent genes and some genes getting expressed. The important discovery was that these suppressions are different in the male and female. It had for years been believed that the chromosomes carried by both were identical. But methylation underlined them in different places. The underlining changes with progressive splitting. This obviously very greatly multiplied the different possibilities for the individual human being. The first cell, the zygote, is the most tremendously specialised of all.

These genetic discoveries described by Jérome Lejeune are indeed very important and very interesting. However what he says is sometimes difficult to understand. That the first cell is programmed so that 'it was written not only what is the genetic message we can read in every cell, but it was written the way it should be read from one sequence to another one', — about that I do have a difficulty to see what the evidence for it can possibly be. I am perhaps willing to believe a BBC announcement that 'they' have discovered a new — i.e. hitherto unrecognised — gene for having cystic fibrosis. Also that the first cell not merely contains all the chromosomes, but all the genes that may be used in the ultimate make-up of the developing human body — this too is intelligible. But that the first cell writes the programme as well as having a programme — this is very difficult to understand. It sounds as if the first cell were a self-constructing computer which — since after all it does not exist after splitting — has — or *has* it not? — turned its progeny cells into lesser computers ready with their programmes and also — perhaps — computer builders in their turn. The discovery that there is a difference between the

DNA carried by the sperm and that carried by the ovum, so that at the time when the two sets of chromosomes are put together, they 'are not as we believed for years identical', because of the phenomenon of methylation: this discovery indeed seems to help account for the uniqueness of the individual human, because the possibilities are so greatly multiplied. And perhaps it also helps to explain the multiple differentiating of cells: the 'underlining system' — i.e. the system of methylation (bits of methyl, CH_3, hooking onto bits of the DNA) which he compares to underlining now this word now that word in a text — 'is progressively changed' so that cells do differentiate, they become specialised 'doing a nail, doing hair, doing skin, doing neurons', doing everything. He must mean making or constituting. One wonders whether some of those things are different according to sex — do I have neurons in some way different from those of any male? The reason for suggesting this is that the methylation was not just a means of suppressing things or bringing them out, but that the difference of methylation — what *gets* methylated — seems to be a matter of contrast between male and female bits of DNA which had previously been supposed to be identical.

I can however now express my difficulty in believing all that Lejeune says. 'I would say', he says, 'that obviously there must be something written in the egg, telling the egg: you split in two; then one of the cells: 'split in two, then you can discuss together all three to know what to do, the three cells together ...'. Individualisation is at the three-cell stage' (p. 52). My understanding falters. He had already said that when there's been one split of the zygote into two cells, and then one split of just one of these into three cells, it's probably at that time that a message goes from one cell to the other cells, comes back to the first one and they suddenly realise: 'We are not a population of cells, we are bound to be an individual!' That is: Individualisation, which makes the difference between a population of cells which is just a tissue culture and an individual which will build himself according to his own rule, is demonstrated at the three-cell stage, that is to say, very soon after fertilisation has occurred.

One wonders why the two cells could not give one another this same message. It seems to have to do, in Lejeune's mind, with the fact that you can get a mouse chimera with two or with three strains of mouse, but three is the limit.

Someone who speaks like this is certainly aware of a problem: How is a set of cells *an* individual? When an amoeba splits into two, the two are not an individual. (Nor are they 'a tissue culture'.) It doesn't seem clear, however, whether the two cells which result from the first splitting of the zygote are *not* at first *an* individual: only their descendant pair of cells plus the one that doesn't split so soon form an individual. This accords ill with the zygote's being itself body and soul, matter and spirit, genetic information and molecular structure, all of which meant that it was, not just the beginning of the new marvel that we call a human, but actually a *homo*, an *anthropos*, a *Mensch*, a man.

I realise that I am discussing Lejeune's evidence in Tennessee from a position of great ignorance of things he knows. Nevertheless, are not the remarks about the 'individual' and the mutual communication at the three cell stage extremely obscure, so that one may be justified in being doubtful about their meaning? Is it foolish to wonder about this, because after all, he was somehow getting through to the court with these exciting-sounding suggestions? — as well as with the extremely interesting information about the real genetic discoveries of the two preceding years. It is evident that he established a *rapport* with the court, i.e. with the judge, and it is likely that he could not have done so if he had expressed it all in the language of genetic discovery by experiments with cells, together with the theoretical knowledge against the background of which the geneticists made the discoveries.

However, my instinct for there being a real problem about the unity of a multicellular organism, an organism moreover which in its developed form consists of many kinds of multi-cellular parts, causes me to think that Lejeune is really speaking to this matter, though I do not understand what he says.

The unity in question is not only that of something composed of many disparate parts, but also that of something identical with an original object. Here something comparatively large and much developed is one and the same living thing with the zygote. Or, if there should be twins, they are two living things and jointly the same with the zygote.

Where we have just a unity of some living thing composed of many disparate parts, there arises the question: how are these different things, which are also various in kind — how are they *one* thing? When we have a unity of a non-living thing like a bicycle, we can answer the parallel question by speaking of the pattern of the thing and the purpose for which it has been put together. But it is not a whole single substance; it is rather an *ens per accidens*. However we continue to identify it as the same bicycle as the original one it began by being, even though various parts of it have been replaced: that is our convention, and we do not pretend that there is any physical identity between this new bit of a pedal and the old bit.

With living things it is otherwise. This was the bone that suffered a crack fracture thirty years ago; this is the foot that I scalded when I was twelve years old. Sometimes people are stupid about this sort of thing and will say solemnly that one has not the same body as one had eight years ago for example, since all its material particles are different from the ones that composed it then. Now that they are making a mistake is not just a matter of a sheddable convention, like the way we would identify the pair of stockings now all wool, which is what an original pair made of silk have become through darning with wool. Here if someone said 'The stockings are not really the same stockings, being made all of different material now', we would sigh and say, 'You are merely shewing what *you* would count as being the same stockings'. But if someone says a parallel thing about a living body, he does not deserve a similar comment: he is not shewing what he would count as the same living body; for what he would call that would not be a living body at all. The identity conventionally acknowledged is not even like that of the bicycle with a new pedal and a new saddle, though so long as we are dealing with a grown-up who has remained much the same in shape and bulk we may be inclined to think what we did say about the bicycle: the *pattern* persists. However, the ways in which a pattern actually does persist in the two cases (the bicycle and the living thing) are not alike. For in the case of a living body it persists through quite gross changes in shape and bulk, even in adult life; and the pattern that we would really have in mind if we said that a living body was an example of a flow of matter through a persistent pattern would be a pattern whose very figure and bulk changed a great deal from tiny babyhood to full grown life: a preborn or newborn terrier is not the same shape, except in a rough sense, as its parents, and similarly of human babies, as you may see if you consider a human conceptus whose gestational age is 10–12 weeks.

Now, speaking more correctly, a living body has a soul, and the soul is the principle of unity of the body. Here I am not speaking quite as modern people usually do; for they would certainly have misunderstood me if I told them that plants have souls. They would think I meant something very sentimental, which I do not. What I mean here hangs together with the fact that the identity of a living body is not normally also the identity of the material particles of which it is composed. It may be quite or nearly that if the living body is a frozen embryo consisting of sixteen cells. But normally the living body metabolises and the material particles are therefore replaceable by other like ones. The pattern of the living thing, in a very ordinary sense of 'pattern', is not going to be the same from first to last; in the case of mammalian reproduction it begins as the pattern possessed by a single cell, and pretty rapidly develops into a multiplicity of cells, some of which will themselves have as their descendant cells cells which actually form the body of the animal, crudely recognisable as such (experts could identify the species long before such crude recognisability has come into being) — and some of which will have as *their* descendant cells cells which form, e.g., the placenta, the conceptus' organ of nutrition and respiration.

Now I can understand Lejeune's saying that at the three-cell stage of a human conceptus, there is a message between them: 'We are an individual'. As I've already said, I do not understand why he should not have said that about the two cell stage — but given that either there is some relevant reason for this, or one need take no notice of it in this context, I would say that the idea of these cells giving and receiving the message 'We are an individual' is Lejeune's acknowledgement that there is a question here: how is a set of cells *an* individual living thing? Well, they marvellously work together in multiplying and becoming differentiated, so as to be the matter of a living thing which is nourished and grows. That they do this essentially by dividing and so multiplying, means that they are governed by a principle of unity as constituting a developing living thing, and this I call a soul. This soul's operations seem offhand only to consist in nutrition and growth by multiplication by division; but Lejeune tells us that it is by a super-programme which was in the first cell. It may be that one can take this account as an account of how the soul — the principle of unity — does operate; I do not understand enough about the first cell as having this staggering programme to know whether one can.

Now for the question whether it is right to say that the zygote and its more immediate descendants as they come to replace it *is* a human being. The argument for this I think, the *serious* argument, is that the whole programme for the coming to be of a human being out of this one cell is there; indeed it is a programme in each case for a quite particular and unique human development. I am not inclined to deny this, though not understanding it fully enough to positively embrace it except as very likely true. Nevertheless I am doubtful about the proposition that this programmed cell *is* itself already a human being. People rest their whole condemnation of procured abortion on the thesis that it is one; so much so, that it sounds as if, were they proved wrong, there would seem to be no room for the condemnation of such abortion. But there is a consideration which seems to operate against the thesis that here you already have a human being, and that is, that this product of conception may become two or more monozygotic twins, triplets etc. The only ways of countering this are to say (with Lejeune) that in these rare cases the doubleness (say) is already there; or to say that an identical twin grows like a sprout out of the original human being that the conceptus was; or that one human being does in this rare case split into two or more human beings like an amoeba which reproduces by splitting into two. This would mean of course that the human being who splits into two at such a splitting, ceases to exist except in his 'descendents', as I would call the cells resulting from cell division 'descendent' cells. Now these positions are held, by the enemies of the Christian attitude to the human conceptus, to involve a contradiction of a logical thesis about identity. Namely, the transitivity of identity: if one thing, call it A, becomes two, call them B and C, then neither B nor C can be identical with A because if they were, they would have to be identical with one another. This is an error on the part of the enemies; if the conceptus is in some unexplained way already double, then there always were B and C, which never were each identical with A, which is itself not a human being. (This would have to be Lejeune's thesis). Or — the sprout theory — B, say, is the original A and C is a new development on B, and never was identical with A. Or — the one human splitting into two — A ceases to exist when he splits, and B and C never were identical with A, so their non-identity with one another would not mean a failure of the transitivity of identity. By all those accounts you would indeed be destroying at least one human being in destroying the conceptus, and by Lejeune's view, two or more. So the objection that you are killing a human being would remain and could be held onto as *the* clear objection to procuring an abortion.

There *is* an objection to maintaining this position, namely that it concedes to someone who believes none of those things, that if *his* opinion is right, the only absolute objection to procuring an abortion in the very early stage of a pregnancy is defeated. Against such a defeat we should notice that the Catholic Christian Church has always objected to procuring abortion, but to this day has not adopted the doctrine of 'immediate animation'. The 'animation' in question is of course the animation with the rational human soul — for, that the living zygote is *alive* no one can rationally doubt. St. Thomas Aquinas thought that the normal product of conception was alive with the vegetative life whose operations are nutrition and growth; that when it had sensation and locomotion it was alive with animal life without being yet alive with the *specific* life of, say, a horse or a human being. But also that the creation of the human soul was special and not a matter of development like the little animal's becoming a horse. That something can be alive with purely animal life without yet being alive with a specific form of animal life is a remarkable doctrine, to be found in the last article of the *Prima Pars* of the *Summa Theologiae*, and also in Aristotle's *Generation of Animals* 736b.

While saluting the recognition of indeterminacy which we find in Aristotle's and Aquinas's account, I would be inclined to doubt whether any conceptus, human or equine, can attain sensation and locomotion without being manifestly of the human or equine form. To be able to swim, for example, it must have a lot of organs and parts; still more must this be so for it to have sensation. At such a stage, of course, it definitely has the appearance of a human, or I take it, a horse. The most one might concede is that inchoate sensation can be called animal life in what does *not* have the appearance of such-and-such a kind of animal except to the expert embryologist.

As I have said, if you have a living thing and it is actually alive, it has a soul — that is, a principle of unity making a single being out of a set of parts. It is this in fact that I take to be expressed by Lejeune's poetic imagination of the message 'We are an individual' or 'We are bound to be an individual', going between the three cells into which the first two cells have split. The soul of the living individual, being its principle of unity, governs the development of the descendant cells; for the unity remains unless there is twinning, when there are two unities.

The operations of the living thing are *of* it in respect of its having this unity. It is here that the teleology I am concerned with comes in.

First, however, some more general observations. In modern times we are disposed to think that if there are final causes, if there is a goal-governed action, this is to be found only in living things and not also in what is inanimate. This indicates a loss of the thesis that *every agent acts for an end* — a thesis that met with strong and contemptuous rejection in the seventeenth century. That theoretical rejection has characterised modern natural sciences. An at least ceremonial expression of it seems to be required etiquette.

That thesis, that every agent acts for an end, does however apply to the action of all substances. It has been argued for by Stephen Makin[1] in the following way: something, G-ing, is the action of a natural agent of kind A — of an acid, for example — only if (i) *either* an A always has a tendency to G and it always does G if it is in a situation to do so, *or* (ii) it does have a tendency to G when it is in the situation to G, though it may still not G. Makin calls a tendency of the first sort a characterising tendency; substances are 'characterised', and therefore identifiable, by *such*

---

[1] 'Aquinas, Natural Tendencies and Natural Kinds', *The New Scholasticism* 63 (1989): 253–274.

tendencies. A substance does not have to act according to its tendencies; an acid may be shut up in a bottle, for example. Its 'being in a situation to G' is being in a situation such that nothing prevents or interferes with its G-ing.

Thus we have an account of 'Every agent acts for an end' which fits in with the argument of Aquinas that if there isn't something determinate that an agent does, it will not do one thing rather than another. Or again, that what is indifferent between just any outcomes does not *produce* one rather than another.

If you want to know what the goal of an inanimate agent is, you have to find out a characterising tendency i.e. one which will be in operation if nothing interferes with it. The way it is in operation may not be a way in which it will always proceed if not prevented. This is because there can be various ways in which it *exercises* its characteristic tendency: Makin gives as an example that a chemical might characteristically react with another one so as to remove one carbon atom; given the chance, therefore, it will do this. But there may be different ways in which it may do this, according to whether it removes this or that carbon atom: chemical analysis will shew the composition of the chemical resulting from the action, which will differ according to which part (so to speak) of the molecule has been deprived of one carbon atom.

I have sketchily mentioned this work because it gives a good clear sense to the notion of action being for an end when it is, for example, chemical action. We may say: when there is not an end in this sense, then there is not a chemical action.

When we come to living things, there is no reason to modify this account until we are considering the actions of free agents. A zygote is not a free agent; given that it is in a situation to grow into a many celled creature, it will do so. That is, if nothing prevents that, it will do so. That in the crudest terms is its life and is the life of the multiple cells which descend from it. Of course there is more to it than that: cell differentiation is crucial, otherwise the multiplication might be like that of cells in a cancer.

Now so long as the developments manifest the kind of life that is being lived by the embryo, we can say that they manifest government by that principle of unity which is the soul of the embryo. At the earliest stage this is a life of growth and nutrition, which includes that differentiation which is going to provide continued nutrition for increasing growth. But when the cell differentiation, as Lejeune puts it, does nails, does skin, does everything, we are teased by an absurd-sounding question: how do the differentiated cells know where to go in the body that is being developed? It sounds absurd only because only a fancy, a poetical fancy perhaps, would represent cells as knowing where to go. They are programmed to go to the right places, you might say. But can this signify the government by the principle of unity which we have postulated?

I would say 'No'. What is governing here is the principle of unity of a new and coming life, the animal life of movement and sensation which is not yet there. But one cannot doubt that what is done — the action of the living embryo in its early stages — is done for the development of that animal life — the production of the beating heart, of the inchoate sense organs, of the limbs and of the brain; the existence of almost all of which is necessary if there is to be the life of an animal. I say 'almost all' because the limbs are an exception. Heart, brain (perhaps only a little of it) and sense organs there must be. But it is possible to be born without limbs.

If what is governing these developments is the principle of unity of a life that is to come, then this principle is a final cause of what is happening. It is not, like the principle of unity in the life of nutrition and growth, the formal cause. The formal cause is the principle that sustains the life as it is going on. That what is going on is in action for such-and-such ends, the skin cells to form the skin, the brain cells to form the brain of an animal — this is manifest in their doing so. But the life which will be manifested in movement and sense when all those things are developed is not yet there. You get to know what something is by getting to know what it is for, but what it is for only appears when it does what it is for. Eyes are for seeing; the beginning of eyes is not accompanied by a beginning of sight. The heart is for pumping blood — is it pumping blood right at the beginning? I don't know, but an embryologist would know. All that I know is that they can tell that something is the beginning of a beating heart, and that calling it that is speaking of what it is for. That is, what it characteristically does in the life of the whole organism of which it is going to be the heart.

Here we can see the difference that does exist between biological concepts and concepts of inanimate things. In the latter we do not find it lying on the surface that what something does, its action, actually belongs to the concept, as we do with concepts such as skin, brain, eye, heart, liver, stomach. Deeper, however, it turns out that, rightly understood, something like that is true of inanimate kinds of stuff and of inanimate lumps of stuff. This will be so also when a lump of stuff cannot be called a substance. I am here not thinking especially of such things as bicycles, but for example of lumps of granite, for granite is not a natural kind of substance but a mixture of some kind of rock and mica, the bits of which you see reflecting light (like bits of tinsel) in a lump of granite.

Returning to my main theme: we are rightly impressed, i.e., rightly *much* impressed, by what the geneticists have discovered. All those chromosomes and genes which determine a lot of the characteristics of a human being — do they not, in the zygote, actually make it *be* a human being? In reply to this, I would beg to distinguish between what plays a part in determining the characteristics of an object, and what constitutes that very object itself, so that when these determinants are there, the object itself must be. Here is the object in question: a human being. I would suggest that those chromosomes and genes provide a marvellous example of the *proximate matter* of a human being.

6*

Knowledge and Reverence for Human Life

This title set me thinking about two different types of knowledge. The one, knowledge of the dignity of human nature, not knowledge of indifferent truth, and most likely an example of knowledge by connaturality. The other, all that is more often called knowledge: mathematics and the natural sciences, logic and psychology, history and the things that have happened within people's personal memories, and so on. Such knowledge one might call knowledge of indifferent truth. It is a prominent feature of philosophy (at least in the English speaking schools) since the time of Hume, to claim that *all* truth is 'indifferent'. 'Reason is and ought to be the slave of passions': there is no such thing as a way reason dictates you should act, except that it can inform you of the ways there are of attaining your ends. But reason cannot give you ends or judge for or against ends. This idea has proved so influential that the notion of non-indifferent truth seems obscure. So also may the idea of connaturality as I have introduced it.

* Lecture given at a Symposium on Human Life in March 1981 at Marquette University, Milwaukee, and subsequently published in R. Hittinger (ed) *Linking the Human Life Issues*. Chicago: Regnery Books, 1986: 170–8. Reprinted by permission of Professor Russell Hittinger.

I did not explain it, and will try to do so now. As I was using the word, it is a character of knowledge. Connatural knowledge is the sort of knowledge someone has who has a certain virtue: it is a capacity to recognise what action will accord with and what ones will be contrary to the virtue. The person who has no meanness in him, but rather generosity, is liable to avoid or reject some course of action, without difficulty perceiving it to be ungenerous. Or it simply won't occur to him as a possibility, and if someone else suggests it he rejects it, brushes it aside, does not deliberate within himself whether to follow that course of action. A clever person might also know that the suggested action was mean, though he lacks generosity himself; he knows it out of a certain sharpness of intelligence. The one with connatural knowledge is inclined against the action and that inclination itself is a sort of peception of the meanness of acting even without the judgments being formulated. (One might compare this to the revulsion which is sometimes part of the perception of something as disgusting, as, for example, if someone were to spit into one's glass.) If the judgment does get formulated, the formulation is an expression of what was already expressed in the rejection.

The word 'connatural' of course has to do with 'nature'. So far as I have been able to notice in St. Thomas, digging around with a lexicon, its principal use in him is to talk of what is readily known by beings of a certain nature. Material substances are connatural objects of knowledge to us, for example. I take it that this is because we are ourselves material beings, embodied intelligences. When Plato says that the soul is 'akin to the forms' he is giving expression to the same idea. I haven't been able to find St. Thomas giving the term the application I have been describing. Indeed, I don't know the source of that application. But it is not difficult to justify; for the virtue of a virtuous person is like a second nature.

Connatural knowledge is thus not necessarily associated with a moral virtue, if human knowledge of natural material kinds is an example of it. Nor is the sort of connatural knowledge which is connatural to one person or class of people and not to another. It is often said for example, 'I know what it is like to ...'. I know what it is like to find one's topic running into the sand, or running away with one in an unintended direction like a badly trained horse. There's reference to *such* connatural knowledge in the exhortation: Deprive not the stranger, for you have been a stranger and you know the heart of a stranger.

Altogether, connatural knowledge is a deeply interesting subject. It contrasts with the other sort of knowledge — what is usually called knowledge — partly in this: it is not something of which there is an accumulating store in the libraries, archives, records, such that with a suitable retrieval system you can go and look any bit of it up. There *are* books that have a lot of it in them, or the fruits of it; but on the whole it is an essentially personal thing, and only if you have it or almost have it — have it in very strong potentiality — will you recognise it in such books.

I wish it were undistractedly my topic, because the connatural knowledge of the dignity of human nature is the most important sort of knowledge of it. However, I have mentioned it as *one* side of the division I made. On the other is what is more familiarly called knowledge. 'Knowledge!' I once heard a woman exclaim in a shop in England, 'I've got all the knowledge I need for the rest of my life'. Her tone of scorn was delightful — she wasn't despising people who want to know things; but she was not to be cajoled with talk of that sacred cow. She was speaking of knowledge in regions where we can speak of pieces of knowledge, or whole subject matters; things one can look up, conduct research into, ask the experts about, found chairs of in universities.

One way in which the contrast between the two kinds may strike one is this: one may think that the second kind — like wealth, health, living under an unoppressive and unmurderous government, having children, and so on — is among the 'goods of fortune'. I take the phrase from Aristotle, who remarks that most people pursue the goods of fortune and pray for them, but that we *ought* to seek what is good for us, and pray that the goods of fortune will be good for us.[1] And again, in the *Eudemian Ethics* he says that the goods of fortune are worth nothing except so far as they help us to worship and contemplate God.[2]

It is at first sight a reasonable thing to say that knowledge is among the goods of fortune. But further reflection gives us pause. If knowledge is so, what is not? One has the luck to have some knowledge of this or that. But may we not even say that heavenly grace itself is one of the goods of fortune, then? There seems to be something wrong with that — divine grace is not distributed by the lottery of chance events. Nor are the virtues and vices of mankind. And indeed certain sorts of knowledge strike one as being like virtues, or even some of them as being virtue: the knowledge that a human being is of more worth than many sparrows, for example. And the knowledge that it is wickedness to do what the Nestlé Company is reported as doing — to persuade poor African women to feed babies their powdered milk instead of suckling them; to value making money far above respecting the lives of human infants.

It is indeed just this sort of knowledge that I've been calling connatural. Connatural, that is, to the just: it belongs with a just way of looking at things; and *it* can't be called a good of fortune. The spirit of such knowledge is what is called a gift of the Holy Ghost; the light of it a light that is there to enlighten everyone who comes into the world. I do not mean that everyone actually has this light on in his mind, for it may have been extinguished or never allowed to come on. It may be there as a mere glimmer, whose sign is the understanding of human language with all its multifarious action and motive descriptions, its machinery for accusing others and excusing oneself.

---

[1]   *Nicomachean Ethics* Book V. 1, 1129b4–7
[2]   *Eudemian Ethics* Book VIII. 3, 1249b16–23

Now there is ground indeed for contrasting the two kinds of knowledge. But it is not that the second kind — what you get from experts, look up in works of reference, ask witnesses of events about — is a good of fortune, and the other kind is not. What is a good of fortune is the *availability* of the second kind, the kind I was calling knowledge of indifferent truth. That only has to be said to be crystal clear. You live in a place where there is a good public library. You know someone who knows something about electricity. Obviously, a good of fortune.

If knowledge, of the sort to be got from experts, well informed sources, etc., is readily available and also is needed to judge correctly and to act well, then the lack of such knowledge on the part of some adult who has to judge and to act is *not* a bit of bad luck, or at least it mostly is not. You would have to construct a case of an unforeseen and not-to-be expected emergency, in which action is necessary and there isn't time to get the knowledge, to make the lack of it out as a case of mere bad luck. The virtuous person will get the knowledge that he needs and which is available to him.

We said that the man who has a virtue — say that of justice — has a connatural knowledge of the worth of a human being, of the dignity of human nature. We may wonder just what that amounts to and what it means to say this. He must act somehow, and abstain from actions too. What actions? He will need, often, information, knowledge of the second kind, in order to know what actions to do and abstain from, not only a connatural 'pro' or 'anti' reaction. That is to say, if he has justice he must also have prudence, practical wisdom, in order to know what *is* just in the particular case, and the prudence will often have to call upon specialist information. That is why people who are up to no good can diddle you in unfamiliar context with specialist *mis*information.

Having practical wisdom thus has two sides to it, the side that connects up with information about what has happened, with scientific information, with knowledge of procedures and so on, and the side that connects up with good inclination, the inclination towards good ends. Without the inclination of a good will the practical purpose of knowing what is just in the particular case will not be there. But the inclination itself will not be there without the virtue, for it is virtue that gives the good inclination. So it seems we have a circle: to have justice our man must have prudence, to have prudence he must have good inclination, to have good inclination he must have justice.

How then does he ever begin? The circle I have described is to be found in Aristotle's ethics; and the answer indicated by Aristotle is this: our man has had a good upbringing and is first trained to do things which in a virtuous person would be acts of this or that virtue — in this case, justice. Getting into the way of doing them makes him *inclined* to do them *qua* just. This is already inchoate virtue and makes him have good inclinations, i.e. inclinations to the ends that a just man has. These then enable him to have the practical purpose of bringing them about. His judgment on the question how will be arrived at with the aid of knowledge of the way things work, the actual situation, and so on, and will be practical wisdom in action. With this the virtue assumes its full-fledged character.

But now we have noticed, or ought to have, that the knowledge of the sort I called 'indifferent' will in fact *not* be indifferent when it has this sort of role in action. I am suggesting that *non*-indifferent knowledge arises from experience of life, of suffering, and above all of moral practice. The knowledge itself, if highly theoretical, is not likely to be anything but rough and crude. Still, there is room for the highly discerning clever villain who is quite sharp in some particular cases; and I am not sure what to say about him.

The sort of knowledge which must be used in calculating what to do certainly includes a great deal which is not included in what I have called 'non-indifferent' knowledge, a great deal which does not *arise* from moral practice and resulting good inclinations, as does the knowledge of human dignity. The recognition that someone is hungry or cold is the merest observation. Someone not interested in helping someone hungry or cold will probably not *make* the observation (though he may do so if he is our clever character, with the habit of observation). Again, there is the phenomenon which the moral theologians oddly called 'affected ignorance' — at least it sounds odd in English. We might rather call it 'politic ignorance'; one does not want to know the things which would mean that one had to reconsider one's investments, say.

More strikingly, people often do not want to know things that are readily available to be known if those things put their own opinions in a bad light. For example, that what is inside a pregnant woman (at least after the first two or three weeks) is undoubtedly a small human being (or more than one). Look at the odd arguments that have been purveyed on this subject. Is a fetus a human being? It's probably not said now, but a dozen years ago you might hear it confidently said that what's there is a jellied lump, an excrescence on part of the mother's body, which she can have removed as readily as a wart. That used to be said. Again, Bronowski published a picture of an infant nearing birth, in one of those big picture books he put his name to, which infant, looking more like an early fetus, must have surprised anyone bright enough to notice. (His interests were to do with evolution.) Favourers of abortion do not want to know what a fetus looks like, that it is active and complete from very early on. It forces itself on nurses' attention that they are helping to destroy for one woman what they are earnestly trying to save for another; but pro-abortionists do not want to know. They invent reasons, which sound like ones belonging to a very special religious position, why someone objects to abortion. 'It is, I suppose', a Polish *aparatczyk* said to me (at a discussion organized by the Polish and British Academies) 'because you think there is a soul that you speak with hostility of abortion.' I replied that the question whether what was inside a pregnant woman was a small human being was the same sort of question as whether what was inside a pregnant mare was a little horse, or what was inside a pregnant cat was a little kitten. Only at the very earliest stage would there (normally) be any dispute about these two cases; there should not be more about the human one. My interlocutor had nothing to say to this; he was obviously taken aback.

There is a sense of non-indifferent truth, which anyone will concede; truth is non-indifferent if it helps or frustrates your purpose to acknowledge it. Here virtue should promote an acknowledgement of the truth, if there is practical wisdom; for a convenient-looking falsehood is likely to do much disservice in the long run and a wise person will know that. Even if the convenient-looking falsehood does not rebound on you in the particular case, the habit of relying on falsehoods certainly will. As habits are created by practices, the wise one will therefore not want to engage in this practice at all. This is a calculation not dependent on his love of truth in itself, or on his unwillingness to offend God by lies.

No truth, then, is indifferent if it affects what is to be done. People who are hell-bent on evil purposes have therefore the strongest inclination of hostility or indifference to the truths, acknowledgement of which would threaten their proceedings. But there is *still* nevertheless the distinction that I started out with, the distinction between knowledge that is got by consulting the well-informed, making observations, checking information, learning history or natural science or mathematics or logic; and the knowledge, which is what I called connatural to a virtuous person: the knowledge, for example, of the dignity of human nature which comes out in the behaviour of one who has it even if he has never formulated it. That knowledge is not unavailable to us who are not virtuous but may be restrained by shame from misusing people we have the power to misuse. But it is strong only in good people.

7

The Dignity of the Human Being

We live in a society — or in societies — where there is an obligatory passion for equality. The prestige of democracy is connected with this.

Marxists, and many other people, regard 'inequality' as a word of reproach against any system. With Marxists, indeed, I have noticed that the various natural inequalities among human beings are not called 'inequalities' but 'differences'. For Marxists, then, an inequality is a 'difference' which is objectionable. To call it an inequality is to imply that it ought to be eliminated.

There *is* a truth of which all this is a distorted reflection. There is just one impregnable equality of all human beings. It lies in the value and dignity of being a human being.

When I call this equality impregnable, I do not mean that it is inviolable. That is, I do not mean that it cannot be violated. It can. Alas, it often *has* been violated, often now *is* violated. It was violated in chattel slavery where the slave had no rights — not even the right to a marriage where husband and wife cannot be sold apart or their small children sold away from them. It is violated every time people are killed for others' convenience as the Nazis killed mental defectives; or as in warfare civilian populations are bombed, or when anyone murders his fellow human, not in anger as deserving death, but for advantage to himself. So too it is

* From undated manuscript. English original of lecture given in German.

violated when an obviously human foetus is deliberately killed in abortion. It is violated by someone who puts his dead or dying mother out into a rubbish bin. I might add to the list but need not.

What do I mean, then, by saying that the value and dignity of a human being is impregnable? I mean that it cannot be taken away.

If there are equal voting rights in a set of people, they may be taken away from part of the set. Then that is an equality you no longer have if you are one of the deprived part. It is not as if you still had that equality, those voting rights, but are prevented from exercising them. No, I am imagining a change in which those rights are taken away from you.

The equality of human beings in the worth and dignity of being human is one that can't be taken away, no matter how much it is violated. Violations remain *violations*.

When I call this an impregnable equality, someone may be tempted to deride me. For are not all cats equal in being cats? Have I said more than that humans are equal in being humans? I have said more, or implied more. There is a special worth and dignity in being a human. The following will bring this out. I implied that angry vengeful killing may not be *eo ipso* a violation of human dignity. This is not meant to suggest that it is an OK sort of thing to do. But here the killer may have an answer to the question: '*For what* did that person have to die?' — an answer which says 'He deserved it'.

To regard someone as deserving death is very definitely regarding him, not just as a human being but as endued with a dignity belonging to human beings, as having free will and as answerable for his actions. I am not defending the murderer I am imagining; he has not the right to kill his victim. But I am *contrasting* him with the murderer who is willing to kill someone for gain or other advantage, to kill as getting rid of this human being suits his plans. *He* is not respecting in his victim the dignity of a human being at all. Similarly with 'active euthanasia' which is non-voluntary on the part of the victim. He is to be killed because of the 'disvalue' of his life; his living is of negative value and so things are better with him dead.

Capital punishment, though you may have reason against it, does not, just as such, sin against the human dignity of one who suffers it. He is at least supposed to be answering for crime of which he has been found guilty by due process.

When capital punishment takes grisly forms, as it often has in various places — like the English hanging, drawing and quartering for high treason, like the French *peine forte et dure*, like the American electric chair or gas chamber, like the Chinese 'death of a thousand cuts', like impalement or burning over a slow fire — then it takes on a character which means that the victim's human dignity is being violated. The ancient Hebrew Law, the Torah, shews us why in an expression restricting punishments: a man was not to be given more than forty stripes 'lest thy brother become vile in thy sight'.*

This warning is connected with other punishments than execution; but it applies to execution too. Sometimes, we learn, an executioner in the past would ask the victim for forgiveness and sometimes the executed would give the executioner something for his pains and freely forgive him. A method of execution which would rule out the possibility of such a request as grotesque because it makes a vile spectacle of the executed, is surely a sin against human dignity. The Athenian cup of hemlock seems the furthest from 'making your brother vile in your sight'. A man might deserve much worse, but inflicting much worse upon him means making him a vile spectacle, as the Romans did those they crucified. It is doing that, even if you cover the spectacle up, as in America they cover the face of the victim in the electric chair with a mask because it becomes horrible to see. The

* Deuteronomy 25: 3

spectacle may be hidden from the physical eye, but so it is emphasised for the eye of the mind.

All my considerations have by implication emphasised the bodily life of man. This is not because disregard of human dignity is always directly connected with attacks on that bodily life. If a state makes it illegal to teach some class of men to read, that is also an assault on human dignity. One can think of others which are similarly directed against mental and spiritual enlargement. Nevertheless in our day — and perhaps in any day — the primary target of assaults on the value and dignity of human nature is man's bodily life. This we see in abortion, in euthanasia, in operations to turn a male or female human being into a pretended member of the opposite sex, in experiments with human embryos. With the latter we approach a sort of attack on the kind of being a human is by playing with developmental possibilities and unnatural modes of reproduction: artificial insemination, in vitro fertilisation, combination of human with non-human gametes; in short, interfering with the human generative powers and elements in such a way as to damage, abuse them *and* the character of human generation itself. This last occurs in *two* ways: one is contraception, whereby what is the generative kind of act is prevented from being so by deliberately rendering it infertile in case it would otherwise have been fertile; the other is by some technical generating or trying to generate human beings otherwise than by procreation. Procreation by the male in the female is intrinsic to the mode of a new human life's coming about by human operation. Why? It is because what the operation is bringing about *is* human life. Fatherhood — which means procreation — and motherhood — which means conception — are a very important part of the human relationships constituting the life of man. Making human zygotes in a dish or test-tube is an enormity because the operator is a manufacturer — even if he uses his own semen — not a father. Remember that we are intellectual animals, whose vegetative and animal life is part of a life framed by our intellectuality: we are nourished, for example, not like plants but like other animals, but our eating is conducted in a specially human way, reason entering into the getting and preparation of food and into the conduct of meals. Similarly our sexual activity and reproduction is all tied up with our intellect, our not merely animal emotions and our aesthetic feelings. Reason and love enter into most, and certainly into all characteristically human exercise of this vital function. Hence marriage and the celebration of and awe before procreation and pregnancy. The child who is conceived by a mother, and who has a father, is not unequal to them. I think people have hardly considered what will be the status of babies who have not even grown inside a woman and been born. Suppose the experimenters succeed with artificial placentas which they are trying to make; suppose they produce children who reach the stage of separation from the placenta. It will take legislation for those children not to be mere scientific property. How far further will our consciences be calloused by that time if it comes in ten or twenty five years?

This helps a bit to make one see that as we respect human dignity by respecting human life, so we violate human dignity by not respecting human sexuality. This means respecting human sexual intercourse as being the means by which human life is propagated into new individuals, not because no other means are imaginable; as we know, they are not merely imaginable but actual; but because procreation is the means belonging to our life as life of the kind we are. That is a very basic aspect of human life, remaining when reproductive sexuality is indulged, without its proper surrounding in marriage. 'Human life' means the human course of life, not just a human's being alive.

We have free will; it is therefore open to us to use our powers wrongly, and it has become open to us to succeed in abusing them essentially. And it is a great temptation to us, the more we can, to arrange to have our pleasures, and have or not have offspring, according to our desires — with recourse to the ingenious technology of our race and time.

If we do this, if we don't stick to human procreation of human beings, we generate further contempt for beginning human life and further alienation from belief in the dignity and value of human-ness. This is clear if we contemplate the experimenter who begged for human ova from gynaecological clinics and fertilised them with his own semen. It will also be clear if you consider how developments make the following possible: human foetuses have a certain commercial value. So a woman of today may find a possibility of becoming pregnant, letting the baby grow to twenty eight weeks (because bigger ones are worth more) and then going somewhere where they will pay her for a late abortion, which yields the foetus for resale, say, as valuable material. If you act so, are you not shewing that you do not regard that human being with any reverence? Few will fail to see that. But the same is true of one who has an abortion so that she can play in a tennis championship; or for any reason for which someone might choose to destroy the life of a new human being.

This lack of reverence, of respect for that dignity of human nature so wonderfully created by God, is lack of regard for the one impregnable equality of all human beings. Lacking it, you cannot revere the dignity of your own human-ness, that is the dignity of that same human nature in yourself. You may value yourself highly as a tennis player or a natural scientist, but without a change of heart you cannot value yourself as being a human, a *Mensch*. For you have shewn the value you set on a human life as such. You are willing to extinguish it as suits you or as suits the people who want you to do so.

Like very many people I have observed something of the celebrations of VE Day, celebrations of the victory of the allies over Nazi Germany. I have been bitterly amused at the solemn pratings about how the human spirit shewed that it *could not* be suppressed; the love of freedom *must* win in the end — but, it was added, we must never forget, because we must be resolved never to let such things happen again. We must remain in the sun of morality triumphant over evil; we must preserve our happy state and be determined to fight against monstrous evils when they threaten. 'Fools!' I thought. 'You talk of being armed in spirit against possible future threats of evil. You seem all unconscious of living in an actually murderous world.' Each nation that has 'liberal' abortion laws has rapidly become, if it was not already, a nation of murderers. There are nearly a million abortions in the United States every year (perhaps more now) and in my own country it is proportionate. I assume that it is about the same in any advanced nation that has embraced abortion.

ACTION AND
PRACTICAL REASON

8

Chisholm on Action

Suppose some phenomenon — e.g. the generation of a salt in muscle fibres, or a pattern of activity in the brain — is associated with voluntary movement. One might make the movement in order to bring the phenomenon about: it is, say, an object of investigation.[1] But it occurs just before the beginning of the movement. Hence it is not itself the effect of the movement; and perhaps the manner of connexion between them convinces us that it belongs in the movement's physical causality.

Chisholm has compared this with the case of a man who wanted to bring about a certain switching in a telephone system.[2] To this end he called Los Angeles, knowing that the connexion with Los Angeles is effected by the desired switching. So, as Chisholm says, he 'caused the telephone to ring in Los Angeles in order to bring about the prior switching in the telephone office in Denver'.[3]

The interest of the comparison lies in contrast no less than in similarity. In both cases one intentionally brings about a cause of an effect by executing an intention of producing that effect. In

* First published in *Grazer Philosophische Studien* [Ernest Sosa (ed) *Essays on the Philosophy of Roderick M Chisholm*] 7/8 (1979): 206–13. Reprinted with the permission of *Grazer Philosophische Studien*.

[1] See G.E.M. Anscombe, *Intention* (Oxford: Blackwell 1957), p. 38.

[2] 'Freedom and Action', in K. Lehrer (ed) *Freedom and Determinism* (New York: Random House 1966), p. 36.

[3] *Ibid,* p. 44.

both cases one is able to do this because of knowing that that effect will have been produced by that cause. *But* in the telephone case one also knows that dialling Los Angeles will work; it will effect the switching. Whereas with the voluntary movement, if we want to align the two cases, it is rather as if 'calling Los Angeles' were an immediate description of something one could do straight off, and not by adopting a method, namely dialling. This is how we'd have to picture 'calling Los Angeles' if we wanted to construe it on the model of a description of the voluntary movement of a limb.

The way people often think about the matter would make the two cases parallel rather by construing the voluntary movement on the model of calling Los Angeles. This involves introducing a cause of those changes in muscles and nerves and brain that produce the movement. If the movement is voluntary, the cause is pictured as an act of intending or something of the kind; a mental event (which a materialist will say is itself a brain event).

Chisholm at first sight appears to follow this line. For he treats *undertaking* to make the movement happen as the analogue of the dialling. He explains undertaking to make an event x happen as: making *something* happen in the endeavour to make x happen. One may not know what this something is, or whether one is succeeding in making x happen — but, he says, one does know that one is undertaking to make x happen.

To see what is persuasive about this, let us recall von Wright's attempt to introduce backwards causation here.[4] He suggested that the movement — raising my arm, say — actually produces the physical events in my brain, nerves and muscles which themselves make the arm go up! For they are explained by what I intentionally do — although they occur prior to my doing it. To this we may object that surely the brain activity and the various chemical changes will take place even if the action is inhibited by

[4]   G.H. von Wright, *Explanation and Understanding* (Ithaca: Cornell University Press 1971), p. 77.

someone's catching my hand. So they must be caused, not by my raising my arm, but by my meaning to do so, or by *something* that I do whether or not I succeed in raising my arm. Chisholm opts for the latter, and calls it 'undertaking'.

Now, however, we shall see the contrast between what may be Chisholm's, and the more conventional view. Chisholm's 'undertaking' is not a prior *event* which causes the changes in the brain, nerves etc. 'Undertaking' to raise my arm, let us remember, was making something happen in the endeavour to make it happen that my arm rises. The 'something' will be those very changes that the conventional view seeks to explain as caused by something else that I do, such as intending or willing to move. In Chisholm's account, the fact that I cause them is just the fact that I 'make them happen in the endeavour to make it happen that my arm goes up'. The making happen seems not to be another event besides them. And how, we ask, do we know that I 'make' them happen? The only possible answer is: by the fact that we *explain* them by their being the relevant physiological events in my endeavour to raise my arm.

In this way Chisholm contrives a specious analogue to the dialling in the telephone case. Just as I knowingly dial, so I knowingly undertake. Since the only events involved are the 'something' that I make happen, we are not confronted with another voluntary movement, mental or physical, itself a distinct event, as the cause of the original one; and the voluntary nature of the original one is preserved.

On the other hand, however pleasing, the analogy seems to be purely verbal. This comes out in doubts we feel about my knowing that I am undertaking to ..., if 'undertaking' is given Chisholm's sense.

Do I know, when I [at least think I] am raising my arm, that I am making something happen in the endeavour to make my arm go up? Let it be a lab experiment in which, like William James' anaesthetic boy, I have no indication that I am raising my arm. I simply do it, or think I am doing it, when they tell me to. If I fail to do it and then they let me look and see this, I am surprised. Must I know that I make something happen? No. Indeed, *must* any candidate exist, for being something that I make happen in this endeavour? The answer to this question too is surely No. And even if something pertinent always does happen, the only reason for saying in Chisholm's way that I make it happen is that it *is* pertinent, i.e. that it had a particular connexion with the fact that I wanted or was trying to raise my arm. The connexion would be this: the events in question are ones of a kind found to go on in successful movement. Here the motion failed to take place, but I thought I was making it, and those events were found to have taken place. *I* do not have to know that there are any such events.

Chisholm's system is an attempt to associate the physiological causes of a voluntary movement with the causality whose concept we use when we explain an action by its intention. On the interpretation that I am giving it here, the account is ingenious in not putting a distinct event of intending or endeavouring or undertaking into a particular slot in a physiological chain of events. Wittgenstein asked 'What is left over if we subtract the fact that my arm goes up from the fact that I raise my arm?' And Chisholm replies: 'What is left over is the fact that I undertook to make my arm go up — the fact that there was something I made happen in the endeavour to make it happen that my arm go up.'[5] Thus the event-type causes are: the relevant events in brain, nerves and muscles. But none of them is my making my arm go up, nor *is* there any event of my making this happen: there is 'agent causality' here, causality by a personal agent, and that isn't event-event causality: no, it simply consists in the fact that I made the events happen in the endeavour.

It is reminiscent of Aquinas's account of creation as a relation to creatures which is real in the creatures but not real in God.

[5]   'The Logic of Intentional Action', in R.Binkley et al (eds) *Agent, Action & Reason* (Toronto: Univ. of Toronto Press 1971), p. 69.

Nothing goes on in 'me', i.e. in the ego, the mind, which stands in the relation of event-event causality to the changes in the muscles, the brain and nerves, and because of which *I* can be said to cause them: no, but all the same those changes have the character of being made to happen by me. Now why should one have the right to say this? And, more particularly: What is left over if we subtract the fact that those events occur from the fact that I make them happen?

We know one thing that motivates Chisholm. [6] Raising my arm is intentional or voluntary. Being so, it must be free. So we cannot be satisfied with an 'event-event' account of the causality; for Chisholm thinks that a cause necessitates its effect, and he is no compatibilist about determinism and freedom. So there must be another kind of causality involved.[7] However, there is some event-event causality too: we know that from physiology. And so Chisholm seizes on this and (presumably) makes some event in that line the immediate bearer of the predicate 'being made by a person to come about'. 'Immediate bearer' is to be understood like this: if *e* is an immediate bearer of that predicate there is no event prior to *e* that also bears it and that is an event-event type of cause of *e*. Here, not entirely digressing, I would like to applaud Chisholm's comment in his footnote on Aune: 'Aune says that "if physiology tells us that a man's actions are caused by physiological changes, it equally tells us that these physiological changes are caused by further physiological changes". But there is a certain ambiguity in the statement that physiology "tell us" this. It may be that certain physiologists have *said* this. But are there any physiologists who have *shown* that it is true, or who *know* that it is

---

[6] See his article in Lehrer's collection, *Freedom and Determinism* and also the chapter 'Agency' in his *Person and Object* (London: G. Allen & Unwin 1976). The motive appears strongest in this work.

[7] In *Person and Object*, p. 70 there is an attempt to describe agent causality *in terms of* event–event causality.

true?'[8] — Chisholm's very charity about Aune's remark is admirable; for of course Aune can't have meant quite what he said: there are external stimuli. When we trace physiological-cum-physical causes back, we mustn't have to stop, having reached a terminus in that line of causality, with a physiological event. Aune would like to exclude, or to say that science excludes, the idea that a person, God-like, initiates a chain of causality. I applaud Chisholm's response for reminding us not to invent knowledge which doesn't exist.

The picture of the physiological events as caused by others, and so on back to a stimulus, does present a very common assumption. To be sure, these events will take place in an immensely complicated mechanism, whose complex processing will account for lack of simple linear explanations. But the assumption itself will have to be modified where no current stimulus is relevant — where, for example, we are thinking of mental activity not at all closely related to the environment. Suppose I sit in my study for a long time thinking about some matter, and at last I jump up and take a book from a shelf. This case might be construed as like what Aune's suggestion sounded like: the physiological events, no doubt brain events, immediately precedent to my getting up will have been caused by others and so on during the hours of my reflection, in which I took no relevant stimulus from outside. And when I did move, if there was any relevant external stimulus, it perhaps occurred twenty years ago when I last read that book, still today in its old place in the book case. Or is the identity of environment, which I know, supposed to be a 'stimulus'? When did this 'stimulus' occur?

Chisholm is right enough to call in question any claims to knowledge of the supposed 'causal chains', either connecting up quickly with a present stimulus or going on for a long time in the internal machinery of the brain.

---

[8]   'The Logic of Intentional Action' in *op.cit.* p. 79.

There are two types of enquiry where we do have a causal chain. I distinguish them as 'back and back' and 'in and in', (where we try to find links *between* established links). It is a mere assumption that where we have a causal chain a back and back enquiry must be fruitful. We may be led a certain distance and then find our object petering out; nothing further belongs to the same process in the way the elements already discovered do. For we ought to recognize that in general we have ever-branching fans, rather than chains, of causality; not just fans as our ancestors fan out, but fans of greatly disparate contributing factors. Nevertheless it can be non-arbitrary to pick a chain out from a branching fan, if we have a unifying concept of a process, whose stages are elements of the chain. Such chains for example could be found in the physiological processes of sight or digestion.

If, given a non-arbitrary chain in connexion with the development of an action, we find it petering out, that is not to say that we have causelessness. We may find significant factors and necessary conditions, but upon the whole the situation may present the appearance of a soup of happenings, which include various kinds of vital process, sensory inputs and transmitted shocks to the system (as when someone runs or walks) — out of which *these* particular preliminaries to a movement arise.

I am not sure that Chisholm has not accepted *too much* of the most conventional philosophic picture at the present day, which leads contemporary philosophers to talk so easily of causal chains. They seem seldom to think of the reality, the ever branching fans. I believe that the talk of these linear chains at least psychologically aids that conception of necessity of the effect, which gives Chisholm *a* starting point. If he rejected this necessity he would perhaps not feel forced to invoke or invent a different kind of causality, the personal initiation of new causal chains. It is not that I want to refuse to believe in any such thing (like Aune). I only question the need for it as a means of escape from determinism.

Solving this problem is however not his only or even his principal concern, and there is no reason to think he would lose interest in his account if it were not needed for this.[9]

Reluctantly, I reject Chisholm's account. But I record a doubt in doing so. It may after all be essentially right. If so, then the flaw which makes me reject it must be reparable. I have already mentioned this flaw in comparing Chisholm's with the more conventional view and pointing out that it is much more unlike the latter than appears at first sight. On the conventional view intending, or perhaps belief-cum-desire, are causes of events in nerves and muscles; and of course one is supposed to know one has these intentions, or these beliefs-cum-desires or whatever is put in here; what goes in here is a distinct item or set of items. Chisholm equally insists that a man knows he is undertaking to make his arm go up. But if undertaking to make his arm go up is *making something happen in the endeavour to make his arm go up,* then when he knows he is undertaking he must know that he is making something happen etc. And it seems clear that one need not know this.

Suppose that this flaw were convincingly repaired. We would still want an account of the connexion between the intentional act, or the intention(s) in the act, and the physiological events preliminary to the initiation of movement: we need a *justification* for saying that the agent makes these happen in the endeavour to … All we have is that they do (pertinently) happen in the endeavour, i.e. when he endeavours to make the movement. To see that our needs are not satisfied, let us remember the question: 'What is left over, if we subtract the fact that these events occur from the fact that I make them happen?' I raised this question but did not answer it on Chisholm's behalf, because I could not see how he could possibly answer it except with the answer: 'Nothing'.

---

[9]   This observation seems more applicable to Chisholm's writings on this subject *before* that chapter 'Agency' of *Person and Object*, than to that chapter.

In *Person and Object* indeed, it looks much more as if he would simply answer that the *undertaking* is left over, and as if the undertaking were supposed to be a distinct event. And *perhaps* he would always have made this reply. Then the 'making happen' is after all an event distinct from the happening of what is made to happen. At one place[10] here he suggests reading 'He undertakes to contribute causally to the occurrence of p', as 'He acts with the intention of bringing about p'. But if we are allowed to ask what the act is, that a man performs with the intention of bringing about p, it appears that there *may* be no answer except 'an act of undertaking or endeavouring'. Is this still to be explained as 'making *something* happen in the endeavour to ...'? How *can* it be, if the act of undertaking can be considered as a distinct event?

Or as anything that combines with, or is an aspect of these happenings *just* when they occur?

To see 'what is left over' we have to look further around. At the fact that what is in question here is the performance of a voluntary act. That is the context of the occurrence of those physiological preliminaries. Without it, they would not be 'made to happen' by the agent.

This is reflected in the fact that Chisholm's 'making --- happen' is a mere extract from 'making --- happen in the endeavour to bring it about that ...'. Thus the question 'Did he, in Chisholm's sense, make --- happen?' cannot be asked independently, i.e. leaving it open whether the context is an 'endeavour' to bring something about. Since Chisholm doesn't mean 'endeavour' to connote either any effort or difficulty, or any longerterm aim, we see that the occurrence of the physiological preliminaries precisely *as* preparation for voluntary movement is what distinguishes their being 'made to happen by an agent' from their otherwise occurrence. So if we subtract the fact that they occur from the fact that the agent makes them happen, what is left over

[10] *Person and Object*, p. 74.

is the voluntary action, the movement to which they are preliminaries — if it happens. And suppose it does not? Well, what
justifies saying that the movement was attempted? — or makes
the subject's profession of this acceptable? *That* will be what is left
over then.

There is one possibility here which I have not considered. I
have supposed that Chisholm's account requires that something
other than the 'undertaking' or 'endeavour' be 'made happen' by
the undertaker. Remember that 'undertaking' and 'endeavour'
are interchangeable; there isn't supposed to be any difference
between them. So 'He undertakes ---' when explained as 'He
makes something happen in the endeavour to ---' is equivalent
to 'He makes something happen in undertaking to ---'. Now in
addition to whatever else (known and unknown to him) the
agent makes happen in an endeavour of his, Chisholm would say
that he *always* makes the undertaking, the endeavour, itself happen. 'If a person undertakes something then he contributes causally to his undertaking something'[11]; and: 'Any instance of "M^t
---,..." implies the corresponding instance of 'M^t (M^t ---,...), ...'
[12]: that is to say, any instance of 'making --- happen in the
endeavour to ...' is an instance of '(making happen that one
makes --- happen in the endeavour to ...) in the endeavour
to ...'. Now it is possible that Chisholm would say: 'There is
always something guaranteed as what the agent (or would be
agent) makes happen in his endeavour to do something, namely
the endeavour itself.' But given the account of 'endeavour' that
would seem to be no answer at all. For it would mean that there is
always something that he makes happen, namely the 'making
something happen in the endeavour to ...'. That is, if the
endeavour is *all* that he makes happen, there isn't at any stage an
answer to 'Namely?' asked about this 'something'. If the *only*

[11] *Ibid.* p. 70.
[12] 'On the logic of intentional action', p. 47.

reply is 'the endeavour' that is equivalent to its having no answer.

If Chisholm would indeed allow 'endeavour' this position in some cases, then his explanations are inadequate. I do not attribute this to him. But some account is needed of the sense in which someone who tries to do something always makes *something* happen; and also of the claim that he knows he makes something happen.

9

The Causation of Action

If we think of some commonplace happening, such as a door's shutting, we can readily imagine a range of different answers to the question 'What made that door shut?' I will mention a few, and to each add some natural questioning that might follow it up.

1. An apparatus attached to the door.

    (a) How does it work?

    (b) Who put it there, why and when?

2. This wedge was propping the door open and got removed.

    (a) How did it get removed?

    (b) Why did the door shut when the wedge was taken away?

3. A blast of air blew it shut.

    (a) Why was there a blast of air there then?

4. Its own weight caused it to shut.

    (a) How do you know — i.e. is that certain?

    (b) How is it hung so as to shut itself like that?

    (c) And why was it open, then?

---

* First published in C. Ginet (ed) *Knowledge and Mind* (New York & Oxford: Oxford University Press 1983), pp.174–90. Reprinted with the permission of Oxford University Press, Inc.

5. A powerful magnet pulled it shut.

   (a) Why could the magnet affect the door?

   (b) How did the magnet come to be there?

6. A sudden vacuum was created in the space beyond the door.

   (a) Why does a vacuum have that effect?

   (b) What created the vacuum?

   (c) (Given certain answers to b) Why was that done?
       or How did that come about?

7. Something flew against the door and banged it shut.

   (a) What?

   (b) What propelled this object against the door?

   (c) Why was that enough to shut the door?

8. The dog pushed it shut.

   (a) What was the dog doing there?

   (b) Was the dog actually trying to shut the door?

9. Jones shut it.

   (a) How?

   (b) By accident or on purpose?

   (c) Why?

I give this list to draw attention to the wide difference of further questions and interests naturally aroused by the different answers to the first, 'simple' question 'What caused the door to shut?' The different answers as it were adjust us to a variety of new enquiries.

All the answers are perfectly appropriate. We can pick out from among them those which name causes which act on the door: the artificial mechanism, the wind, the dog, the projectile, the magnet, the human. By contrast, the removal of the wedge was a 'causa removens prohibens' — a cause that removes a hindrance; the creation of the vacuum produced an imbalance of air pressure, as a result of which what moved the door — acted on it — was the air on the other side of it. And what would one say about the weight of the door, which caused it to shut 'of itself'? Neither that the weight moved the door nor that it did something that led to something else's moving it.

This brings out how a general enquiry into the nature of *a cause* is rather like a general enquiry into the nature of *a factor*. We may be reminded of Aristotle's four causes: he at least recognized some variety. But four is not enough. E.g. the door's weight does not belong under any of Aristotle's headings. We certainly need to remember often repeated warnings against using the expression '*the* cause'. We shall prefer expressions of the form '*p* because *q*' and '*p* because of *x*'. When the magnet pulled the door shut, the door shut because of the magnet, but possibly also because the wedge was removed and certainly also because of the way the hinges were seated.

We don't ask *how* the wind blows the door shut. It shuts the door by blowing it shut. Long since, we grasped that rapidly moving air *presses*, and the citation of the wind, blowing against the door as cause of its shutting, does not evoke questions as to the mechanics of its action.

The first question about the apparatus, 'How does it work?', might be echoed about the magnet. Here we want a *theory* of magnetism, a general theory of natural science. Comparably, a theory of gravity seems to dissolve our question what sort of cause weight is, whereas our question 1 (a) 'How does it work?' is a question what sort of apparatus *this* is — magnets and weights might come into it. Now compare 'How did the apparatus work?' with 'How?' asked of Jones' shutting the door. 'It exerted a pushing action' would be a very inadequate answer to 'How did the apparatus shut the door?', a mere slight specification of the type of action in answer to a question which is naturally a request to be told something about the inner working of the mechanism. By contrast 'by pushing it' may be an adequate answer to 'How did

Jones shut the door?' and doesn't mean: He's a door-shutting mechanism which works by a pushing action.

Nevertheless, there *is* a question 'How does that work?' to be asked about someone's pushing a door with his hand, say; about, that is, likely answers to 9 (a). And we are *also* inclined to ask verbally the same question about likely answers to 9 (c): 'Why did he shut the door?', e.g. 'So as to have a private conversation'. How does *that* work? But first let us attend to this follow-up of answers to 9 (a).

To repeat, we don't ask how the wind works; pressure we feel we understand as a cause of new motion. But, familiar as we are with the capacity of a human to give a push, still our curiosity is aroused how *this* mechanism may operate. The answer treats of impulses in efferent nerves, of the contraction of muscles, of the pull of muscles on tendons and bones, of ball-and-socket joints, and so on. Now our enquiry is like that into the artificial mechanism.

There are two quite distinct directions of enquiry here. In the *first* we are interested in picking out 'chains' of causality going back in time. (*Chains* are picked out from *fans*.)

The door moved because of the push from the arm of the mechanism; that happened because of the expansion of a spring; that, because of the previous compression of the spring; that, because of the previous movement of the door in the other direction; that, because of the push of a hand; that, because of the placing of the hand and the extension of the arm; that, because of the contraction of the muscles; this last because of the message down the efferent nerves; and that because of — what? No one knows in this line of causes unless he is helped by information of a different sort: it can be told that the man shutting the door was, say, obeying an order or had caught sight of something that made him want to shut the door. If so, we can go on where we broke off: that, because of the afferent nerve impulses leading to the sensory cortex and other parts of the brain; these, because of the impact of vibrating air on the ear drum etc.

Here one wants to say: there was a gap. What came between the impulses in the efferent and the afferent nerves? Well, not much is known. But — and this makes plain our *second* direction of enquiry — is there not also a gap between, say, the impulses in the efferent nerves and the contraction of the muscles? This gap, as it happens, is easier to work at filling in. The question is: how? How does the nerve affect the muscle? Such-and-such happens — a change in the character of a calcium salt, say. How does that come about, and how does it make this bit of tissue slide over that? This 'how' about the connexion between *established* links is the second of the two directions of enquiry.

When we want to know how a human being — or other animal — works in doing such things as pushing doors, we are usually asking for answers to questions of this latter sort. A set of questions tracing causal chains, not back and back, but in and in: until we reach, if we ever reach, elementary links — links not themselves chains.

To know that the impulses in these afferent nerves are relevant, we have to make a judgment that the action was an immediate reaction to an external stimulus; was, e.g., obeying an order just given. That is the clue that makes us attend to these particular processes of perception here, to the impulses in those nerves. Recognizing that is recognizing a pattern of a different sort from the patterns of elementary physical causation.

An analogy to illustrate this: suppose that for some purpose or other you were plotting relations of colour spots in a *pointilliste* picture. Something gives you a line of spots to trace up. This something corresponds to the push of this object, the hand, against the door, and to whatever tells you to look inside the hand and arm as, in like case, you would *not* look inside a block of wood. You pursue your line of dots up to a certain point. Then you can't pursue it any further unless you step right back and see the *figure* that is painted. Doing so gives you your clue, it tells you to connect your line with *these* other spots elsewhere within the figure. Eventually, you hope, you may be able somehow to join up the two lines. But recognizing the figure was necessary; if your new line did not hang together with that, it could not be a right line. Recognizing the figure was a different sort of observation from noting the relations of the particular spots. But the concern is simply to find where to continue tracing your line of spots. Similarly the interest *here* in recalling or noting that the animal was, say, obeying an order lies in our learning from this where to look in order to continue our line of causality back from the impulses in the efferent nerves. Knowing this is of course essential to knowing what gap we have to fill in when our interest is not so much in tracing causes back and back but in asking 'How does this effect that?'

There is, however, a different sort of enquiry 'How does that work?', when that question was elicited by answers to 9 (c), 'Why did he shut the door?'; and equally when it is elicited by answers to 8 (b), 'Was the dog trying to shut the door?' And accordingly a different sort of answer. How does a human — or other similar — animal work? By looking for food, by recognizing danger and responding with flight or fight, by obeying orders, by calculating how to attain various ends. But now: what sort of 'ways of working' are these?

Here someone may say: 'In connection with these things we can certainly ask what goes on in the brain and nervous system; what is their state, when an animal is in one of these psychological states — looking for food, for example. We can already sometimes get an answer to this. And if here too we did have to 'step back' as you put it, and 'recognize a pattern of a different sort', that is just a methodological point about our present situation. When we have the information we want, there will be no need of 'stepping back' and that especially striking gap in our causal chain, which we found in the physiological enquiry, will be filled, in some case, presumably, with the brain states corresponding to beliefs and wants. These will be states of the system either just produced or pre-existing and such that the impulses in the afferent nerves mesh in with them in discoverable ways and the impulses in the efferent nerves are then produced. In this way we are after all *not* engaged in a different sort of enquiry.'

This is a position, or complex of positions, which I will show to be wrong.

It makes the assumption that the explanation of the coming about of actions by volition and intention is what thinkers of modern times call 'causal' explanation and that this is just *one* single sort of explanation. And similarly for reference to what someone believes, when this comes into explanation of his action.

Not that the existence in a man of a belief, a desire, an aim, an intention, may not be causes of various things that later come about. Indeed they may, and the effect of an intention may even be an action in execution of that intention! E.g. suppose I have a standing intention of never talking to the Press. Why, someone asks, did I refuse to see the representative of *Time* magazine? — and he is told of that long-standing resolution. 'It makes her reject such approaches without thinking about the particular case.' This is 'causal' because it says 'It makes her ...': it derives the action from a previous state.

The mistake is to think that the relation of *being done in execution of a certain intention,* or *being done intentionally,* is a causal relation between act and intention. We see this to be a mistake if we note that an intention does not have to be a distinct psychological state which exists either prior to or even contemporaneously with the intentional action whose intention it is. E.g. someone applies some extra force to a telephone dial-piece because it is a bit jammed. Is not his application of extra force perfectly intentional? — as opposed, let us say, to a case where he moves his hand (with the finger already in one of the holes) somewhat violently as involuntary recoil from a sting. But there was, we *can* suppose, no prior formation of intention, nor is the intention a mental state that accompanies the action. *That* the action under this description, 'applying a bit of force', was intentional, comes out in his explanation, in what he says if someone asks him why. 'To unjam it,' he says. So the application of the extra force was a means to the end which he mentions. But that this was so was formulated *after* the event. Was what was formulated not there before? All introspection or observation can tell him, we may suppose, is that *it seemed jammed* and then he acted. He doesn't find e.g. that the *thought* of the need to unjam it 'went through his head.' But didn't he *want* it to move? Well, what was that supposed to be like? Did he *feel* something which he could call a desire that it should move, as when he is showing someone an experiment in which something is supposed to move and he watches it with anxiety? No. This is what he was doing — dialling a number. Of course he wanted it to move! But saying so does not add a new event to the record. The teleology of conscious action is not to be explained as efficient causality by a condition, or state, of desire. Remembering that *that* was 'what I did ... for,' does not have to involve remembering such a state.

Suppose you say at this point 'I admit in such a case I may not recall such a *thought*, or any feeling of desire, but the action's being 'to unjam it' imparted a certain atmosphere, a certain character, which I *now* recall its being suffused with, and *that* was the intention.' Was that then a separable mental experience which you want to say *caused* the action? For that was what we were arguing about: whether there being such-and-such an intention — in this case, of applying force, since that is what the intentional action is — causes the action which is described as intentional. And in this conception a cause has to be thought of as a distinct thing, which is found to have this effect: as, e.g., the evocation of solemn feelings may keep me from laughing in some game. You didn't find that when you experience *this* atmosphere it turns out that there is an action of applying extra force to a slightly stuck telephone dial. When you introduced the atmosphere, you thought of it as something *in*separable, an indefinable character intrinsic to an action when it is intentional; or rather, definable only by the description of the intentional action. But such is not a cause of the action.

At this point someone may say: 'Now wait! Why all this *phenomenological* investigation? Your point of departure had nothing to do with the phenomenology of intention. Remember where we were. We were talking about tracing the physiological casual chain which leads up to the door's getting pushed. You said, and we admitted, that we have to "step back" and "recognise a pattern of a different sort" — i.e. see that the human is acting in obedience to an order — before we know where to look to continue the causal chain back beyond the impulses in the efferent nerves. When we know that, we can find the impulses in the afferent nerves produced by the impact of sound waves on the ear-drum. We granted that this was true, but said it was a methodological fact about our present situation. When we've got the information we want, we shan't need to step back. The gap will be filled with the *brain-states* corresponding to beliefs and wants. We know that it used to be suggested that there will always be a gap, however close we get to closing it, in this chain of physical causality, and that this gap is filled by a mental, spiritual event of choice, will, intention, which determines the further physical processes, the messages down the efferent nerves. We have not stopped smiling at this naïveté, Your argument is surely directed against just such a view (long since outmoded) and has nothing to do with us.'

On the contrary: it has plenty to do with that position. For that position assumes that that gap is to be filled with brain-states, or something meshing in with pre-existing brain-states, that *correspond* to beliefs and wants (some would say, *are* beliefs and wants, but that controversy does not interest us). Now there's no reason to say that, unless one is convinced that the explanation of the coming about of action by volition and intention is (a) true, (b) 'causal' in character.

What is meant by saying that explanation of actions by intention is *true*? Not, of course, that every explanation of an action by an intention that may be offered is true — clearly there are both lies and mistakes. But that there is such a thing as intentional action and when there is, the intention or intentions involved in it *belong in an account* of such action. But the explanation is rather in terms of the future than the past. It would be too absurd to reject the notion of intention altogether as having a place in our account of action — to say that 'He applied extra force to the dial on purpose, to free it, because it was stuck' is not a possible true account and partial explanation of an occurrence. At this point someone says that that is true of course, but the 'ordinary language' in which it is couched embodies a 'mentalistic theory' which we want to reject. And *that* is why we want (roughly speaking) to put those brain-states into the gap.

But if it was a complete mistake to think of those explanations and accounts as 'causal,' then there is no reason to think of 'the gap' as being filled with something corresponding to or correlated with beliefs and desires. Fill 'the gap' if you can: that means, see if you can find a continuation of the chain of causality that bridges the gap. It is no more than another of those investigations that I called the second direction of causal enquiry — how do impulses in the afferent nerves in these circumstances produce impulses in the efferent nerves? It is no doubt a difficult and intractable problem, but it *is* mere naïveté after all to think that it must be filled by brain-states corresponding to beliefs and desires.

For there can be no such brain-states except in the particular case. I mean: there can be no such kind of brain-state as *the* kind of brain-state corresponding to such-and-such a belief in the sense of being a sufficient condition of it. 'Why not? There are untold millions of possible states of the brain. So it may well be that among these is a set of states which all are, and which are the totality of, states of a brain whose owner for example believes that such-and-such.' But even on that supposition the brain-state is still not a sufficient condition for the belief. Why not? Because the belief might, be, say, a belief about banks, and a human whose brain might get into that state might never have heard of a bank. 'Well,' it may be replied, 'the brains of such people never do get into any of these states. The causal conditions for getting into them exist in nature only where there are banks etc.' But let us suppose a way of producing one of these states artificially, i.e. outside the circumstances in which the causal conditions occur 'naturally.' And now, consider the inference that if such a state has been so produced the subject is then in a state of belief that, say, 'such-and-such a bank in – cester is open at 5.00 p.m. on Thursdays', though neither – cester nor banks nor clocks nor days of the week ever came into his life before, nor did he ever hear of them. The absurdity of the inference brings it out that even on the initial supposition – which there is no evidence for anyway – the brain-state is not a sufficient condition for the belief.

Nor is any other state of the person. Here we may be tempted to revert to the discarded position: 'No other *physical* state, perhaps, but why not a *mental* state?' But in reply we can repeat the argument. We take it that a state is supposed to be something holding of its subject here and now, or over a period of time, without reference to anything outside that of which it holds or the time at which it holds: in particular, without reference to the history of the thing whose state it is. If that is how we understand a state, we can suppose the same state of an object in quite different circumstances and with a completely different history. If the argument does not apply to mental states that must be because they are not 'states' in this same sense. But however we decide about that, we cannot ascribe a belief like that about the bank's opening hours, to someone not living in a world of banks and clocks. Indeed we are implicitly looking *away* from the individual and into his world if we ascribe *any* belief to him. This we don't have to do for the ascription of a brain-state.

The same point holds for wants, aims; the same argument would have gone through if for a belief about the bank we had put wanting to rob the bank or be president of the bank. And the same goes for intentions, decisions, and thoughts — I mean thoughts in the sense of one's thinking something to oneself, say, on an occasion.

So: fill up that gap how you will. I mean, of course, *suppose* it filled up how you will. No way of filling it up, whether with brain-states or (the fanciful) supposed correlates of expressions of Cartesian *cogitationes,* will fill it up with intentions, beliefs, wants, aims, volitions, or desires. For you are in pursuit of a type of causal history in which those things do not belong *at all.* I am not saying such a causal history is impossible — good luck to you in your pursuit of it if it is a serious scientific pursuit. Nor am I saying that it must be inadequate, 'leave something out', always have 'the gap'. The kind of enquiry that looks for it might be completed. There might come a point at which there is no further puzzle about *how* each link in the causal chain produces the next one. And still nothing has been said about intentions, beliefs, thoughts or decisions.

But wait — did I not grant that the existence in a man of a belief, a desire, an aim, an intention, may be a cause of something that happens later, of actions of his for example? Certainly I did. Henry VIII longed for a son; the death of many children made him believe he had sinned in marrying Queen Catherine; he formed the intention of marrying Anne Boleyn. All this led to, helped to produce, the Act of Supremacy, to his decision to break with Rome. This is a causal history. It is merely a causal history of a different type from the physiological one. And indeed the physiological one touches it, but only at certain points. Henry signed something, let us say, and this was an episode in the above history. Ink got on a page in a certain pattern. It was deposited on the paper by a pen pushed by the royal hand. At the other end of the chain perhaps there was a noise — a courtier saying 'Here, Sire' and messages up the afferent nerves. Etc. The causal histories of the two types aren't rival accounts.

But to repeat: it is one thing to say that a distinct and identifiable state of a human being, namely his having a certain intention, *may* cause various things to happen, even including the doing of what the intention was an intention to do; and quite another to say that *for* an action to be done in fulfilment of a certain intention (which existed *before* the action) is *eo ipso* for it to be caused by that prior intention.

It may seem that the case is analogous to that of an action's being done in obedience to an order. The order's being given is then a cause of the action — who would deny it? But here one points to the order's *having* been given, in explanation of how it was brought about that this was done. Now if one can justly point to the prior existence of the intention as an influencing condition, in an account of how the action was brought about, then it can indeed be called a cause (as in the case of the refusal to see the *Time* magazine interviewer). The mere fact of priority is insufficient. One is tempted to think it sufficient because one does appeal to the *intention* to explain the action, and in the supposed case the intention existed before. But explanation by intention does not get a new character just because the intention existed before. It is just the same as when the intention is, so to speak, embodied in the action, and is not ever or only afterwards distinctly thought of. Contrast the case where, to my own irritation, I do something which I now don't mean to do — because I *had meant* to do it! Here the 'explanation by intention' is indeed a causal explanation. But it is not really an explanation by intention at all as we usually understand that expression — for the action is *un*intentional.

It is important here that the physical investigation of action takes as its object, i.e. as the system whose workings are being investigated, the individual human being. If, somewhat fancifully, a whole society were the unit system of physical investigation, then 'A believes that the bank is open on Thursday at 5 p.m.' might be supposed translatable into a statement, relating to any among a lot of possible histories of configurations of atoms whose totality added up to the existence of a society of people with A among them, with banks and with education in 'knowledge' of them. But the unit of physical investigation of the action of a human being is the unit of physiological investigation — the individual human. And whether what a human being is doing is, say, signing a check, a petition, or a death warrant is not to be revealed by a physical investigation of what goes on within him: such descriptions are not a physiologist's concern, and so neither can he deal with the intentions implied by them.

When we consider 'the causation of action' we need to decide which sort of enquiry we are engaged in. Is it the physiological investigation of voluntary movements? I.e. do we want to know how the human mechanism works when, at a signal, the hand pushes a pen, or perhaps a door shut? It is an enormously interesting enquiry. But that will not be our enquiry into the causation of action where our interests are in the following sort of question: What led to Jones' shutting the door then? We ascertain that he shut the door in order to have a private conversation with N. What history of actions, i.e. dealings of Jones and N with each other and with other people, of beliefs and wishes and decisions, led up to this action of shutting the door? That might be another interesting enquiry, an historical one to which knowledge of the detailed results of the first one is hardly ever pertinent.

If we now think in terms of, say, some sort of elementary particles and the operation of the fundamental forces recognized by physics, the very descriptions which occur in physiology may seem to be descriptions of shadows. I mean that the movement of a shadow has not any reality that has been left out once you have described the successive occlusion of light from a continuum of areas of a surface. Now what are we to think of the causal histories of human dealings of such a kind as we have mentioned? Are they so to speak shadows on shadows?

It may indeed be a handy way of speaking to say that a shadow with such and such a shape moved across the surface. Perhaps a more forcible analogue is that of a wave. No one attributes causal efficacy to a shadow. In a Disney cartoon, again, perhaps the mouse shatters a tea-pot with a hammer: but the reality is the successive complicated states of illumination of the screen, and we have, not efficacy, but a *picture* of efficacy on the part of a mouse with a hammer. But we really do find it scientifically convenient to speak of the causal efficacy of waves; they not only move but 'interfere' with each other. All the same, everyone will admit that this is just a convenient manner of speaking: if they are water waves, the description of the water masses bobbing up and down will be equivalent to the description of the waves, and the causal efficacy belongs rather to the masses of water particles in these up-and-down motions.

My question, then, is: are we to consider the causality of action, when we are talking about histories of human dealings, as just a highly convenient, nay indispensable, *façon de parler*, such as we use also when we speak of waves as interfering with one another?

I shall call descriptions in terms which in this way merely amount to a convenient *façon de parler: supervenient descriptions.*

Let us first consider the supposition of strict and complete determinism in relation to the particles of which we and all things are composed, and the forces acting between them. I do not equate being caused with being determined. For a result to be determined is for no other result to have been antecedently possible. (A result might thus *become* determined at a point in time before it occurs, but not have been yet determined before that point.) Therefore in speaking of actions as being caused, brought about, by antecedent factors in the human history, I am not already settling the question of their being pre-determined. But given a strict and total determinism relative to the particles of which all things are composed, I think two things follow: one, that these descriptions of action and their causation in human (and animal) histories *are* supervenient descriptions, and two, that actions *are* 'determined,' in the sense that I have explained for that term.

The physicist David Bohm (in *Causality and Chance in Modern Physics*[1], ch. 2, sec. 14) interestingly characterized what he called 'the philosophy of mechanism' in such a way that 'mechanism' might be deterministic *or* indeterministic. In my own language, his characterization is this: there is some basic level of physical description such that all 'higher-level' descriptions are supervenient. Let the basic level be that of particles and fundamental physical forces. Then the forms of substances and animals and all sorts of actions and happenings will, as he puts it, be comparable to shadows.

We take Bohm's point and see that 'the philosophy of mechanism' — there *is* undoubtedly such a thing — may be either deterministic or indeterministic. On the other hand the position is not symmetrical. If you are a determinist at any level, it appears to me that you *must* be a 'mechanist' in relation to 'higher level' descriptions: you must regard them as supervenient. Thus if you are a determinist about particles and forces you must regard as supervenient the descriptions of the actions and reactions of chemical substances, and of the actions of humans and other animals. And you must also regard them — the actions and reactions that in fact take place — as in truth determined from any previous point of time.

---

[1]   London: Routledge & Kegan Paul 1957.

If, however, you are indeterminist at any level, you may or may not be a mechanist in relation to higher-level descriptions. Thus determinism settles the question of mechanism, indeterminism leaves it open.

It is perfectly possible to be an indeterminist about some kind of particles (called 'fundamental') and their forces, while not being a mechanist in relation to certain higher-level descriptions; but nevertheless to be a *determinist* in relation to them. Thus one might think that the descriptions of chemical or animal forms were not merely supervenient. But that the existence and actions of all chemicals and animals that ever exist were determined — i.e. causally *necessitated* — from any previous point of time.

Something like this position, indeed, has perhaps been adopted as a result of the triumph of indeterministic physics. It manifests what I believe to be an itch for determinism which exists in the human mind. It is entertaining to read the last chapter of Richard von Mises's book, *Probability, Statistics and Truth*, and see what the intellectual position was fifty years ago. Granted that, macroscopically, determinism did not seem to be true, he tells us, still people had felt confident that *fundamentally* it was so; at the microscopic or submicroscopic level it would turn out to be true, and the macroscopic appearances would be revealed as illusory. But behold! at the submicroscopic level this turned out to be false. Thus von Mises. But what has happened since? At the submicroscopic level, people will say, to be sure physics has revealed a basic indeterminism. But no matter — macroscopically determinism can hold. For the macroscopic is the overall result of processes which are statistically constant. The *statistical* laws can't be infringed.

This little bit of thought-history does surely reveal a deterministic itch. What has got lost is the recognition, mentioned by von Mises, that in various ways the macroscopic appearances are not of things being deterministic. However, it must be acknowledged that the position sketched is *possible:* at the macroscopic level determinism *may* hold in some immensely complicated fashion. But why should one believe it does? *Here* the itch calls to its aid a fallacious argument. Namely: the statistics are constant — therefore, determinism at the macroscopic level *must* be true; otherwise the statistics would be infringed by the operation of new, higher-level, indeterministic causes. Now this does not follow at all. The statistical laws would not have to be infringed by the operation of new higher level causes, even if these were indeterministic.

I mean: we just do not know whether, for example, the course taken by an animal is predetermined any time it runs about some area where the causal factors are constant. The appearance is otherwise; but that may be illusory — we ought to admit that *we do not know*. There can be no argument from the necessary preservation of statistical laws governing any submicroscopic processes that might be involved. The supposition of a large variety of possibilities is perfectly compatible with that. And the supposition of causal factors of a 'new' sort (a psychological sort, let us say), sometimes predetermining which of these possibilities is actualized, is equally compatible with it. It would only be incompatible if the same train of submicroscopic events were necessary for the same animal motion, described perhaps as one of attraction towards an object. Then indeed the supposition of 'new' causes would seem incompatible with the supposed statistical laws, as the 'new' causes would keep reflecting just *these* out of the previously random outcomes.

I hope it is now clear that there is no need to regard the causal histories of human dealings as supervenient descriptions: we *must* do this only on the basis of a radical physical determinism. Nothing is settled by saying this, however, as to the possibility of holding deterministic views in relation to 'human' causality. That question is left entirely open.

I have not at all dealt with something I have briefly indicated — the explanation of action by intention. This topic is indeed important, but it is big, and there would hardly be room to develop it here. In any case, I have indicated that it does not properly come under my title, 'The causation of action' — at any rate as moderns, rather than Aristotelians, understand the term 'causation'.

Let us end by considering the causalities especially involved in a history of people's dealings with one another. When such dealings concern or constitute great events, important in the history of nations, they are the greater part of what is called 'History', where this is treated as the name of a subject of traditional lore and of academic study, a special discipline. But public or private, great events or small, the causalities concerned in them are much the same type. The first thing to note is: these causalities are mostly to be understood derivatively. The derivation is from the understanding of action as intentional, calculated, voluntary, impulsive, involuntary, reluctant, concessive, passionate, etc. The first thing we know, upon the whole, is what proceedings are parleys, agreements, quarrels, struggles, embassies, wars, pressures, pursuits of given ends, routines, institutional practices of all sorts. That is to say: in our descriptions of their histories, we apply such conceptions of what people are engaged in. In the context of such application, then, the causalities to which we ascribe such events can, so to speak, get a foothold. Given the idea of an engagement to marry, say, you can look for its causal antecedents. Or again, this man was travelling from Aix to Ghent. What for? He was a messenger taking news. So in the situation in which the news was generated, and in which there was a requirement that he should take it, together with the instructions of whoever sent him off, and the exigencies of route or difficulties posed by his means of carrying out the purpose, together with accidental encounters and concatenation of events with aspects of temperament and facts of people's excitements — all these will contribute causalities of various kinds to the event of his arrival or non-arrival at his destination. The causalities will, for example, include negations. Because this man did not know this language, he went this way rather than that: a very different sort of causality from that of the issuing of a certain order to him at a certain moment. Or again: *because* he was quick tempered, he got into a rage *because* of a supposed insult, and *because* of that all unawares escaped certain dangers or involuntarily fell into other ones.

10

Practical Inference

Logic is interested in the UNASSERTED propositions.

(Wittgenstein)

I will write in appreciation of, but some dissent from, this paragraph of von Wright's:

> Now we can see more clearly, I think, wherein the claim to logical validity of the practical inference consists. Given the premises
>
> > *X* now intends to make it true that *E*
>
> He thinks that, unless he does *A* now, he will not achieve this
> and excluding, hypothetically or on the basis of investigations,
> that he is prevented, then his actual conduct, whatever it may
> 'look like', either is an act of doing A or aims, though unsuccess-
> fully, at being this. Any description of behaviour which is logi-
> cally inconsistent with this is also logically inconsistent with the
> premises. Accepting the premises thus forces on us this under-
> standing of his conduct — unless for some reason we think that a
> preventive interference occurred right at the beginning of his
> action.[1]

* This paper, written in 1974 as a contribution to P.A.Schilpp and L.E.Hahn (eds)
The Philosophy of Georg Henrik von Wright. Library of Living Philosophers Series
Volume XIX (La Salle, Ill: Open Court 1989), originally appeared under the title
'Von Wright on Practical Inference'. It was reprinted under the title 'Practical
Inference' in R. Hursthouse, G. Lawrence and W. Quinn (eds) *Virtues and Reasons:
Philippa Foot and Moral Theory* (Oxford: Clarendon Press 1995), pp. 1–34. It is
reprinted here by permission of Open Court Publishing Company, a division of
Carus Publishing Company, Peru, IL, copyright © 1989 by The Library of Living
Philosophers.

[1]   G.H. von Wright, 'On So-Called Practical Inference', *Acta Sociologica*, **15/1** (1972): 49.

1

If there is practical inference, there must be such a thing as its
validity. Validity is associated with necessity. I take it that this is
what leads von Wright always to consider only the 'unless'
forms, giving

> I want to achieve *E*;
>
> Unless I do *A*, I shall not achieve *E*

as a scheme in the first person. Suppose, having that end and that
opinion, I do *A*, 'What sort of connexion would this signify
between want and thought on the one hand, and action on the
other? Can I say that wanting and opining *make* me act? If so,
would this be a form of causal efficacy? Or would it be more like a
logical compulsion?'[2]

Donald Davidson opts for 'causal efficacy' here, on the ground
that there is a difference between my having a reason and its
actually being my reason. I act because ... We need an account of
this 'because'. The psychological 'because', he supposes, is an
ordinary *because* where the *because* clause gives a psychological
state. The solution lacks acumen. True, not only must I have a reason, it must also 'operate as my reason': that is, what I do must be
done *in pursuit* of the end and *on grounds* of the belief. But not just
any act of mine which is caused by my having a certain desire is
done in pursuit of the object of desire; not just *any* act caused by
my having a belief is done on grounds of the belief. Davidson
indeed realized that even identity of description of *act done* with
act specified in the belief, together with causality by the belief and
desire, isn't enough to guarantee the act's being done *in pursuit of
the end* and *on grounds of the belief.* He speaks of the possibility of
'wrong' or 'freak' causal connexions. I say that any recognizable
causal connexions would be 'wrong', and that he can do no more
than postulate a 'right' causal connexion in the happy security
that none such can be found. If a causal connexion were found we

_____

[2]   *Ibid.* 40.

could always still ask: 'But was the act done for the sake of the end and in view of the thing believed?'

I conjecture that a cause of this failure of percipience is the standard approach by which we first distinguish between 'action' and what merely happens, and then specify that we are talking about 'actions'. So what we are considering is already given as — in a special sense — an action, and not just any old thing which we do, such as making an involuntary gesture. Such a gesture might be caused, for example, by realizing something (the 'onset of a belief') when we are in a certain state of desire. Something I do is not made into an intentional action by being caused by a belief and desire, even if the descriptions fit.

Von Wright has no taste for this explanation by causal efficacy, but is drawn to the alternative which he gives — logical compulsion. He has difficulties with this which lead him to substitute 'intend' for 'want' and the third person for the first, prefixing 'he believes' to the second premise. Even so, there is still a time gap; so he closes the gap with a 'now' which is to be quite narrowly understood. He must also exclude instant prevention. But he now has a rather obscure difficulty about the 'instantaneous' application of the argument. 'Is there explanation of action only on the basis of what is *now* the case — and is there intentional action which is *simultaneous* with the construction of a justification of it?' He thinks not; but he does not explain why not.

He *seems* to conceive the application like this: one *makes use* of an argument. Now one can hardly be said to make use of an argument that one does not produce, inwardly or outwardly. But the production takes time. If I do *A* 'on the instant', there isn't time. Given time, the argument or calculation will look to a future action. Or, if I have done the action, I may be justifying it. I cannot *be reaching* the action as a conclusion. (This is interpretation on my part; I hope not unjust.)

This raises the interesting question: is inference a process? Is 'infer' a psychological verb? Is 'reasoning' a psychological concept? If so, it is perhaps curious that people don't usually put inference and reasoning into lists of mental phenomena. Bernard Williams once wrote that an inference must be something that a person could conduct. What has one in mind, if one speaks of someone as 'conducting an inference'? Presumably not repro- ducing an argument, but rather: thinking first of one proposition, say, and then another, which is seen to follow from the first. Is there something else which one could call not just *seeing* that the second follows from the first, but actually *inferring* it? I take it, no. That is, it is of no importance that I 'wouldn't have produced the one except because I had produced the other'. One may feel inclined to say such a thing in a particular case, but one wouldn't say 'You didn't infer, if the second proposition merely flashed into your mind; you saw it followed from the first and added "then" to it!' Nor need one even have added 'then'. If inferring is a particular mental act, one might suppose that it was 'conceiving the second proposition under the aspect *then* in relation to the first'. But now, how is it that when one considers or examines inferences, one has no interest in whether anything like that has gone on in someone's mind, i.e. whether he has experienced some- thing which he would like to express in that way? It is because we have no such interest that it does not come natural to classify infer- ence as a mental content, 'infer' as a psychological verb.

Von Wright's observation about the simultaneous construc- tion of a justification comes in a passage where he is asking 'what uses has the type of argument which I here call practical infer- ence?' and it therefore seems entirely fair. Construction, produc- tion, going through, all these take some time; therefore no 'instantaneous' use. And yet it appears as if something deeper had been said. Has he perhaps not exhausted the 'uses' of this type of argument? ✕

Practical inference was delineated, as anything called 'infer- ence' must be, as having validity. The validity of an inference is supposed to be a certain formal character. The appreciation of validity is connected with the evaluation of grounds *qua* grounds. Therefore, one use (which von Wright has not mentioned) of his type of argument will be not to get at a conclusion or explain or justify an action, but to form an estimate of an action in its relation to its grounds. Now can a person act on grounds upon the instant? For example, he steps behind a pillar to avoid being seen, as soon as he sees someone enter the building. If so, the setting forth of the grounds, displaying the formal connexion between description of the action and propositions giving grounds, will indeed take time but will relate to something instantaneous.

Von Wright's investigation has led him to the curious position that there is such a thing as the validity of a practical inference, but that when it *is* valid, it has no use as an argument — that is to say, as an inference. Its use is connected, rather, with understanding action. Where it is of use as an argument it lacks validity because of the time gap: 'with this gap there is also a rift in the logical connexion between the intention and epistemic attitude on the one hand and the action on the other'. Thus when we obliterate the time gap we 'obliterate the character of an argument or an inference': we obliterate it from the propositional connexions which we were investigating.[3]

2

If there is such a thing as practical inference, it is surely exhibited not only by the 'unless' form:

I want to attain *E*

Unless I do *A* I shall not attain *E*

after considering which I do *A*.

It is also exhibited by the 'if' form:

I want to attain *E*

If I do *A* I shall attain *E*.

---

[3]   *Ibid*. 50.

I have conjectured that von Wright does not consider this latter form because with it there is no shadow of a sense in which doing the action *A* is necessitated by the premises. With the 'unless' form, the action is required if my desire is not to be frustrated. However, we have seen the difficulty in making out a necessity about *its being true that the action happened,* which I take to be his picture of making out the *validity* of inference here. He looked for the relation to be 'one of logical compulsion'.

He notices my remark that the conclusion of a practical syllogism is not necessitated; perhaps he thought I said this because of these difficulties. But in fact my view was completely different: I thought that the relation between the premises and the action which was the conclusion was this: the premises shew what good, what use, the action is.

If someone acts on the premises, that shews that he is after — or perhaps that he wants to avoid — something mentioned in the first premise. In 'On So-called Practical Inference', von Wright says: 'According to Anscombe the first premise ... mentions something wanted', and he claims that this doesn't fit Aristotle's version of practical inference, which 'subsumes a particular thing or action under some general principle or rule about what is good for us or is our duty'.[4] He contrasts with this the inference in which the first premise mentions an end of action, and the second some means to this end.

He seems to think that 'mentioning an end of action' or 'mentioning something wanted' is saying that a certain end is wanted. Otherwise, he would not contrast the well-known Aristotelian forms with the form 'in which some end of action is wanted'.

Pure water is wholesome

This water is pure

[4]   *Ibid.* 39–40.

— followed by drinking the water, would be an example on the most frequent Aristotelian pattern. It mentions the wholesome, and this is shewn to be what the person wants by his acting on these propositions as grounds for drinking the water. It seems to me incorrect to call such a premise 'A general rule about what is good for us'. It is a general statement about what is good for us, not a rule.

It is true that Aristotle's first premises in these forms are always some sort of 'general principle'. But 'principle' here only means 'starting-point'. This generality is indeed important, and I will return to it. However, an end calculated for certainly might be very particular and no general considerations about the kind of end be stated. Let us concentrate for the moment on the question whether the wanting or intention of the end *ought to figure in the premises*.

As I formerly represented that matter, 'I want' does not go into the premises at all unless indeed it occurs as in the following example. (I owe the point and example to A. Müller.)

> Anyone who wants to kill his parents will be helped to get rid of this trouble by consulting a psychiatrist. [5]
>
> I want to kill my parents.
>
> If I consult a psychiatrist I shall be helped to get rid of this trouble.
>
> NN is a psychiatrist.
>
> So I'll consult NN.

Here my wanting to kill my parents is among the facts of the case; it is not that wanting which we picture as, so to speak, constituting the motor force for acting on the premises. *That* is evidently the desire to get rid of the trouble. The decision, if I reach it on

---

[5] This is the Aristotelian general premise which does not appear in von Wright's examples. It is easily supplied; e.g. 'Unheated huts in cold climates are uninhabitable by humans' or 'Unheated huts are not rendered inhabitable unless they are heated'. But the hypothetical statement seems to make the general one redundant and vice versa. See Section 4.

these grounds, *shews* that I *want* to get rid of the trouble. It is clear that the roles of these two statements of wanting are different.

If a set of premises is set out without saying what the person is after who is making them his grounds, then the conclusion might be unexpected. It might be opposite to what one would at first expect. For example, in the given case: 'So I'll avoid consulting *NN*'. This seems perverse and pointless; why then get as far as specifying *NN*, at least if it is a thing one would be in little danger of doing inadvertently? On the other hand identical considerations:

> Strong alkaloids are deadly poison to humans.
>
> Nicotine is a strong alkaloid.
>
> What's in this bottle is nicotine

might terminate either in careful avoidance of a lethal dose, or in suicide by drinking the bottle.

That being so, there is a good deal of point in having the end somehow specified if we want to study the form. This at least is true: if you know the end, you know what the conclusion should be, given these premises. Whereas if you do not know the end, (1) the conclusion may be either positive *or* negative. Aristotle, we may say, assumes a preference for health and the wholesome, for life, for doing what one should do or needs to do as a certain kind of being. Very arbitrary of him. But also (2) how do we know where the reasoning should stop and a decision be made? For example, note that in the case above we left out a premise, 'I am human'. As Aristotle remarks somewhere, this premise is one that would seldom be formulated, even by someone who was actually going through the considerations of a practical inference, and though 'strictly' that premise belonged among them. Replacing it by '*NN* is a human' can suggest a different tendency altogether for the reasoning! However, in saying that, we are betraying our actual guess what the reasoning is for. Our idea of where the reasoning should terminate depends on this guess.

Thus the end ought to be specified, but the specification of the end is not in the same position as a premise.

A rather pure example of practical reasoning, as we are at present conceiving it, is afforded by the search for a construction in geometry. In Euclid all we are given is the problem, the construction, and then the proof that it does what is required. That saves space, but it does not represent the discovery of the construction.

We have the requirement stated, e.g. *To find the centre of a given circle*. We may then reason as follows, reaching Euclid's construction.

> If we construct the perpendicular bisector of a diameter, that will give us the centre.

> If we construct the perpendicular bisector of a chord, and produce it to the circumference, that will give us a diameter.

We can draw a chord, and we can construct the bisector of any given line. So we conclude by drawing a chord, bisecting it, and bisecting the resultant diameter.

This is different from most of Aristotle's examples. It is of the form:

> Objective: to have it that *p*.

> If *q*, then *p*.

> If *r*, then *q*.

Whereupon, *r* being something we can do, or rather immediately make true, we act. But this form is something like one once sketched by Aristotle:

> The healthy state comes about by reasoning as follows: since health is such-and-such, it is necessary, if health is to be, that such-and-such should hold, e.g. homogeneity, and if that, then heat. And so one goes on considering until he comes to some last thing, which he himself can do.[6]

---

[6] Aristotle, *Metaphysics* Z. 1032b7–10.

This last thing, Aristotle indicates, may be rubbing: 'In treatment, perhaps the starting-point is heating, and he produces this by rubbing'. Here 'starting-point' evidently means the thing the doctor starts by considering how to procure.[7]

In the geometrical example, the construction of a diameter is not the only possible construction for finding the centre of a circle, but in Aristotle's example, the 'homogeneity' is said to be *necessary* for restoration of health, and heating for homogeneity. Friction, however, is merely a way of producing heat. What is important is surely that the end will be attained by the means arrived at, not whether it is the only means.

The relation between the premises given for the more usual type of Aristotelian reasoning, and these 'if, then' premises, is an obvious one. 'The healthy is such-and-such' is rather of the standard type. Somewhat tediously, we could put the two side by side. For 'such-and-such' I put 'X':

Being healthy is being X.	Only if this patient is X will he be healthy.
Only the homogeneous is X.	Only if he is homogeneous will he be X.
Only by heating does the unhomogeneous become homogeneous.	Only if he is heated will he become homogeneous.
Rubbing is heating.	If he is rubbed, he will be heated.

Similarly, we could equip our 'if, then' propositions in the geometrical search with accompanying justifications. 'The centre of a circle is the mid-point of a diameter.' 'The perpendicular bisector of a chord, produced to the circumference, is a diameter.' These might have stood by themselves as premises on which the

---

enquirer acts by constructing a chord, etc. Aristotle's 'light meats' syllogism again can be cast in the 'if, then' form:

Light meats suit so-and-sos.

I am a so-and-so.	If I eat light meat, I'll be eating what suits me.
Such-and-such a kind of meat is light.	If I eat such-and-such, I'll be eating light meat.
This is such-and-such a kind of meat.	If I eat this, I'll be eating such-and-such.

There is an interesting difference between the forms. I said that the first premise mentions, not *that* one wants something, but something that one wants. Applying this to the left, it claims that what is wanted (by someone acting on these grounds) is something that suits beings of a certain kind — to which, indeed, he belongs. Applying it to the right, it claims that what is wanted is to eat something that suits oneself.

Suppose we refashioned the right-hand column in an attempt to avoid this apparent difference:

If a so-and-so eats light meat, he eats what suits him.

If a so-and-so eats such-and-such, he eats light meat.

If I eat this, a so-and-so eats such-and-such.

This would make it look as if the objective were the somewhat abstract or impersonal one, that a being of a certain kind should eat suitable food. This is, after all, not what is suggested by the left-hand column together with the comment that if these are premises of practical reasoning, what is wanted is something that suits beings of a certain kind. I shall return to this matter when I take up the topic of the nature of the *generality* of Aristotle's first premises.

For the moment, it is only necessary to say first that the considerations on the left justify (prove) those on the right, a point
that we saw also for the geometrical example; and also that the
'abstract' aim would seem to be an absurdity. I do not mean,
however, that all aims must concern one's own doing or having
something. That there should be adequate food in prisons, or a
Bible in every hotel room, or fireworks on every New Year's Day,
are possible aims in which the reasoner's doing or having something are not mentioned. I mean only that *in this case* the abstract
aim is absurd. In other cases, indeed, one might do something so
that *someone* of a class to which one belongs shall have done a
thing of a certain kind. But that is evidently not what is in question in Aristotle's 'light meats' syllogism.

3

The previous section has shewn not what practical reasonings
are, but at any rate what are practical reasonings, and how great
is the contrast with reasonings for the truth of a conclusion. Practical grounds may 'require' an action, when they shew that *only*
by its means can the end be obtained, but they are just as much
grounds when they merely shew that the end *will* be obtained by
a certain means. Thus, in the only sense in which practical
grounds *can* necessitate a conclusion (an action), they need not,
and are none the less grounds for that.

The difficulty felt is to grasp why this should be called 'inference'. Inference is a logical matter; if there is inference, there must
be validity; if there is inference, the conclusion must in some way
follow from the premises. How can an action logically follow from
premises? *Can* it be at all that, given certain thoughts, there is
something it logically *must happen* that one does? It seemed no
sense could be made of that. Von Wright indeed came as near as
he knew how to making sense of it, but he did not succeed. He
was indeed assured of failure by the move which ensured that he
was speaking clearly in speaking of logical necessity — namely

by going over into the third person. What — hedged about by various saving clauses — became the logically necessary conclusion was not the doing, but merely the *truth* of the proposition that the agent would do something. But in this way the practical inference degenerated into a theoretical inference with the odd character of being invalid so long as it was truly inferential!

I have given a very different account, but the question remains outstanding: in what sense is this *inference*? One speaks of *grounds* of action indeed, as of belief; one says 'and so I'll ...' or 'therefore I'll ...', and we understand such expressions. But are they more than mere verbal echoes? The frequent non-necessity of the 'conclusion' is a striking feature. In order to eat *some* suitable food, one eats *this*. Or again: either A or B will do, and so one does A.

Some philosophers have tried to develop an account of 'imperative inference' — inference from command to command, or from command to what to do in execution of a command, conceived as self-administration of a 'derived' command by one who seeks to obey the first command. This has some bearing on our topic. If someone has the objective of obeying an order which does not tell him to do what he can simply do straight off, his problem is a problem of practical inference: he has to determine on doing something, in doing which he will be carrying out the order. The picture of this as reasoning from a more general to a more specific command, or from a command to achieve something to a command to do such-and- such with a view to this, is of some interest to us.

R.M. Hare maintained that imperative inference repeated ordinary inference; if one proposition followed from another, the corresponding imperatives were similarly related. And also, from an imperative *p!* and a proposition *if p then q,* there would follow an imperative *q!*

Anthony Kenny was struck by the 'non-necessary' character of many Aristotelian inferences. He suggested that there was a 'logic of satisfactoriness' by reasoning within which one could move from 'kill someone' to killing a particular individual, from a disjunctive command to obeying one of the disjuncts, and from a requirement that q, with the information that p then q, to the decision to effect p. All these reasonings would be fallacious in the logic of propositions. Accordingly, Kenny suggested that this logic was the mirror image of ordinary logic; what would be conclusions in ordinary logic figure as premises in this logic — premises of the form Fiat $p!$ — and the reasoning proceeds to conclusions, also Fiats,[8] which are what in the indicative mood would be premises in ordinary logic. To see whether an inference in the 'logic of satisfactoriness' is valid, you check whether the reverse inference is valid when instead of Fiats you have the corresponding propositions.

Hare's 'imperative inference' of course does not allow of such inferences as these. Also, as had earlier been pointed out by Alf Ross, such a 'logic' admits the inference of $(p$ or $q)!$ from $p!$ Kenny's system allows many natural moves, but does not allow the inference from 'Kill everyone' to 'Kill Jones!' It has been blamed for having an inference from 'Kill Jones!' to 'Kill everyone!' but this is not so absurd as it may seem. It may be decided to kill everyone in a certain place in order to get the particular people that one wants. The British, for example, wanted to destroy some German soldiers on a Dutch island in the Second World War, and chose to accomplish this by bombing the dykes and drowning everybody.[9] (The Dutch were their allies.)

This 'logic', however, curiously and comically excludes just those forms that von Wright has concentrated on. Expressing the end as a 'Fiat', and given that unless one does such-and-such the

---

[8] In a special sense: not that the 'conclusion' has to be fulfilled or implemented. But the proposition is given the 'Fiat' form to shew that it is not being asserted or supposed, but proposed as something to make true.

[9] Alf Ross shews some innocence when he dismisses Kenny's idea: 'From plan *B* (to prevent overpopulation) we may infer plan *A* (to kill half the population) but the inference is hardly of any practical interest.' We *hope* it may not be.

end will not be achieved, it seems obvious that if there is such a thing as inference by which a command or decision can be derived, there must here be an inference to 'do such-and-such'. It also seems absurd that $(p \& q)!$ for *arbitrary q*, follows from $p!$ Effecting two things may indeed often be *a way of* effecting one of them; but the admission of arbitrary conjuncts is one of those forced and empty requirements of a view which shew that there is something wrong with it. It is in this respect like the derivation of $(p \lor q)!$ from $p!$ in Hare's system.

Kenny's suggestion has this value: it suggests that we consider a passage *from* what would be a conclusion of inference from facts *to* what would be premises of such a conclusion, when the conclusion is something to aim at bringing about, and the premises are possibly effectable truth-conditions of this, or means of effecting them. A truth-condition is a circumstance or conjunction of circumstances given which the proposition is true. Execution-conditions for commands are truth-conditions for the corresponding propositions. A proposition implies that *a* (some or other) truth-condition of it holds, but the truth of a given truth-condition of it does not usually follow from its truth. If we find a conjunctive truth-condition, it may be that the truth of one of the conjuncts follows from the truth of the proposition, but this need not generally be so.

In reckoning how to execute an order, one may be looking for straightaway practicable execution-conditions. Also, perhaps, for practicable conditions whose falsehood implies that the order is not carried out. If there is something of this sort, the proposition stating that it is true *will* follow from the proposition corresponding to the original order. But there may be no particular condition of that sort. Thus, one may not be looking for anything, and certainly will not be looking for everything, which will necessarily have been made true if the original order is carried out.

Let us illustrate. An administrator for a conquering power gives the order 'Bring all the members of one of these committees before me'. There are a dozen or more committees in question. So if all the members of any one of them are brought before him, the order is obeyed. But there is no committee that must be brought before him. If, however, there is someone who is a member of all the committees, then if *he* is not fetched the order has not been obeyed. Let there be such a man. The executor of the order picks up this man and one by one a number of others, until he knows he has a set among them that comprises a committee. He may not aim at any particular committee but let chance decide which one he makes up as he gets hold of now this man, now this pair of alternatives, now that man. All the time he is calculating the consequences of his possible moves as contributions to the achievement of his goal, and acting accordingly.

This brings out the relation we have mentioned between the idea of practical inference and imperative inference. The one seeking to obey this order has a goal, expressed by what the order requires should become the case.

But now, it appears that all the reasoning is ordinary 'theoretical' reasoning. It is, for example, from potential elements of truth-conditions for the attainment of his goal. 'If he does this, he will have that situation, which has such-and-such relevance to the attainment of the goal.' Such conditionals and such relevance will themselves be established by 'ordinary' inference from various facts. What he is trying to do is to find a truth-condition which he can effect, make true, (practicable ways of making not straightaway practicable truth-conditions true). As he does so, or as he finds potential conjuncts of a truth-condition which he can effect, he acts. Where in all this is there any other than 'ordinary' reasoning — i.e. reasoning from premises to the truth of a conclusion?

Let us suppose that the order is placed at the beginning of a set of considerations, but is cast in the form of a 'Fiat' ('May it come about that') adopted by the executive.

Fiat: some committee is brought before X.

He now reasons:

> If I get all the members of some committee rounded up, I can bring them before X

and adopts a secondary Fiat:

> ∴ Fiat: I get all the members of some committee rounded up.

He reasons further:

> Only if A is rounded up will all the members of any committee be rounded up.

And he can pick up A, so he does. Let us verbalize this action:

> ∴ Let me pick up A. (Or: So I pick up A.)

He reasons further:

> If the occupants of this bar are rounded up, several members of committees will be rounded up.

> If several members of committees are rounded up, we may be able to pick a whole committee from among them, together with A.

And he can round up all the occupants of the bar, so he does. Verbalized:

> ∴ Let me round up all the occupants of this bar. (Or: So I round up all the occupants of this bar.)

He now finds he hasn't yet got all the members of any one committee, but he reasons:

> If I pick up B and C, or D, or E and F, or G or H, then, with what I have already I shall have a whole committee.

He now gets an opportunity to pick up B, C, and G. Verbalizing his action as before, we have:

> ∴ Let me pick up B, C and G. (Or: So I pick up B, C and G.)

or: ∴ Let me pick up B and C. (Or: So I pick up B and C.)

or: ∴ Let me pick up G. (Or: So I pick up G.)

Now, what is the relation between the original Fiat and the secondary Fiat, and between the secondary Fiat and the actions (or, if you like, their verbalizations)? The relations, if the man is right, are severally given in the reasoning; that is, in the conditionals that I prefaced with the words 'he reasons'.

What, then, does the *therefore* signify? 'Therefore' is supposed to be a sign of reasoning! But what we have been calling the *reasoning* was the considerations. These will just be truths (or, if he is wrong, falsehoods). If they in turn were conclusions, the reasoning leading to them wasn't given. If we say 'He reasons. . .', should it not run 'He reasons. . . ($\therefore$) . . .'? We gave a 'therefore' indeed, but it is just what we are failing to understand. The therefores that we'd understand are these:

(a) I pick up B and C.

$\therefore$ I have a complete committee rounded up.

(b) I get all members of some committee rounded up.

$\therefore$ I can bring some committee before X.

(c) A will not be picked up.

$\therefore$ No complete committee will be rounded up.

(d) A will not be picked up.

$\therefore$ It will not be possible to bring a complete committee before X.

whereas the corresponding ones that we actually gave were:

(a^1) Let me get a complete committee rounded up.

$\therefore$ Let me pick up B and C.

(b^1) Let me bring some committee before X.

$\therefore$ Let me get all the members of some committee rounded up.

(c^1) Let me get a complete committee rounded up.

$\therefore$ Let me pick up A.

(d^1) Let me bring a complete committee before X.

$\therefore$ Let me pick up A.

Now first note this: what I implicitly called the 'reasoning' — by putting 'he reasons' in front of the examples — were considerations which would be the same in corresponding cases; I mean that the same conditional propositions mediate between 'premise' and 'conclusion' for a and a^1, for b and b^1, for c and c^1, *for d and d^1.*

For a and a^1 it is:

> If I pick up B and C, with what I already have I shall have a whole committee.

For b and b^1:

> If I get all the members of some committee rounded up, I can bring some whole committee before X.

And so on. Criticism of the transition as incorrect, whether in the 'Fiat' or the 'ordinary' form, will be exactly the same, e.g. 'What makes you think that if you round such people up, you will be able to bring them before X?'

Let us also note that the 'reasoning' that we seemed to understand, where there was 'ordinary' inference, was purely supposititious. The premises were not asserted; they concerned future possible happenings, and were merely supposed.

With these observations we have already indicated the relation between the different 'Fiats' and between them and the decisions. Where this relation exists, *there* we have the practical 'therefore'.

We should note, however, that to the transition

> Fiat q!
>
> ∴ Fiat p!

or ∴ I'll make p true

there corresponds not one but four different patterns of supposititious inference:

p will be.	$\sim$ (p will be).	p will be.	$\sim$ (p will be).
∴ q will be.	∴ q will not be.	∴ q will be possible.	∴ q will not be possible.

The hypotheticals 'If p will be, q will be' etc. prove the correctness of the inferences 'p will be, $\therefore$ q will be' etc. Such a hypothetical may be true, either because p is or is part of a truth-condition
of q, or because the coming about of p will bring about the truth of
q, or of at least part of some truth-condition of q. The difference
between these is not reflected in the schemata. That is quite as it
should be. In his reasonings our executive considered execution-
conditions and ways of bringing about the truth of execution-
conditions all in the same way. Nor in 'ordinary' inference, when,
for example, we use 'if p, then q' in *modus ponens,* do we have to
ask ourselves whether p is a truth-condition of q, or q is some
other sort of consequence of p.

And now we can say in what sense there is, and in what sense
there is not, a special 'form' of practical inference. We can represent any inference by setting forth a set of hypothetical considerations:

If p, q.

If q, r.

The question is: what are these considerations *for*, if they are not
idle? There may be at any rate these uses for them: We may be
able to assert p, and go on to assert r. Or we may want to achieve r,
and decide to make p true — this being something we can do
straight away. In either case we may appeal to considerations.
Looked at in this way, we find no special form of practical inference; we have a set of propositions connected with one another the
same way in the two cases. The difference lies in the different service to which they are put.

Not that these two are the only uses. These hypotheticals might
of course be used to make a threat or offer a warning. But we are
interested in cases where the first and last propositions get
extracted from the hypothetical contexts, and the hypotheticals
get used to mediate between them. In the cases we have consid-

ered, the extracted propositions are either asserted or made the topic of a Fiat.

But again, those are not the only cases. There is also a use in seeking an explanation; we have it given that *r*, and the hypotheticals suggest *p*, which we will suppose is something we can check for truth. If *p* turns out true, it may perhaps explain *r*.

The hypotheticals can be put to *practical* service only when they concern 'what can be otherwise', that is: what may happen one way or the other, that is: future matters, results which our actions can affect. Then the hypothetical mediates between will for an objective and decision on an action.

A passage in von Wright's 'On So-called Practical Inference' is relevant here:

> The conclusion of the first person inference, we said, is a declaration of intention. This intention may not have been formed until we realised practical necessities involved in our aiming at a certain end. So its formation may come later, after the first intention was already formed. We can speak of a *primary* and a *secondary* intention here.
>
> The connexion between the two intentions is, moreover, a kind of logically necessary connexion. The second (epistemic) premise can be said to 'mediate' between the primary intention of the first premise and the secondary intention of the conclusion. One can also speak of a transfer or *transmission of intention*. The 'will' to attain an end is being transmitted to (one of) the means deemed necessary for its attainment.[10]

I have taken cases where the means chosen aren't supposed to be necessary. Yet here too there can be a 'transmission of intention'. Von Wright finds 'a kind of logically necessary connexion' between the primary and secondary intentions. Now can we not say that there is logical connexion — but beware! this does not mean 'a relation of logical necessitation' — between the truth-connexion of *p*, $p \supset q$, and *q* on the one hand, and the transmission (1) of belief from *p* to *q* and (2) of intention from Fiat *q*! to

---

[10]   von Wright, *op.cit.* 45.

Fiat p!? But the logical necessity involved is only the truth-connexion of p, $p \supset q$, and q; this truth-connexion is common to both kinds of inference.

'But the logical necessity is *the justification* of assertive inference from p to q, and its apprehension *compels* belief!' That is a confusion. The justification is simply the truth of p and $p \supset q$: where there is such a justification, we *call* the connexion one of 'logical necessity'. And how can belief be 'compelled'? By force of personality, perhaps, or bullying. But that is not what is in question. One may also *feel* compelled, but again, that is not what is in question. What is claimed is that the belief is 'logically' compelled. But what can that mean except that there is that 'logical necessity', the truth-connexion? But it was supposed to be not *that* necessity, but a compulsion produced by perceiving that necessity. Once again: if it is a feeling, a felt difficulty so strong as to create incapacity to refrain from belief, that is still not 'logical'. And the same would hold for any other 'state of the subject'. As soon as we speak of 'logical' compulsion, we find that we can mean nothing but the 'necessity' of the truth-connection.

(Von Wright would here slide into the third person: 'X consciously believes p and consciously and simultaneously believes $p \supset q$ and the question whether q is before X's mind' *entails* 'X believes q'. But how do we know this? Only as we know 'Treason doth never prosper': if X doesn't then believe q, we won't *allow it to be said* that those other three things are true of him.)

I conclude that transmission of intention and transmission of belief should be put side by side; that there is no such thing as the transmission's being 'logical' in the sense that the 'necessity' of the truth-connexion has an analogue in a 'logical compulsion' to be in one psychological state once one has got into another. And therefore that there never was a problem of how the action or decision could be 'logically compelled'. This is obscured for us if we make the assumption that there is such a thing in the case of belief, and that *it* at least is unproblematic. I believe this is a common scarcely criticized assumption.

Nevertheless, we cannot *simply* say: practical inference is an inference, a transition, that goes in the direction from q (Fiat q!) to p (Fiat p!) when, for example, we have the truth-connexion of p, $p \supset q$, and q. For that is not the whole story. We have observed that when the propositions are turned into Fiats they are restricted in their subject-matter to future matters which our action can affect. But we have also noticed that not just any effectable truth-conditions are of practical relevance. That is, that $p \& q$ may be a condition of r *merely* because p is so, merely a truth-condition. If there is a way of effecting $p \& q$ jointly, that may be a practical conclusion, however outrageous, for one who wants to effect r (like burning the house down to roast the pig). But what if the only way of effecting $p \& q$ is to effect them separately?

In such a case, 'if $p \& q$, then r' may still have practical relevance; namely, that effecting q as well as p does not impede r. 'If p then r, and if p and q then still r' the agent may say. The consideration is of service to him if, for example, he independently wants to effect q. (Or someone else does). But there is here no 'transmission of intention' *via* $(p \& q) \supset r$, from the primary intention that r to a secondary intention that p and that q. That is, the truth-connexion of $(p \& q)$ and $(p \& q) \supset r$ does not 'mediate' such a transmission.

We cannot state *logical* conditions for this restriction on the relevance of effectable truth-conditions. We cannot do it by saying, for example, that $p \& q$ won't be a relevant effectable truth-condition of r if $p \& \sim q$ too is an effectable truth-condition of r. For that may be the case, and effecting $(p \& q)$ *still* be *a* way of effecting r. For example, I invite a married couple to dinner; I really want to just see the wife and I could invite her alone, but (for some reason or none) the way of getting to see her that I choose is to issue a joint invitation.

What is in question here is something outside the logic that we are considering, namely whether there is 'one action' which is a way of effecting (p & q) and therefore a way of effecting p. But what counts as 'one action' may be very various in various contexts and according to various ways of looking at the matter.

We have now given the sense in which there is *not* a special 'form' of practical inference. The considerations and their logical relations are just the same whether the inference is practical or theoretical. What I mean by the 'considerations' are all those hypotheticals which we have been examining, and also any propositions which show them to be true. The difference between practical and theoretical is mainly a difference in the service to which these considerations are put. Thus, if we should want to give conditionals which are logical truths, which we might think of as giving us the logically necessary connexions which 'stand behind' the inferences, *they will be exactly the same conditionals* for the practical and for the corresponding 'theoretical' inferences.

I must therefore make amends to Aristotle, whom I formerly blamed for speaking of practical inference as 'just the same', as theoretical. I wanted to say it was a *completely different form*. I believe Aristotle might have had a difficulty in understanding the debate that has gone on about 'whether there is such a thing as practical (or imperative) inference'. For what I believe has lurked in some of our minds has been something which his mind was quite clear of.

That is the picture of a logical step: an act of mind which is making the step from premise to conclusion. Making the step *in logic*, making a *movement* in a different, *pure*, medium of logic itself. So the dispute seemed one between people who all agreed there was such a thing as this 'stepping' for assertions or suppositions; but some thought they could see such a 'step' also in the case of practical inference, while others just couldn't descry it at all. But there is no such thing in any case!

There is, however, a distinct 'form' of practical inference, if all we mean by the 'form' is (1) the casting of certain propositions in a quasi-imperative form, and (2) how the matters are arranged. What is the starting-point and what the terminus? The starting-point for practical inference is the thing wanted; so in representing it we put that at the beginning. Then there are the considerations (to which I formerly restricted the term 'premises') and then there is the decision, which we have agreed to verbalize. So:

Wanted: that *p*. (Or: Let it be that *p*)

If *q*, then *p*.

If *r*, then *q*.

Decision: *r*!

While for theoretical inference the starting-point is something asserted or supposed:

r. (Or: Suppose *r*.)

If *r* then *q*.

If *q* then *p*.

p.

The change of mood and different order of the same elements give what may be called a different form. But that is all. We would have as much right to call 'a different form' that search for an explanation which we noticed. In arrangement it is just like practical inference. The mood is not changed, and the reasoning is towards a hypothesis proposed for investigation.

Given: *p*.

If *q*, then *p*.

If *r*, then *q*.

To investigate: *r*. (Is '*r*' true?)

For example, we may either seek to attain something, or to explain it when given it as a phenomenon:

To attain:	Spectacular plant growth	To explain:	Spectacular plant growth
	If plants are fed with certain substances, there will be spectacular plant growth. If these substances are in the soil, the plants will be fed with them.		
Conclusion:	To put those substances in the soil.	Conclusion:	To examine the soil so as to check whether those substances are present.

Both of these uses are different from the 'theoretical' use to reach the truth of a conclusion:

Premise: There are certain substances in the soil.

If those substances are in the soil, the plant will be fed with them.

If the plants are fed with those substances, there will be spectacular plant growth.

Conclusion: There will be spectacular plant growth.

If the common characteristics of these three patterns are recognized, and it is also clear wherein they differ, then it seems a matter of indifference whether we speak of different kinds of inference or not.

Those, however, who have objected to the idea of 'practical inference' have this speaking for them: though there is a 'validity' of practical inference, it is not of a purely formal character. By that, I mean one that can be displayed by the use of schematic letters, such that any substitution instance of the forms so given will be valid. The restriction of subject-matter to future contingents may be formally characterizable. The restriction, which we have mentioned, on inferences to *bringing it about that p and q*, apparently cannot be.

The transmission of belief can be called 'logical' in a derivative sense: if *r* follows from *p and q* and one *believes r 'because p and q'*. Given the truth-connexions of the propositions, *any* such belief will be 'logically transmitted' in our derivative sense. A parallel sense of 'logical transmission' for practical inference would be empty and vain, failing to catch the idea of 'transmission of intention'. For there *is* such a thing, but it is excluded in the case where *p* will be relevant to the end and we add just any arbitrary conjunct *q*, whose truth would have to be effected 'separately'.

In his earlier 1963 article on practical inference, in the *Philosophical Review*,[11] von Wright mentions a form in which the second premise says that the end won't be attained unless someone *else*, *B*, does something. With his assumptions, he cannot give an account of a reasoning whose conclusion is *B*'s action; 'the agent who is in pursuit of the end and the agent upon whom the practical necessity is incumbent must be the same'.

Nevertheless, there are such forms. They will be practical (rather than idle) if the considerations on the part of *X*, whose objective is mentioned in the first premise, lead to the other's doing the required thing. But this might be because *X forces B* to do it! If so, then the terminus is that action on *X's* part which compels *B* to do *A*. But it might also exemplify some relation of affection or authority or co-operation. Then we could treat the action on *B's* part (without verbalization) as the conclusion. At any rate, we can do so just as much as where the person who acts is the same as the person whose objective is promoted.

If the reasoning terminates in the utterance of an order, then of course *B* does not have to derive that conclusion; he is already given it. That will not be a case that interests us; the cases we are after are ones where *B* makes the inference. Now in discussion of 'imperative inference', people have usually had in mind the derivations to be made by someone obeying other people's orders. I

---

[11] 'Practical Inference', *Philosophical Review* 72 (1963): 159–79.

described this as a problem of practical inference: such a person, I supposed, has the objective of executing an order. But what have people in mind who discuss whether '*Do r!*' follows from '*Do r or q*', or conversely? I think that either the initial order is supposed to be accepted, in the sense that the one who accepts it as it were administers it to himself, after which he 'infers' derivable orders, or he is conceived of as ascribing the derivable orders to the person giving the initial order. In either way of looking at it there is a supposed or putative inference on the part of someone who seriously means the first order, to the derived order.

Reverting to von Wright's first-person form, suppose I say to you:

> I want to get this message to N by four o'clock. Unless you take it
> to him, I shan't get it to him by four o'clock.

And suppose I then hand you the message with nothing more said, whereupon you carry it to N. (Such is our relationship.) So *you* act on *my* grounds. I state the premises (as premises are conceived by von Wright); you draw the conclusion.

Now if it were 'theoretical' reasoning, i.e. reasoning to the truth of a conclusion, you might 'draw the conclusion' without believing it. I make assertions, you produce a statement that is implied by them. If you did believe what I said, and are clear about the implication, very likely you will believe the conclusion. But you may not have believed me. Nonetheless, you can still produce the conclusion precisely as a conclusion from the premises without asserting it and without believing it.

How is it with action? The way we are looking at the matter, drawing the conclusion in a practical sense is acting. Then you act in *execution* of my will. But what are you after yourself?

You may be after promoting my objectives. If so, we might represent the matter by setting forth *your* 'practical grounds':

> I want what she wants to be attained.

> Unless I do *A*, what she wants won't be attained.

So … But may it not be that you have no objective of your own here? That you are functioning as an instrument? Asked for the grounds of your action, you point to *my* grounds, as a man may point to his orders.

You are then speaking as one who had a certain role, but whose own objectives do not yet come into the picture.

Do you, for example, have to believe the 'second premise'? No! Then you act, but perhaps woodenly or even as it were ironically. Surely slaves and other subordinates must often act so.

Not aiming at what the directing will aims at, not believing his premises, but still drawing the conclusion in action: *that* will be what corresponds to not believing the assertions and not believing the conclusion but still drawing the conclusion in the theoretical case.

These considerations make a distinction between what a man is up to and what he is after. In the case imagined, what he is up to is: being the executive, the instrument, a kind of rational tool, and *so* acting as a subordinate. But this does not show what, if anything, he is after: it does not show *for the sake of what* he acts. It might be objected that he *has* the objective of 'acting as a subordinate'; this no doubt is an intermediate end, for him, pursued perhaps for the sake of getting by, of not getting into trouble. This may be so sometimes. Then the man does not merely act as a subordinate, *he thinks* he had better do so in order to keep out of trouble. But it would be a mistake to think this must always be the situation. We can go directly from taking the message in these circumstances to the end of not getting into trouble. The means, acting as a subordinate, are not required as an intermediate term. That he acts as a subordinate in the way I have described is a true characterization or summary description of his thus acting under the will of his master or superior. But perhaps his 'consciousness has not been raised' sufficiently for the idea to enter into his calculation.

Now I can at last bring out the objection to von Wright's putting wanting and believing — the psychological facts of wanting and believing — into the premises. It is as incorrect as it would be to represent theoretical inference in terms of belief. No doubt we could argue that '*A* believes that *p* and that if *p* then *q*' entails '*A* believes that *q*'. I have already remarked on a certain emptiness in this contention when it is decked out with such saving clauses as are needed to make it true. One will then take the failure to believe *q* as a criterion for the falsehood of the statement of conjunctive belief: we won't *call* it 'really' believing that *p* and if *p* then *q*. Similarly for '*X* intends to attain *E* and believes that unless he does *A* he will not' — if he does not now do *A*. Yet the objection may not impress. For if *p* entails *q*, then of course *not-q* will entail *not-p*, and one may not be sure of the weight of the notion of a 'criterion' here.

But there is a clearer objection. We would never think that the validity of '*p*, if *p* then *q*, therefore *q*' was to be expounded as the entailment of '*X* believes *q*' by '*X* believes that *p* and that if *p* then *q*'. It is, we feel, the other way around.

Belief is the most difficult topic because it is so hard to hold in view and correctly combine the psychological and the logical aspects. Beliefs are psychological dispositions belonging in the histories of minds. But also, a belief, a believing, is internally characterized by the proposition saying what is believed. This is (mostly) not about anything psychological; its meaning and truth are not matters of which we should give a psychological account. Propositions, we say, are what we operate the calculi of inference with, for example the calculus of truth-functions; and here is the calculus. We then display it. Certainly what it is *for* is, for example, to pass from beliefs to beliefs. But we should throw everything into confusion if we introduced belief into our description of the validity of inferences. In setting forth the forms of inference we put as elements the propositions or we use propositional variables to represent them.

Just the same holds for the patterns of practical inference. I have argued that the *logical facts* are merely the same as for theoretical: e.g. the truth-connexions of p, if p then q, and q; and of *not-p*, only if p then q, and *not-q*. But the patterns are different; the elements are put in a different order; and the propositions are not asserted but propounded as possibilities that can be made true.

There would be no point in the proof patterns, if they were never to be plugged into believing minds, if nothing were ever asserted; and equally no point in patterns of practical inference if nothing were aimed at. But *still* one should not put the wanting or intending or believing into the description of the inferences.

Now this point about the inference itself appears to me capable of demonstration from the cases we have just been considering. Just as, without believing it, I can draw a conclusion from your assertions, so our ironical slave can draw a conclusion in action from the specified objective and the assertion made by his master. In both cases the inference is something separable from the attitude of the one who is making it. The elements of the inference must all be in one head, it is true: that is, they must be known to whoever makes the inference; but the cognate believing and willing do not have to exist in that soul. So the inference patterns should not be given as ones in which these psychological facts are given a place.

Theoretical inferences do essentially concern objects of belief, and practical ones do concern objects of will and belief. This can put us on the wrong scent if we think that belief and will are themselves experienced soul or mind states, happenings, actions or activities, as are pains, feelings of all sorts, images, reflections, and, sometimes, decisions. It is easy to think this. Then 'I believe p' would mean, say, 'I get assent feelings about the idea that p'. But if one does adopt such a view, one will find the greatest difficulty in maintaining that there is anything at all in the entailment: 'X believes that p and that if p then q, therefore X believes q'; Or by the same token, anything at all in the argument 'X intends to attain end E: X believes that unless he does action A now he will not attain E; so X is just about to do action A'.

4

One of von Wright's moves, which helped to obtain necessity in the conclusions of practical inferences, was to change 'want' to 'intend': X intends to make the hut inhabitable. This has the effect of restricting his first premise to definitely accomplishable objectives. A man may hubristically say that he intends to be rich, healthy, happy, glorious, to attain the knowledge of things worth knowing, or to enjoy life. Whether he will do so is very much on the knees of the gods. If we speak, as I am willing to speak, of an *intention of the end* even for such ends, intention here means nothing but 'aiming at', and the verb 'intend' remains inept.

We have seen that the pursuit of necessary connexion or logical compulsion is pursuit of a Will-o'-the-wisp. So we need not limit ourselves to such restricted ends. Von Wright himself did not stress the purpose of securing some kind of necessity of a conclusion; nevertheless, that purpose was served by the restriction in the following way: when ends are of such a diffuse character as the ones I have just mentioned, it is rare for some highly specific action here and now to be quite necessary in pursuing them. Not that it is out of the question. I might, for example, have the end of leading an honourable, unblemished life, and then there will sometimes be situations in which, as we say, some 'quite particular' act is necessary for me. All the same, the case is exceptional. But it is a quite frequent one for the attainment of such very specific objectives as I can properly be said to *intend to bring about*.

Von Wright gives a different reason for the restriction: a man may want incompatible things. But his purpose of ruling out incompatible ends is not guaranteed success by changing 'want' to 'intend'. Although no doubt a man can intend only what he at least thinks he can achieve, still the objective is always at a remove from the action: it is thus quite possible for him in his actions seriously to intend to achieve things which are severally possible, but not possible together; nor does he have to *think* that they are compossible; he may never have brought them together in his mind – if he had, he would perhaps have realized at once that they were not possible together. Thus he may do one thing to help bring it about that two people meet, and another to help bring it about that one of them travels overseas, though this will prevent their meeting.

We may therefore confidently abandon this impoverishing restriction. This allows us to consider an important fact of human nature, namely, that men have such 'diffuse' ends. They are not merely concerned to bring about such circumstances as that object *A* be moved to point *B*. They want, for example, happiness, glory, riches, power.

We might call these ends 'generic'. But here we must avoid a confusion: 'generic' does not mean the same as 'general'. The generic is contrasted with the more specific: what *form* of wealth, for example, is a man who wants to be wealthy aiming at in his calculations, when he has worked out something to do in order to be wealthy? The possession of lands, or of a regular income, or of a large sum of money? His heart may just be set on being wealthy, but if he is to achieve this it must take a more specific form, per-haps determined for him by his opportunities.

An end may be called 'particular' either by contrast with being generic or by contrast with being general. It will be convenient to avoid this ambiguity. When I call an end *particular,* I will hence-forth mean that the end is that something shall hold about a given individual. *This hut* is to be inhabitable, *I* am to be rich or happy. Thus all these generic ends of health, wealth, knowledge, etc. are in this sense particular. That *this hut* is to be inhabitable is particu-lar but not very specific. More specific is that it is to be warm, or furnished. Still more specific: that it is to be warmed with a coke stove. We descend from the merely specific to the particular on the side of *what is to be done* to the hut if I make it my objective that it be warmed with the stove I found in a certain shop; at least, if I mean the very example of the stove, and not the type.

Ends can be general. I may not be aiming at *NN*'s doing or being something, but have, for example, the aim that some men know classical Greek, or again that men be free. This last is not merely general but generic. But if my aim is: that there be a copy of the Bible in every hotel room, that is a general but specific end.

It is human to have generic ends. These are particular when they are ends that one shall oneself be or do something. I don't know if it is humanly possible to have no *general* ends. I suppose that a good man will be likely to have some. (Though I don't mean that it *takes* a good man to have any.)

Having thus far cleared the ground, we can make some observations on the role of 'general principles' in practical inference.

If, as in Aristotle, 'principle' means 'starting-point', we might first think that a starting-point is wherever you happen to start. But this would not be quite satisfactory, since you might happen to *start* with some quite particular fact, as, that *N* is married to *M*. It is not a historical order of actual consideration that is meant; a man's considerations leading to an action can be arranged in an order that displays a progress from something mentioning an end to the particular action adopted. This is so whether the first thing merely mentions an end as 'pure water is wholesome for humans to drink' mentions the wholesome to drink, or specifies it *as* an objective, as 'Health is to be restored' does. In either case we can call the thing aimed at the starting-point. If the objective is not specified *as* an objective, then the statement mentioning it which we put first in an orderly arrangement *may or may not be a general statement*. Thus, 'Only if this hut is heated will it be habitable' is not a general statement; yet it might be the first in a set of considerations which we give as the grounds of an action.

However, its truth will be connected with general facts as well as a particular one. For example, 'Humans need a certain degree of warmth in their habitations' as well as 'This hut lacks such a degree of warmth as it is'.

Aristotle's 'general' or 'universal' premises are of that kind. It is a reasonable view that such premises are always, in some sense, in the offing. But maybe only in the sense that they ought to be reachable. '*This* hut needs heating if *you* are to live in it' might be the judgment of a sensible person who had not formulated a general statement — for perhaps another person rather hardier could manage well without heat in this hut. 'General propositions derive from particular ones'[12] Aristotle remarks, and an experienced person may just have good particular judgement. He has just spoken of 'intelligence' (*nous*), which in practical considerations — and here I will translate with the uncouthness of a close rendering of the Greek — 'is of the particular, of the possible and of the second premise; for these are starting-points of that for the sake of which'. Here 'starting-points' does not mean *considerations* or things put in some arrangement of propositions; it means rather *causes*. That for the sake of which something is done has its source, if it does get achieved, in perfectly particular contexts, where there is possibility of things turning out one way *or* another, and in the particular premise, which is the immediate ground of action. Thus the general premises may be dispensable. But if we could not simply and directly judge the particular '*You* need *this* hut to be heated' we might reach it from generalization, as also if we heard it and looked for a justification of it. Somewhat vague generalizations like 'Humans need a certain degree of warmth in their dwellings' are of course readily available.

So much for the relation of general and particular premises. I now turn to what is much more important, the matter of generic ends.

---

[12] *Nicomachean Ethics* 1143[b] 4ff.

Aristotle has a teaching which is useful to mention because of the contrast that it offers with von Wright's. I stick to my principles of close translation:

> Of theoretical thinking which is neither practical nor productive, the *well* and *badly* is the true and false, for this is the business of any thinking; but of what is practical and intellectual, [it is] truth in agreement with right desire.[13]

By contrast, we may say: in von Wright's picture the business of practical thinking is simply *truth in agreement with desire,*[14] *i.e. getting things the way you want them to be without the qualification that Aristotle puts in 'getting things a way it's all right to want them to be'.*

This may be a little unfair to von Wright, who after all has not addressed himself to the question. But we can ask: is not the truth about it a necessary component of the essential characterization of practical inference?

I claimed that in practical inference the relation between the premises and the conclusion (the action) is that the premises show what good, what use, the action is. Now if, following von Wright, we put 'I want' into the first premise, this aspect assumes insignificance. It could be admitted, but it would be of no consequence. Of course the premises show what use the action is — it is that of bringing about something one wants, which has to be achieved, if it is achieved, by some means.

But in Section 2 I shewed that the wanting, the drive towards the end, does not properly go into the reasoning at all. This 'I want' is not a reason; a reason must shew or be connected with further reasons that show what good it is to do the thing. Now does this mean merely what it will effect or help to effect — which, as it happens, one wants?

---

[13] *Ibid.* 1139ᵃ 27–30.

[14] I mean truth which you make true by acting. For some reason, people find this idea very difficult. In lecturing I have sometimes tried to get it across by saying: 'I am about to make it true that I am on this table.' I then climb on the table. Whether I have made it true that my hearers understand, I do not know.

Admittedly, that is how I have been presenting it so far. There are strong reasons for doing so. If an end, an objective, is specified, then how is correctness of calculation to be judged? By whether it indicates an action that is necessary for, or will secure, that objective. Not *only* by this, indeed, since an effective means may be cumbersome or clumsy or difficult, and a better means may be available. But a criticism of the means on any other ground, for example on grounds of outrageousness, makes an appeal to other ends which ought not to be violated in pursuing this one. If you don't mind burning the house down to roast the pig, and it is easy and effective, the pig getting well roasted that way, then why not do it?

Criticism of means which are good purely in relation to the given end, must be in the light of other ends which it is assumed that you have or ought to have. If you have them, we can put them in and criticize the calculation for failure in relation to its ends. If not, then this criticism of means is a criticism of ends and can be considered together with a possible criticism of the given end, either as such or in those circumstances. Now the question becomes: what has a criticism of ends got to do with an evaluation of practical reasoning as such?

Aristotle discusses an intellectual virtue, *euboulia*, which is translated 'good counsel'. This does not imply that one is a giver or receiver of advice, only that the actions of one who has it are, as we might say, 'well-advised', of one who lacks it 'ill-advised'. He observes that it is a certain kind of correctness of calculation; not every kind, because 'the self-indulgent or bad man will get what he purposes by calculation if he is clever, and so he will have calculated correctly, but will obtain for himself a great evil' — whereas good counsel will not produce such a result. We can now say: hitherto we have been considering that 'correctness of calculation' which can be common to the well-advised and the ill-advised. That correctness of calculation which produces 'truth in agreement with desire', i.e. things as one wants them to be.

It is easy to say at this point: 'Ah, what is in question here is *moral* criticism, and that is something else. It is not a criticism of practical inference as such.' But I cannot accept this observation: I have long complained that I don't know what 'moral' means in this sort of use. 'Perfectly sound practical reasoning may lead to bad actions.' Yes, that is true, in just the same sense as it is true that 'Perfectly sound theoretical reasoning may lead to false conclusions'. If we limit what we mean by 'soundness' to what is called 'validity', both observations are correct. And in our philosophical training we learn carefully to use this idea of soundness of reasoning and to make the distinction between truth and validity and we are right to do so. Equally right, therefore, to distinguish between goodness and validity; for in the sphere of practical reasoning, goodness of the end has the same role as truth of the premises has in theoretical reasoning.

This the great Aristotelian parallel: if it is right, then the goodness of the end and of the action is as much of an extra, as external to the validity of the reasoning, as truth of the premises and of the conclusion is an extra, is external to the validity of theoretical reasoning. *As* external, but not *more* external.

We know that the externality is not total. For truth is the object of belief, and truth-preservingness an essential associate of validity in theoretical reasoning. The parallel will hold for practical reasoning.

In the philosophy of action we often hear it debated to and fro whether something, *p*, 'is a reason' for action. We sometimes hear it said that 'moral considerations' *just are* 'reasons'. But what does all this mean? It seems to be discussed independently of anybody making the thing *his* reason. With our present insight, we can clarify. '*p* is a reason', in theoretical contexts, assumes that some proposition *q* is in question. It may mean that *if p* is true to believe, then *q* is true to believe or is probable. And that someone believing *p* would intelligibly believe *q* 'because *p*'. Or it may mean that *p is* true, and that anyone would be right to believe *q*, absolutely or with more or less confidence, 'because *p*'. Similarly in practical contexts '*p* is a reason' assumes that some act *A* is in question, and then it may mean one of two things. Either that *p* mentions an end *E* or states something helping to shew that *A* will promote an end *E*, such that *if p* is true *and E* is good to pursue, *A* is good to do. And that someone who had the end *E* would intelligibly do *A* 'because *p*'. Or, that *E is* good to pursue, that *p* is true, and someone would be right to do *A* 'because *p*'.

What sort of proposition is 'that *E* is good to pursue'? There are two types of case: one, where one can ask 'good for what?' As, for example, if I am proposing to do various things to build a bonfire. Building a bonfire is my aim — what's the good of that? In the second type of case *E* is already specified as some good, for example as health is the good state of the body, knowledge of what is worth knowing the good of the intellect. Pleasure is a specially problematic concept, pleasantness therefore as a terminal characterization especially problematic and I won't concern myself with that question here.

But may not someone be criticizable for pursuing a certain end, thus characterizable as a sort of good of his, where and when it is quite inappropriate for him to do so, or by means inimical to other ends which he ought to have?

This can be made out only if man has a last end which governs all. Only on this condition can that illusory 'moral ought' be exorcised, while leaving open the possibility of criticizing a piece of practical reasoning, valid in the strict and narrow sense in which in theoretical contexts validity contrasts with truth. The criticism will be of the practical reasoning as not leading to the doing of good action. An action of course is good if it is not bad, but being inimical to the last architectonic end would prove that it was not good.

Now, that practical reasoning so understood should be of use in understanding action, including the action of a society, I can accept.

11

Practical Truth

A stone can't lie in ambush waiting to trip you up. A cracking branch of a tree doesn't aim at the cups and glasses it breaks in falling. A monkey can't open a bank account. A cow can't pay debts.

Now, there is a special kind of multiplicity of levels of description of human acts of which I want to speak. I put ink on paper in the form of letters. I'm writing something. I am in fact signing something with my name. And I'm thereby joining in a petition to the governor of the state — or prison — where I am an inhabitant. I am taking part in a campaign to get people tortured under interrogation. In doing this I am keeping a promise. I am avoiding trouble with some conspirators who have got me to promise to do that.

What I'm now wanting to remind you of is just this kind of different levels of description. I don't mean every list of different things that might suitably be called 'different levels'. *That* might apply to the branch of the tree falling. It breaks the glasses it falls on. It infuriates the owner of the glasses. It makes him behave crossly to the people he is with. So it causes him to lose a contract he was hoping to make. This is a sequence of effects, each effect a cause of the next one. Like in the lines:

* This paper was the first in a series of *Working Papers in Law, Medicine and Philosophy* (edited by John M. Dolan) published by the Program in Human Rights and Medicine of the University of Minnesota in 1993. It was subsequently reprinted in the journal *Logos* 2/3 (Summer 1999): 68–76. It is reprinted here with the permission of Professor John M. Dolan.

For want of a nail, a shoe was lost.

For want of the shoe, the horse was lost.

For want of the horse, the rider was lost.

For want of the rider, a message was lost.

For want of the message, a battle was lost.

And all for the want of a horse-shoe nail.

But the kind of different levels of description of a human action that I want to attend to here takes as examples descriptions of the same act under which the agent is *responsible* (guilty or praise-worthy). In many cases all the descriptions are descriptions under which the action is intentional. In these cases, the series of descriptions is connected with a special sort of developing series of true answers to the question 'What for?' You were writing your name on a piece of paper — what for? The answer is 'I was signing a contract of sale of a car'. What for? 'So as not to own the car, so as to be able to avoid its being taken from me by bailiffs to contribute to a fine I don't want to pay — that is, to avoid paying a fine.' What for? 'Oh, because I regard the fine as unjust and am therefore unwilling to pay it, and I don't want property taken from me to meet it.' Why won't you give up your property to pay a fine you think unjust? 'Simply because I think it unjust and I can reasonably avoid loss of property in this way.'

This sort of series showing one's intentions in respect of a series of descriptions of some one action is not indeed the only type of example where the agent is responsible. For a true answer to 'Why did you do this?' might be 'I didn't notice such-and-such features of the situation'. But such an answer raises complicated issues which I don't want to cover here, so I will stick to the type I have exemplified in some detail, where the action-descriptions form a related series and were shown by the true answers to the questions as being descriptions under which the action was intentional.

My purpose in discussing such cases is to explain the notion of practical truth.

So far as I know, Aristotle was the first to formulate this concept. The place to find it formulated is the second chapter of Book VI of the *Ethica Nicomachea*, within the numbers 1139a–b. Aristotle tells us that as positive and negative predication are in thought, so are pursuit of and flight from in desire. This comparison is rendered pretty clear if we remember that predicating something, *S*, of some object *O* is equivalent to rejecting a contrary negation of *S* in respect of the same object. Comparably, going after something can be equated with the willful rejection of *not* having it. To speak in terms of propositions, we note the equivalence of *p* and *not-not-p*, and see it paralleled by an equivalence of 'Yes' to possible health and 'No' to prospective sickness.

We note that Aristotle is not comparing *attraction* and contrary affects of the psychic faculty of desire to affirmation and negation: no, he compares pursuit and flight, which are possible *actions*, to positive predication and negation. That is to say, he *considers* desire (ὄρεξις) and in connection with it he identifies actions of pursuit and flight as saying 'Yes' or 'No', one to what is sought, the other to what is fled. This, I take it, is because avoidance of avoidance is equivalent to seeking-to-have. The comparison with positive and negative judgmental[1] predication is of course made *à propos* reactions of human beings who have language and are well advanced in the use of it. This fits the fact that his topics are πρᾶξις and προαίρεσις, *action* and *decision*, in a sense in which neither can be attributed to children or beasts.

Aristotle is therefore writing about men, ἄνθρώποι, not counting children, and also excluding other animals. This is apparent from the rest of the passage. His next sentence begins 'so that',

---

[1]   I think we have to take Aristotle's positive and negative predication as signifying *assertive* predication; otherwise the comparison of pursuit and avoidance with it would not be apt.

which shows that he is drawing a conclusion from the comparison he has made.

'So that, since moral virtue, i.e., virtue in actions and passions, is a disposition of decision making, and decision is deliberative will, this means that for decision to be sound the reasons must be *true*, the will *right*, and the same things must be named by the one and pursued by the other.' This is implied by the parallel he has pointed to between thought and will (ὄρεξις) given his account of decision, which involves both thought and will.

Thus, by identification of their roles in will with those of positive and negative predication in thought, the sort of 'Yes' and 'No' involved in decisions is claimed to be specifically human and not generically animal. Aristotle draws his conclusion not only from that identification, but, given it, from the character of a virtue as a disposition of the faculty of decision.

He tells us that, for purely theoretical thinking the 'well and badly' are truth and falsehood. This is indeed what thinking does, well or badly, truly or falsely, and so these are the business (the ἔργον) of *any* thinking. But he has also said, in speaking of the conditions of 'sound' *decision*, that the thinking and truth *here* are '*practical* thought and truth'. Here we have the explicit formulation 'practical truth'. And now he adds to the general characterization of any thinking at all, that the 'business', the 'job', of thinking that is practical is 'truth in agreement with right desire'. This does not exclude the possibility that practical thinking may be bad, and its badness partly lie in falsehood. Still, we *shall* want to know what falsehood is special to practical thinking. However, at this point of the text Aristotle is most concerned to say that there is no decision-making, no deciding without mind, thought, and *some* ethical disposition. This, he insists, applies also to 'poetic', i.e. *productive*, thinking. For every producer or maker is producing for the sake of something, and the product itself is not his end *simpliciter*: that is, not his end. 'For doing well is the end, and the desire in decision is for that. So decision is desiring thought or thinking desire — and *the* cause of this kind is man.' Note the importance of this final sentence of the passage. There is this special kind of cause operating in the world, and it is man.

We need now to consider what Aristotle means by 'truth in agreement with right desire'.

It is clear what 'truth in agreement with desire' would be. It would be: things being as a desirer wants them to be. Remember in Edward Fitzgerald's translation of Omar Khayyam where he (Fitzgerald, at least) speaks of a longing 'to break this sorry scheme of things entire' and 'remake it nearer to the heart's desire'.

'Truth in agreement with right desire', then, will mean 'things (i.e. whatever is in question to bring about in action) being as rightly desired'. We ask: 'With *what* rightness?' It must be rightness of the 'right desire' in the decision of the agent when that is sound. That decision, Aristotle has said, ought to be to pursue what true thinking names.

To understand this, we look further in our text and come to the desire being ultimately a desire of doing well (εὐπραξία). In Book VI, Aristotle writes as if this were always the last objective here and now of a human 'action'. Therefore of the action of a wicked man no less than of a good one. At some level of characterization of his action, the wicked man's will be false. The falsehood may be in an earlier identification — for example, helping your neighbours *is* doing well, but killing someone for them is not helping them. And the desire or will in choice will be for this end, doing well, whether the choice is that of the good or of the bad man.

At this point someone may say to me: 'Either Aristotle is inconsistent here with what he says about decision in Book III or you have got him wrong. For in Book III he is quite clear that a decision, a choice, relates to means, not ends. But by your understanding of this passage in Book VI he thinks that the will in decision is a will for an end.'

The question is relevant, but the suspicion is wrong. Aristotle does indeed not think that choice is of ends. But he does think that the will or desire *in* choice is primarily of the end. We should not forget that the choice of means is choice of them *as* means. Therefore, though we may not choose what to make our ends, the decisions we make must *contain* willings of ends.

In modern philosophy of the Anglo-American tradition there is a great fault: I call it 'the monolithic conception of desire, or wanting, or will'. It is readily seen what you want by what you do. This is simplistic. It is, for example, *as* possible to want not to get something you want as it is to believe that not everything you believe is true. If so, there are different levels and kinds of wanting, and this the ancients, certainly Aristotle, did know. The wanting of the thing you choose is in your decision. But there is also wanting what you choose it *for*, and this wanting is in the decision too, even though it may be that you have never chosen, never decided, to *make* it your objective.

However, Aristotle does not write as if he needed to look only at sound practical thinking. He does not speak of a 'well or badly' of thinking in determining actions. It comes in implicitly a few lines on, when he speaks of the dependence of doing well *and* its opposite, on thought and moral character. I think he could not have launched into *discussion* of 'the opposite' without getting into questions too complicated for the balance of the passage — for example, the argument, which Plato puts into the mouth of Socrates in the *Meno*, that no man ever wills evil.

However this may be, there is something further that my imaginary opponent may say: 'There is a statement in Aristotle's *Rhetoric* (1367b) which can't be true to Aristotle: namely that it is a property of — i.e. is peculiar to — the sound man that what accords with his decision, το κατα προαίρεσιν, happens. But now: if Aristotle meant that, would he not have to think that the wicked man (the ακολαστος) was incapable of choosing, or at any rate of doing so effectually? Yet we know from numerous passages that Aristotle thinks that the wicked man does choose, does act, i.e. choosing and deciding he does what he does. Also, that if he's clever enough to bring about what he has chosen, then, lacking good counsel (ευβουλία), 'he obtains for himself a great evil'.

That is all quite true and in fact it contains the solution to the problem felt when presented with that passage in the *Rhetoric*: the wicked man *does* choose, and acts badly if he is effective. But does 'things being according to his choice' characterize him? In a sense yes, if he's clever. He robs and seduces successfully, let us say. But 'things being according to his choice' is more than that. It is evidently part of Aristotle's understanding that everyone (once grown-up) acts, if he does act, choosing, i.e. deciding what to do, in the belief that in so acting he is doing well — doing well for himself.

Suppose a man does *not* act according to that conception — he is not wicked, only *weak-willed*. So he is bad, but not in his moral decisions, only in his failure to act according to them. This man perhaps has the right — i.e. true — conception of what doing well is; in action, however, he fails to pursue that objective. But the wicked man does act in the belief that, in his very action, he *is* doing well. It is at least in *this* that his thinking is false.

This enables us to understand why Aristotle said that if a choice is to be sound, not only must the thought be true, but the thinking must name and the desire pursue the same things. The 'names' in the relevant thoughts will finally and most importantly include 'doing well', but also names like 'getting wealth', 'avoiding taxation', 'making friends', or again 'paying bills', 'fighting a duel'. The 'names' must all be true of what is actually done and if they are not, then the agent's thoughts are not true, and his will may not be right.

Finally, we may note that we have given an explanation of 'practical truth'. This is truth that one produces in acting according to choice and decision.

There is often resistance to the idea that one can produce truth, i.e. make something true. But can it not be that one brings it about that p? And are not p and the truth of p equivalent. I.e.

It is true that $p \equiv p$.

If, then, one can bring it about that p, then one can make it true that p. This, however, does not satisfy people who are outraged by the notion that one can make truth. Truth, they say, is always truth and unchangeable and cannot be *brought about*. Whatever *is* true always *was* so; we just make a change of tense. Suppose it is true that I am signing a contract now. Then 10,000 years ago it *was* true that I was going to be signing that contract now. Or, perhaps more correctly, the following proposition was true 10,000 years ago: 'Elizabeth Anscombe will sign such-and-such a contract in 10,000 years'. (Perhaps we don't want to be bothered by questions of dates and chronology — so we can say instead 'Any amount of time ago this was true: "Elizabeth Anscombe will sign such-and-such a contract that time ahead".') A consequence of this is *not* a pure logical determinism; it does not mean that my action is not free. It does *not* mean that when today comes I *have* to make it true that I sign that contract today. As if I *had* to 'make it true' all that long time ago that I would sign the contract today. After all, I wasn't there to do it, was I? There is here no proof that I don't make it true that p. If I make it true that p, and q follows from $p - q$ being, say, '10,000 years ago it was true that NN would make it true that p', and I being NN, then when I make it true that p, I make it have been true 10,000 years ago that q. I make it so *now*.

I have been given an objection to this, that it is contrary to the distinction between practical and theoretical knowledge — for if one knows that one made it to have been true 10,000 years ago, that's theoretical knowledge, whereas knowing one is signing a contract is practical knowledge. But this is not a sound objection. We — and, according to St. Thomas, God too — can have theoretical knowledge of what our present practical knowledge is of.

Why then, it may be asked, the peculiarities of Aristotle's investigation? We already have the answer: practical truth is the truth *brought about* in sound deliberation leading to decision and action, and this *includes* the truth of the description 'doing well'. Then, *if* the decision is sound, what happens — the action — does accord with it as I have described — right up to the description 'doing well'.

Reverting to my opening, it may have seemed that I must attribute 'making true' to any cause. If a branch falls and breaks a tea-pot, the falling branch has made it true that the tea-pot is broken. If a dog bites my hand and it bleeds, the dog has made it true that my hand is bleeding. One might indeed say these things, but they would be trivial and pointless. Practical truth is truth created by action in a sense in which neither branches nor dogs nor children are capable of action. It might be called 'praxistic truth' in order to emphasise that it is truth brought about by a praxis resulting from deliberation — i.e. by an action (in fulfillment of a choice) which satisfies the description 'doing well'. That is a final description of what every praxis — every 'action' in this limited sense — aims at being. This makes clear what 'practical falsehood' would be. The agent chooses and he wants and believes the action that he chooses to be a *case* of doing well; and it is not. Plato's Socrates would say that his wanting to be doing well shows that he does *not* choose evil, but rather good, just because he wants to do well. But Plato's Socrates ought to admit that wanting to do what is in fact doing badly

(a) does not amount to doing well just because one wants to be doing well, and

(b) that it does not then even amount to *wanting to be doing well*.

He would admit (a) but deny (b). He would deny (b) because he would attribute the correctness of the description 'doing badly' to mere ignorance on the part of the agent, and would persuade his companions that such ignorance would not falsify the

description of the will in question as will for what is good —
namely, doing well.

ETHICS

12

Does Oxford Moral Philosophy Corrupt Youth?

A review in the periodical called *Mind* once reported that there are people who think that moral philosophy in one of its current fashions 'corrupts the youth'. The moral philosophy in question is the one connected with linguistic analysis, which has various exponents in the English speaking world. They might not like being lumped together, but their work looks roughly alike from the outside, and none of it stands above and apart from the rest, marked out as original with the others as derivations. Some forms of it are current at Oxford, and it is especially up-to-date Oxford moral philosophy that I have been asked to consider here.

I will say straight away that I do not think the accusation is correct. I will explain why later. First, however, I will note a remark by that same reviewer, who was discussing a book by Mr Hare, that no one could think him a corrupter in view of his obvious moral earnestness. This does not seem good evidence. There was an Archbishop of our time — Archbishop Temple[1] — who was always saying such things as that Christian business men and

---

* A talk given on the BBC Third Programme and subsequently printed in *The Listener* Vol. 57 (14 February 1957): 266–7, 271.

[1]   In *Christian Faith and the Common Life*, pages 58–60.

politicians must 'compromise' with their ideals because otherwise they would be driven out of their fields which would then
be left to people who had no ideals; 'the actual purification of
commerce depends on the continuance in business of those who
have ideals'. This, he explained, means sinning — 'all is sin that
falls short of the glory of God'. And *his* moral earnestness is
unsurpassed. If you really wanted to corrupt people by direct
teaching of ideas, moral earnestness would, in fact, be an important item of equipment. But I should also suspect that direct
teaching of ideas is not, nowadays, the best way of setting about
changing people; public action is much more effective. A good
deal was done, for example, by arranging trials of war criminals
on the bad side with judges from the good and victorious side
making up their law as they went along; this educated people out
of old-fashioned over-legalistic conceptions of justice. There is a
moral law above any positive enactments, and it was an inspiring
thing that horrible sinners against it should be brought before its
bar — so I have had it explained to me by young men at Oxford
who, I felt, had learned more definite, new moral theory from this
than from any teaching of moral philosophy.

However, as I have said, if you want to corrupt people by direct
propagation of ideas, moral earnestness is pretty well indispensable. Another important thing is to keep away from facts other
than ones which it is standard practice to mention — unlike, for
instance, that communist witness before a Royal Commission on
the armaments trade who read out a list of the holdings in armaments shares of members of the commission. The irrelevance of
facts (stressed on this occasion by the chairman of the commission) might be agreed to in a certain sense by moral philosophers
with whom it is a regular dogma that no fact can entail an ethical
proposition, and that people might agree on all the facts (and, I
suppose, on their mention) and still disagree in ethics. I suppose
they might, but the situation is an ideal one; a logical model, as
people say. A third point of method which I would recommend

to the corrupter would be this: concentrate on examples which are either banal: you have promised to return a book, but … and so on; or fantastic: what you ought to do if you had to move forward and stepping with your right foot meant killing twenty-five fine young men while stepping with your left foot would kill fifty drooling old ones. (Obviously the right thing to do would be to jump and polish off the lot.)

But it is in my opinion an entirely unfair and absurd accusation that such moral philosophy as is now dominant at Oxford corrupts the youth; I am surprised to learn that such a charge has been made, and it is my purpose to rebut it. In order to show that a certain teaching corrupts people you must obviously show that they have (or would have come to have) better ideas without this teaching. One way of doing this would be to say that you knew of examples: I know of none, which is at least negative evidence, for what it is worth. But another way is to look at the ideas which are specially characteristic of our society — ones, that is, which are both fairly standard and pretty much in the van — and compare them with the teaching of up-to-date university teachers. For they are presumably what most of the youth would be absorbing without the aid of those teachers; and if they are better than the teachers' ideas, and these are really influential, then they are corrupting the youth; but if they are about equal, or not so good, then no such accusation is fair.

It seems to me evident that there is no difference at all: Oxford moral philosophy is perfectly in tune with the highest and best ideals of the country at large, and this can be demonstrated in a few instances. It is a matter of dead level, no more and no less.

First, there is what I may call an anti-Platonic view of justice — anti-Platonic, I mean, in one detail. Plato seems to have thought that a just society would be one in which people were just. But this, you can learn at Oxford, may conceal a fallacy; it is not at once clear whether 'just' is a term like 'healthy' (you could not call a community healthy unless its members were individually healthy) or rather a term like 'well-arranged', which obviously does not apply to the individual. I should think that Plato was not analysing — and therefore possibly fallacious, but maintaining a thesis — and therefore possibly wrong. But is not this teaching, as to the fallacy that may lie concealed here, very much in line with one of the most important insights of modern times: that injustice may be nobody's fault, and that what is required is good arrange- ment? With this goes preference for policy — which is an effort to calculate and promote the general good — over archaic and metaphysical conceptions of justice. One can cite the unquestion- ably correct decisions of courts that, for example, certain tribu- nals need take no account of what is called 'natural justice' in their decisions; and that local authorities' proceedings in certain matters are not challengeable on grounds of fraud and bad faith on their part.

Then, again, there is a high conception of responsibility which is certainly imparted at Oxford and which is in tune with the time. If something seems in itself a bad sort of action, but you calculate that if you do not do it then the total situation (some say the total state of the world) will be worse than if you do it — then you must do it; you are answerable for the future if you can affect it for the better. This is familiarly echoed outside the university; for example, it was right to massacre the Japanese because it was (or at least was thought to be) productive of a better total state of affairs than not doing so would have been. Of course, it takes a don to give one formulation of the idea that I have heard, namely: if, unless you do A someone else will do B, then if you do not do A, you can yourself be said to *do* B (you bring it about that B is done, for the other man would not have done it if you had done A). It sounds a bit odd in the case of adultery, but the general idea is a common one.

There is, further, a gentle, tolerant, and civilised idea of responsibility for things once they have been done, which in fact goes with the high one I have mentioned. Responsibility is causality; for to hold someone in good standing responsible for what he did is to ascribe the whole causality of it as an event to him — and that is unfair; you must not make him a scapegoat for something that obviously had all sorts of causes. Thus I must face the future with a recognition of limitless responsibility; no letting myself off this; I cannot, for example, take the easy way out by saying that certain courses of action are excluded by their badness; but towards the past I need feel only that degree of responsibility indicated by my share in bringing about whatever situation was brought about. With this also goes the merciful and humane attitude towards criminals characteristic of the best liberal minds. For an agent is himself the victim of causality, so it is better to treat and train him than to blame and punish him. *Bien entendu*, treatment may take longer than punishment. That may even be the only difference, as in the case of 'corrective training'.

Thus, both in the university and outside, people are surely getting rid of the merely legalistic and unphilosophical notion of the 'nature and quality of an act'. It survives in our older laws and hence in the minds of our judiciary, but newer laws are putting this right so far as concerns the essential business of calculating the improvement of the general state of affairs, as is shown by the correct legal decisions that I have cited; and that this is the correct procedure in making moral decisions is constantly taught in the university. A frequent occurrence that is much in the same spirit is the removal by authority of elderly widows from their dwellings, which anyone can see they are not keeping in accordance with the standards of hygiene which are desirable for their own and general welfare. How remote and alien — and indeed totally irrelevant — sounds the remark of Solomon 'The tender mercies of the wicked are cruel'.

Another instance can be found in the intense feeling for cruelty and suffering. This is *the* topic on which there is an automatic pressure of general moral opinion in Oxford discussions. If anyone should try saying that some kind of action was bad, a case (however fantastic) is at once imagined in which a consequence of doing that action is that some horrible suffering is averted, and that settles the question. Is not this feeling for suffering a common feature of our time: one of the strongest standard things to appeal to in common talk and in newspapers, outside the university too? Think how strongly we feel about the need for preventive measures in regard to cruelty to children (very widely interpreted). I do not know if any vulgar minds ever have the thought: Preventive measures means they want to go into people's homes and push them around not because they have 'done anything', but just in case they do. But, if so, they would be wise to keep this sentiment to themselves. With this too goes the idea that what is dreadful in war is purely the 'use of force', aggression, the amount of suffering; who, for example, is made the object of attack, with what justification, does not make much difference.

There is also the realisation in moral philosophy that what you have to do is to choose your way of life and act the way that fits in with this. *De finibus non est disputandum*. In discussion common standards are assumed – 'our' standards, shown by 'what we say' in judging others. These are tacitly assumed to be good, and indeed the general picture conjured up is one of people free of crime, behaving nicely (they always tell lies to avoid betraying friends, for example), and also looking for improvement, both of the state of the world and of standards themselves – in the direction towards which they already point. 'Way of life' talk is not a university invention; it is the staple of our time (no one, obviously, is going to persuade us to give up anything, like contraception, which goes with our way of life). It universally carries with it these connotations both of satisfactoriness and arbitrariness; nor does it lack the upward-looking glance.

Finally, there is the immensely serious question of the upbringing of children. Everybody knows that we have long since discarded the hideous conception of parental authority.

The business of parents is to do the best for their children, whom they therefore confront fearfully. The disservice of imposing their own standards, which may become outmoded, is evident. In a changing world, with changing conditions, standards must change; and you must cut your morals according to your purposes and the conditions, so that your actions will promote the effects you choose to pursue. (For your actions show what your morals are, no matter what you say.) Clearly, all we can do is to equip our children as thinking human beings, capable of forming and indefinitely improving their own standards of action without impediment. Is not this the general, as well as the university, opinion?

I hope that I have said enough to show that the famous imputation of 'corrupting the youth' is undeserved. This philosophy is conceived perfectly in the spirit of the time and might be called the philosophy of the flattery of that spirit.

13

Modern Moral Philosophy

I will begin by stating three theses which I present in this paper. The first is that it is not profitable for us at present to do moral philosophy; that should be laid aside at any rate until we have an adequate philosophy of psychology, in which we are conspicuously lacking. The second is that the concepts of obligation, and duty — *moral* obligation and *moral* duty, that is to say — and of what is *morally* right and wrong, and of the *moral* sense of 'ought', ought to be jettisoned if this is psychologically possible; because they are survivals, or derivatives from survivals, from an earlier conception of ethics which no longer generally survives, and are only harmful without it. My third thesis is that the differences between the well-known English writers on moral philosophy from Sidgwick to the present day are of little importance.

Anyone who has read Aristotle's *Ethics* and has also read modern moral philosophy must have been struck by the great contrasts between them. The concepts which are prominent among the moderns seem to be lacking, or at any rate buried or far in the background, in Aristotle. Most noticeably, the term 'moral' itself, which we have by direct inheritance from Aristotle, just doesn't seem to fit, in its modern sense, into an account of Aristotelian

* First published in *Philosophy* 53 (1958): 1–19. Reprinted with the permission of the Director of The Royal Institute of Philosophy, Professor Anthony O'Hear, and of the original publishers, Cambridge University Press.

ethics. Aristotle distinguishes virtues as moral and intellectual. Have some of what he calls 'intellectual' virtues what *we* should call a 'moral' aspect? It would seem so; the criterion is presumably that a failure in an 'intellectual' virtue — like that of having good judgement in calculating how to bring about something useful, say in municipal government — may be *blameworthy*. But — it may reasonably be asked — cannot *any* failure be made a matter of blame or reproach? Any derogatory criticism, say of the workmanship of a product or the design of a machine, can be called blame or reproach. So we want to put in the word 'morally' again: sometimes such a failure may be *morally* blameworthy, sometimes not. Now has Aristotle got this idea of *moral* blame, as opposed to any other? If he has, why isn't it more central? There are some mistakes, he says, which are causes, not of involuntariness in actions, but of scoundrelism, and for which a man is blamed. Does this mean that there is a *moral* obligation not to make certain intellectual mistakes? Why doesn't he discuss obligation in general, and this obligation in particular? If someone professes to be expounding Aristotle and talks in a modern fashion about 'moral' such-and-such, he must be very imperceptive if he does not constantly feel like someone whose jaws have somehow got out of alignment: the teeth don't come together in a proper bite.

We cannot, then, look to Aristotle for any elucidation of the modern way of talking about 'moral' goodness, obligation, etc. And all the best-known writers on ethics in modern times, from Butler to Mill, appear to me to have faults as thinkers on the subject which make it impossible to hope for any direct light on it from them. I will state these objections with the brevity which their character makes possible.

Butler exalts conscience, but appears ignorant that a man's conscience may tell him to do the vilest things.

Hume defines 'truth' in such a way as to exclude ethical judgements from it, and professes that he has proved that they are so excluded. He also implicitly defines 'passion' in such a way that aiming at anything is having a passion. His objection to passing from 'is' to 'ought' would apply equally to passing from 'is' to 'owes' or from 'is' to 'needs'. (However, because of the historical situation, he has a point here, which I shall return to.)

Kant introduces the idea of 'legislating for oneself', which is as absurd as if in these days, when majority votes command great respect, one were to call each reflective decision a man made a *vote* resulting in a majority, which as a matter of proportion is overwhelming, for it is always 1 – 0. The concept of legislation requires superior power in the legislator. His own rigoristic convictions on the subject of lying were so intense that it never occurred to him that a lie could be relevantly described as anything but just a lie (e.g. as 'a lie in such-and-such circumstances'). His rule about universalizable maxims is useless without stipulations as to what shall count as a relevant description of an action with a view to constructing a maxim about it.

Bentham and Mill do not notice the difficulty of the concept 'pleasure'. They are often said to have gone wrong through committing the naturalistic fallacy; but this charge does not impress me, because I do not find accounts of it coherent. But the other point — about pleasure — seems to me a fatal objection from the very outset. The ancients found this concept pretty baffling. It reduced Aristotle to sheer babble about 'the bloom on the cheek of youth' because, for good reasons, he wanted to make it out both identical with and different from the pleasurable activity. Generations of modern philosophers found this concept quite unperplexing, and it reappeared in the literature as a problematic one only a year or two ago when Ryle wrote about it. The reason is simple: since Locke, pleasure was taken to be some sort of internal impression. But it was superficial, if that was the right account of it, to make it the point of actions. One might adapt something Wittgenstein said about 'meaning' and say 'Pleasure cannot be an internal impression, for no internal impression could have the consequences of pleasure'.

Mill also, like Kant, fails to realize the necessity for stipulation as to relevant descriptions, if his theory is to have content. It did not occur to him that acts of murder and theft could be otherwise described. He holds that where a proposed action is of such a kind as to fall under some one principle established on grounds of utility, one must go by that; where it falls under none or several, the several suggesting contrary views of the action, the thing to do is to calculate particular consequences. But pretty well any action can be so described as to make it fall under a variety of principles of utility (as I shall say for short) if it falls under any.

I will now return to Hume. The features of Hume's philosophy which I have mentioned, like many other features of it, would incline me to think that Hume was a mere — brilliant — sophist; and his procedures are certainly sophistical. But I am forced, not to reverse, but to add to this judgement by a peculiarity of Hume's philosophizing: namely that, although he reaches his conclusions — with which he is in love — by sophistical methods, his considerations constantly open up very deep and important problems. It is often the case that in the act of exhibiting the sophistry one finds oneself noticing matters which deserve a lot of exploring: the obvious stands in need of investigation as a result of the points that Hume pretends to have made. In this, he is unlike, say, Butler. It was already well-known that conscience could dictate vile actions; for Butler to have written disregarding this does not open up any new topics for us. But with Hume it is otherwise: hence he is a very profound and great philosopher, in spite of his sophistry. For example:

Suppose that I say to my grocer 'Truth consists in *either* relations of ideas, as that 20s. = £1, *or* matters of fact, as that I ordered potatoes, you supplied them, and you sent me a bill. So it doesn't apply to such a proposition as that I *owe* you such-and-such a sum.'

Now if one makes this comparison, it comes to light that the relation of the facts mentioned to the description 'X owes Y so much money' is an interesting one, which I will call 'brute relative to' that description. Further, the 'brute facts' mentioned here themselves have descriptions relatively to which *other* facts are 'brute' — as, e.g., *he had potatoes carted to my house* and *they were left there* are brute facts relative to 'he supplied me with potatoes'. And the fact X *owes Y money* is in turn 'brute' relative to other descriptions — e.g. 'X is solvent'. Now the relation of 'relative bruteness' is a complicated one. To mention a few points: if xyz is a set of facts brute relative to a description A, then xyz is a set out of a range some set among which holds if A holds; but the holding of some set among these does not necessarily entail A, because exceptional circumstances can always make a difference; and what are exceptional circumstances relatively to A can generally only be explained by giving a few diverse examples, and *no* theoretically adequate provision can be made for exceptional circumstances, since a further special context can theoretically always be imagined that would reinterpret any special context. Further, though in normal circumstances, xyz would be a justification for A, that is not to say that A just comes to the same as 'xyz'; and also there is apt to be an institutional context which gives its point to the description A, of which institution A is of course not itself a description. (For example, the statement that I give someone a shilling is not a description of the institution of money or of the currency of this country.) Thus, though it would be ludicrous to pretend that there can be no such thing as a transition from, e.g., 'is' to 'owes', the character of the transition is in fact rather interesting and comes to light as a result of reflecting on Hume's arguments.[1]

---

[1] The above two paragraphs are an abstract of the paper 'On Brute Facts', *Analysis* 18/3 (1958); reprinted in G.E.M Anscombe, *Collected Philosophical Papers, Volume III: Ethics, Religion and Politics* (Oxford: Basil Blackwell, 1981), pp. 22–5.

That I owe the grocer such-and-such a sum would be one of a set of facts which would be 'brute' in relation to the description 'I am a bilker'. 'Bilking' is of course a species of 'dishonesty' or 'injustice'. (Naturally the consideration will not have any effect on my actions unless I want to commit or avoid acts of injustice.)

So far, in spite of their strong associations, I conceive 'bilking', 'injustice' and 'dishonesty' in a merely 'factual' way. That I can do this for 'bilking' is obvious enough; 'justice' I have no idea how to define, except that its sphere is that of actions which relate to someone else, but 'injustice', for its defect, can provisionally be offered as a generic name covering various species, e.g. bilking, theft, (which is relative to whatever property institutions exist), slander, adultery, punishment of the innocent.

In present-day philosophy an explanation is required how an unjust man is a bad man, or an unjust action a bad one; to give such an explanation belongs to ethics; but it cannot even be begun until we are equipped with a sound philosophy of psychology. For the proof that an unjust man is a bad man would require a positive account of justice as a 'virtue'. This part of the subject-matter of ethics is, however, completely closed to us until we have an account of what *type of characteristic* a virtue is — a problem, not of ethics, but of conceptual analysis — and how it relates to the actions in which it is instanced: a matter which I think Aristotle did not succeed in really making clear. For this we certainly need an account at least of what a human action is at all, and how its description as 'doing such-and-such' is affected by its motive and by the intention or intentions in it; and for this an account of such concepts is required.

The terms 'should' or 'ought' or 'needs' relate to good and bad: e.g. machinery needs oil, or should or ought to be oiled, in that running without oil is bad for it, or it runs badly without oil. According to this conception, of course, 'should' or 'ought' are not used in a special 'moral' sense when one says that a man should not bilk. (In Aristotle's sense of the term 'moral' — ἠθικός

— they are being used in connection with a *moral* subject-matter: namely that of human passions and [non-technical] actions.) But they have now acquired a special so-called 'moral' sense — i.e. a sense in which they imply some absolute verdict (like one of guilty/not guilty on a man) on what is described in the 'ought' sentences used in certain types of context: not merely the contexts that *Aristotle* would call 'moral' — passions and actions — but also some of the contexts that he would call 'intellectual'.

The ordinary (and quite indispensable) terms 'should', 'needs', 'ought', 'must' — acquired this special sense by being equated in the relevant contexts with 'is obliged', or 'is bound', or 'is required to', in the sense in which one can be obliged or bound by law, or something can be required by law.

How did this come about? The answer is in history: between Aristotle and us came Christianity, with its *law* conception of ethics. For Christianity derived its ethical notions from the Torah. (One might be inclined to think that a law conception of ethics could arise only among people who accepted an allegedly divine positive law; that this is not so is shown by the example of the Stoics, who also thought that whatever was involved in conformity to human virtues was required by divine law.)

In consequence of the dominance of Christianity for many centuries, the concepts of being bound, permitted, or excused became deeply embedded in our language and thought. The Greek word 'ἁμαρτάνειν', the aptest to be turned to that use, acquired the sense of 'sin', from having meant 'mistake', 'missing the mark', 'going wrong'. The Latin *peccatum* which roughly corresponded to ἁμάρτημα was even apter for the sense 'sin' because it was already associated with *culpa* — 'guilt' — a juridical term. The blanket term 'illicit', 'unlawful', meaning much the same as our blanket term 'wrong', explains itself. It is interesting that Aristotle did not have such a blanket term. He has blanket terms for wickedness — 'villain', 'scoundrel'; but of course a man is not a villain or a scoundrel by the performance of one bad action, or a few bad actions. And he has terms like 'disgraceful', 'impious'; and specific terms signifying defect of the relevant virtue, like 'unjust'; but no term corresponding to 'illicit'. The extension of this term (i.e. the range of its application) could be indicated in his terminology only by a quite lengthy sentence: that is 'illicit' which, whether it is a thought or a consented-to passion or an action, is something contrary to one of the virtues the lack of which shows a man to be bad *qua* man. That formulation would yield a concept co-extensive with the concept 'illicit'.

To have a *law* conception of ethics is to hold that what is needed for conformity with the virtues failure in which is the mark of being bad *qua* man (and not merely, say *qua* craftsman or logician) — that what is needed for *this*, is required by divine law. Naturally it is not possible to have such a conception unless you believe in God as a law-giver; like Jews, Stoics and Christians. But if such a conception is dominant for many centuries, and then is given up, it is a natural result that the concepts of 'obligation', of being bound or required as by a law, should remain though they had lost their root; and if the word 'ought' has become invested in certain contexts with the sense of 'obligation', it too will remain to be spoken with a special emphasis and a special feeling in these contexts.

It is as if the notion 'criminal' were to remain when criminal law and criminal courts had been abolished and forgotten. A Hume discovering this situation might conclude that there was a special sentiment, expressed by 'criminal', which alone gave the word its sense. So Hume discovered the situation in which the notion 'obligation' survived, and the word 'ought' was invested with that peculiar force having which it is said to be used in a 'moral' sense, but in which the belief in divine law had long since been abandoned: for it was substantially given up among

Protestants at the time of the Reformation.[2] The situation, if I am right, was the interesting one of the survival of a concept outside the framework of thought that made it a really intelligible one.

When Hume produced his famous remarks about the transition from 'is' to 'ought', he was, then, bringing together several quite different points. One I have tried to bring out by my remarks on the transition from 'is' to 'owes' and on the relative 'bruteness' of facts. It would be possible to bring out a different point by enquiring about the transition from 'is' to 'needs'; from the characteristics of an organism to the environment that it needs, for example. To say that it needs that environment is not to say, e.g., that you want it to have that environment, but that it won't flourish unless it has it. Certainly, it all depends whether you *want* it to flourish! as Hume would say. But what 'all depends' on whether you want it to flourish is whether the fact that it needs that environment, or won't flourish without it, has the slightest influence on your actions. Now *that* such-and-such 'ought' to be or 'is needed' is supposed to have an influence on your actions: from which it seemed natural to infer that to judge that it 'ought to be' was in fact to grant what you judged 'ought to be' influence on your actions. And no amount of truth as to what *is* the case could possibly have a logical claim to have influence on your actions. (It is not judgement as such that sets us in motion; but our judgement to get or do something we *want*.) Hence it *must* be impossible to infer 'needs' or 'ought to be' from 'is'. But in the case of a plant, let us say, the inference from 'is' to 'needs' is certainly not in the least dubious. It is interesting and worth examining; but not at all fishy. Its interest is similar to the interest of the relation between brute and less brute facts: these

---

[2]   They did not deny the existence of divine law; but their most characteristic doctrine was that it was given, not to be obeyed, but to show man's incapacity to obey it, even by grace; and this applied not merely to the ramified prescriptions of the Torah, but to the requirements of 'natural divine law'. Cf. in this connection the decree of Trent against the teaching that Christ was only to be trusted in as mediator, not obeyed as legislator.

relations have been very little considered. And while you can contrast 'what it needs' with 'what it's got' — like contrasting *de facto* and *de iure* — that does not make its needing this environment less of a 'truth'.

Certainly in the case of what the plant needs, the thought of a need will only affect action if you want the plant to flourish. Here, then, there is no necessary connection between what you can judge the plant 'needs' and what you want. But there is some sort of necessary connection between what you think *you* need, and what you want. The connection is a complicated one; it is possible *not* to want something that you judge you need. But, e.g., it is not possible never to want *anything* that you judge you need. This, however, is not a fact about the meaning of the word 'to need', but about the phenomenon of *wanting*. Hume's reasoning, we might say, in effect, leads one to think it must be about the word 'to need', or 'to be good for'.

Thus we find two problems already wrapped up in the remark about a transition from 'is' to 'ought'; now supposing that we had clarified the 'relative bruteness' of facts on the one hand, and the notions involved in 'needing', and 'flourishing' on the other — there would *still* remain a third point. For, following Hume, someone might say: Perhaps you have made out your point about a transition from 'is' to 'owes' and from 'is' to 'needs'; but only at the cost of showing 'owes' and 'needs' sentences to express a *kind* of truths, a *kind* of facts. And it remains impossible to infer '*morally ought*' from 'is'.

This comment, it seems to me, would be correct. This word 'ought' having become a word of mesmeric force, could not, in the character of having that force, be inferred from anything whatever. It may be objected that it could be inferred from other 'morally ought' sentences: but that cannot be true. The appearance that this is so is produced by the fact that we say 'All men are φ' and 'Socrates is a man' implies 'Socrates is φ'. But here 'φ' is a dummy predicate. We mean that if you substitute a real predicate for 'φ' the implication is valid. A real predicate is required; not just a word containing no intelligible thought: a word retaining the suggestion of force, and apt to have a strong psychological effect, but which no longer signifies a real concept at all.

For its suggestion is one of a *verdict* on my action, according as it agrees or disagrees with the description in the 'ought' sentence. And where one does not think there is a judge or a law, the notion of a verdict may retain its psychological effect, but not its meaning. Now imagine that just this word 'verdict' *were* so used — with a characteristically solemn emphasis — as to retain its atmosphere but not its meaning, and someone were to say: 'For a *verdict*, after all, you need a law and a judge'. The reply might be made: 'Not at all, for if there were a law and a judge who gave a verdict, the question for us would be whether accepting that verdict is something there is a *Verdict* on'. This is an analogue of an argument which is so frequently referred to as decisive: If someone does have a divine law conception of ethics, all the same, he has to agree that he has to have a judgement that he *ought* (morally ought) to obey the divine law; so his ethic is in exactly the same position as any other: he merely has a 'practical major premise'[3]: 'Divine law ought to be obeyed' where someone else has, e.g., 'The greatest happiness principle ought to be obeyed in all decisions'.

I should judge that Hume and our present-day ethicists had done a considerable service by showing that no content could be found in the notion 'morally ought'; if it were not that the latter philosophers try to find an alternative (very fishy) content and to retain the psychological force of the term. It would be most reasonable to drop it. It has no reasonable sense outside a law conception of ethics; they are not going to maintain such a conception; and you can do ethics without it, as is shown by the

---

[3] As it is absurdly called. Since major premise = premise containing the term which is predicate in the conclusion, it is a solecism to speak of it in the connection with practical reasoning.

example of Aristotle. It would be a great improvement if, instead of 'morally wrong', one always named a genus such as 'untruthful', 'unchaste', 'unjust'. We should no longer ask whether doing something was 'wrong', passing directly from some description of an action to this notion; we should ask whether, e.g., it was unjust; and the answer would sometimes be clear at once.

I now come to the epoch in modern English moral philosophy marked by Sidgwick. There is a startling change that seems to have taken place between Mill and Moore. Mill assumes, as we saw, that there is no question of calculating particular consequences of an action such as murder or theft; and we saw too that his position was stupid, because it is not at all clear how an action *can* fall under just one principle of utility. In Moore and in subsequent academic moralists of England we find it taken to be pretty obvious that 'the right action' means the one which produces the best possible consequences (reckoning among consequences the intrinsic values ascribed to certain kinds of act by some 'Objectivists'[4]). Now it follows from this that a man does well, subjectively speaking, if he acts for the best in the particular circumstances according to his judgement of the total consequences of this particular action. I say that this follows, not that any philosopher has said precisely that. For discussion of these questions can of course get extremely complicated: e.g. it can be doubted 'such-and-such is the right action' is a satisfactory formulation, on the grounds that things have to exist to have predicates — so perhaps the best formulation is 'I am obliged'; or again a philosopher may deny that 'right' is a 'descriptive' term, and then take a roundabout route through linguistic analysis to reach a view which comes to the same thing as 'the right action is the one

---

[4]   Oxford Objectivists of course distinguish between 'consequences' and 'intrinsic values' and so produce a misleading appearance of not being consequentialists. But they do not hold — and Ross explicitly denies — that the gravity of, e.g., procuring the condemnation of the innocent is such that it cannot be outweighed by, e.g., national interest. Hence their distinction is of no importance.

productive of the best consequences' (e.g. the view that you frame your 'principles' to effect the end you choose to pursue, the connection between 'choice' and 'best' being supposedly such that choosing reflectively means that you choose how to act so as to produce the best consequences); further, the roles of what are called 'moral principles' and of the 'motive of duty' have to be described; the differences between 'good' and 'morally good' and 'right' need to be explored, the special characteristics of 'ought' sentences investigated. Such discussions generate an appearance of significant diversity of views where what is really significant is an overall similarity. The overall similarity is made clear if you consider that every one of the best known English academic moral philosophers has put out a philosophy according to which, e.g., it is not possible to hold that it cannot be right to kill the innocent as a means to any end whatsoever and that someone who thinks otherwise is in error. (I have to mention both points; because Mr Hare, for example, while teaching a philosophy which would encourage a person to judge that killing the innocent would be what he ought to choose for over-riding purposes, would also teach, I think, that if a man chooses to make avoiding killing the innocent for any purpose his 'supreme practical principle' he cannot be impugned for error: that just is his 'principle'. But with that qualification, I think it can be seen that the point I have mentioned holds good of every single English academic philosopher since Sidgwick.) Now this is a significant thing: for it means that all these philosophies are quite incompatible with the Hebrew-Christian ethic. For it has been characteristic of that ethic to teach that there are certain things forbidden whatever *consequences* threaten, such as: choosing to kill the innocent for any purpose, however good; vicarious punishment; treachery (by which I mean obtaining a man's confidence in a grave matter by promises of trustworthy friendship and then betraying him to his enemies); idolatry; sodomy; adultery; making a false profession of faith. The prohibition of certain things simply in virtue of their description as such-and-such identifiable kinds of action, regardless of any further consequences, is certainly not the whole of the Hebrew-Christian ethic; but it is a noteworthy feature of it; and, if every academic philosopher since Sidgwick has written in such a way as to exclude this ethic, it would argue a certain provinciality of mind not to see this incompatibility as the most important fact about these philosophers, and the differences between them as somewhat trifling by comparison.

It is noticeable that none of these philosophers displays any consciousness that there is such an ethic, which he is contradicting; it is pretty well taken for obvious among them all that a prohibition such as that on murder does not operate in face of some consequences. But of course the strictness of the prohibition has as its point *that you are not to be tempted by fear or hope of consequences.*

If you notice the transition from Mill to Moore, you will suspect that it was made somewhere by someone; Sidgwick will come to mind as a likely name; and you will in fact find it going on, almost casually, in him. He is rather a dull author; and the important things in him occur in asides and footnotes and small bits of argument which are not concerned with this grand classification of the 'methods of ethics'. A divine law theory of ethics is reduced to an insignificant variety by a footnote telling us that 'the best theologians' (God knows whom he meant) tell us that God is to be obeyed in his capacity of a *moral* being. ἡ φορτικός ο ἔπαινος; one seems to hear Aristotle saying: 'Isn't the praise vulgar?' (*Eth. Nic.* 1178b16). But Sidgwick *is* vulgar in that kind of way: he thinks, for example, that humility consists in underestimating your own merits — i.e. in a species of untruthfulness; and that the ground for having laws against blasphemy was that it was offensive to believers; and that to go accurately into the virtue of purity is to offend against its canons, a thing he reproves 'medieval theologians' for not realizing.

From the point of view of the present enquiry, the most important thing about Sidgwick was his definition of intention. He defines intention in such a way that one must be said to intend any foreseen consequences of one's voluntary action. This definition is obviously incorrect, and I dare say that no one would be found to defend it now. He uses it to put forward an ethical thesis which would now be accepted by many people: the thesis that it does not make any difference to a man's responsibility for something that he foresaw, that he felt no desire for it, either as an end or as a means to an end. Using the language of intention more correctly, and avoiding Sidgwick's faulty conception, we may state the thesis thus: it does not make any difference to a man's responsibility for an effect of his action which he can foresee, that he does not intend it. Now this sounds rather edifying; it is I think quite characteristic of very bad degenerations of thought on such questions that they sound edifying. We can see what it amounts to by considering an example. Let us suppose that a man has a responsibility for the maintenance of some child. Therefore deliberately to withdraw support from it is a bad sort of thing for him to do. It would be bad for him to withdraw its maintenance because he didn't want to maintain it any longer; *and* also bad for him to withdraw it because by doing so he would, let us say, compel someone else to do something. (We may suppose for the sake of argument that compelling that person to do that thing is itself quite admirable.) But now he has to choose between doing something disgraceful and going to prison; if he goes to prison, it will follow that he withdraws support for the child. By Sidgwick's doctrine, there is no difference in his responsibility for ceasing to maintain the child, between the case where he does it for its own sake or as a means to some other purpose, and when it happens as a foreseen and unavoidable consequence of his going to prison rather than do something disgraceful. It follows that he must weigh up the relative badness of withdrawing support from the child and of doing the disgraceful thing; and it may easily be that the disgraceful thing is a less vicious action than intentionally withdrawing support from the child would be; if then the fact that withdrawing support from the child is a side effect of his going to prison does not make any difference to his responsibility, this consideration will incline him to do the disgraceful thing; which can still be pretty bad. And of course, once he has started to look at the matter in this light, the only reasonable thing for him to consider will be the consequences and not the intrinsic badness of this or that action. So that, given that he judges reasonably that no *great* harm will come of it, he can do a much more disgraceful thing than deliberately withdrawing support from the child. And if his calculations turn out in fact wrong, it will appear that he was not responsible for the consequences, because he did not foresee them. For in fact Sidgwick's thesis leads to its being quite impossible to estimate the badness of an action except in the light of *expected* consequences. But if so, then *you* must estimate the badness in the light of the consequences *you* expect; and so it will follow that you can exculpate yourself from the *actual* consequences of the most disgraceful actions, so long as you can make out a case for not having foreseen them. Whereas I should contend that a man is responsible for the bad consequences of his bad actions, but gets no credit for the good ones; and contrariwise is not responsible for the bad consequences of good actions.

The denial of *any* distinction between foreseen and intended consequences, as far as responsibility is concerned, was not made by Sidgwick in developing any one 'method of ethics'; he made this important move on behalf of everybody and just on its own account; and I think it plausible to suggest that *this* move on the part of Sidgwick explains the difference between old-fashioned utilitarianism and that *consequentialism*, as I name it, which marks him and every English academic philosopher since him. By it, the kind of consideration which would formerly have been regarded as a temptation, the kind of consideration urged upon men by wives and flattering friends, was given a status by moral philosophers in their theories.

It is a necessary feature of consequentialism that it is a shallow philosophy. For there are always borderline cases in ethics. Now if you are either an Aristotelian, or a believer in divine law, you will deal with a borderline case by considering whether, doing such-and-such in such-and-such circumstances is, say, murder, or is an act of injustice; and according as you decide it is or it isn't, you judge it to be a thing to do or not. This would be the method of casuistry; and while it may lead you to stretch a point on the circumference, it will not permit you to destroy the centre. But if you are a consequentialist, the question 'What is it right to do in such-and- such circumstances?' is a stupid one to raise. The casuist raises such a question only to ask 'Would it be *permissible* to do so-and-so?' or 'Would it be permissible *not* to do so-and-so?' Only if it would *not* be permissible *not* to do so-and-so could he say '*This* would be *the* thing to do'.[5] Otherwise, though he may speak *against* some action, he cannot prescribe any — for in an *actual* case, the circumstances (beyond the ones imagined) might suggest all sorts of possibilities, and you can't know in advance what the possibilities are going to be. Now the consequentialist has no footing on which to say 'This would be permissible, this not'; because by his own hypothesis, it is the consequences that are to decide, and he has no business to pretend that he can lay it down what possible twists a man could give doing this or that; the most he can say is: a man must not *bring about* this or that; he has no right to say he will, in an actual case, bring about such-and-such unless he does so-and-so. Further, the consequentialist, in order to be imagining borderline case at all, has of course to assume some sort of law or standard according to which this is a borderline case. Where then does he get the standard from? In practice the answer invariably is: from the standards

---

[5] Necessarily a rare case: for the positive precepts, e.g. 'Honour your parents', hardly ever prescribe, and seldom even necessitate, any particular action.

current in his society or his circle. And it has in fact been the mark of all these philosophers that they have been extremely conventional; they have nothing in them by which to revolt against the conventional standards of their sort of people; it is impossible that they should be profound. But the chance that a whole range of conventional standards will be decent is small. Finally, the point of considering hypothetical situations, perhaps very improbable ones, *seems* to be to elicit from yourself or someone else a hypothetical decision to do something of a bad kind. I don't doubt this has the effect of predisposing people — who will never get into the situations for which they have made hypothetical choices — to consent to similar bad actions, or to praise and flatter those who do them, so long as their crowd does so too, when the desperate circumstances imagined don't hold at all.

Those who recognise the origins of the notions of 'obligation' and of the emphatic, 'moral', *ought*, in the divine law conception of ethics, but who reject the notion of a divine legislator, sometimes look about for the possibility of retaining a law conception without a divine legislator. This search, I think, has some interest in it. Perhaps the first thing that suggests itself is the 'norms' of society. But just as one cannot be impressed by Butler when one reflects what conscience can tell people to do, so, I think, one cannot be impressed by this idea if one reflects what the 'norms' of a society can be like. That legislation can be 'for oneself' I reject as absurd; whatever you do 'for yourself' may be admirable; but it is not legislating. Once one sees this, one may say: I have to frame my own rules, and these are the best I can frame, and I shall go by them until I know something better: as a man might say 'I shall go by the customs of my ancestors'. Whether this leads to good or evil will depend on the *content* of the rules or of the customs of one's ancestors. If one is lucky it will lead to good. Such an attitude would be hopeful in this at any rate: it seems to have in it some Socratic doubt where, from having to fall back on expedients, it should be clear that Socratic doubt is good; in fact rather generally it must be good for anyone to think 'Perhaps in some way I can't see, I may be on a bad path, perhaps I am hopelessly wrong in some essential way'. The search for 'norms' might lead someone to look for laws of nature, as if the universe were a legislator; but in the present day this is not likely to lead to good results: it might lead one to eat the weaker according to the laws of nature, but would hardly lead anyone nowadays to notions of justice; the pre-Socratic feeling about justice as comparable to the balance or harmony which kept things going is very remote to us.

There is another possibility here: 'obligation' may be contractual. Just as we look at the law to find out what a man subject to it is required by it to do, so we look at a contract to find out what the man who has made it is required by it to do. Thinkers, admittedly remote from us, might have the idea of a *foedus rerum*, of the universe not as a legislator but as the embodiment of a contract. Then if you could find out what the contract was, you would learn your obligations under it. Now, you cannot be under a law unless it has been promulgated to you; and the thinkers who believe in 'natural divine law' held that it was promulgated to every grown man in his knowledge of good and evil. Similarly you cannot be in a contract without having contracted, i.e. given signs of entering upon the contract. Just possibly, it might be argued that the use of language which one makes in the ordinary conduct of life amounts in some sense to giving the signs of entering into various contracts. If anyone had this theory, we should want to see it worked out. I suspect that it would be largely formal; it might be possible to construct a system embodying the law (whose status might be compared to that of 'laws' of logic): 'what's sauce for the goose is sauce for the gander', but hardly one descending to such particularities as the prohibition of murder or sodomy. Also, while it is clear that you can be subject to a law that you do not acknowledge and have not thought of as a law, it does not seem reasonable to say that you can enter upon a contract without knowing that you are doing so; such ignorance is usually held to be destructive of the nature of a contract.

It might remain to look for 'norms' in human virtues: just as *man* has so many teeth, which is certainly not the average number of teeth men have, but is the number of teeth for the species, so perhaps the species *man*, regarded not just biologically, but from the point of view of the activity of thought and choice in regard to the various departments of life — powers and faculties and use of things needed — 'has' such-and-such virtues: and this 'man' with the complete set of virtues is the 'norm', as 'man' with, e.g., a complete set of teeth is a norm. But in *this* sense 'norm' has ceased to be roughly equivalent to 'law'. In *this* sense the notion of a 'norm' brings us nearer to an Aristotelian than a law conception of ethics. There is, I think, no harm in that; but if someone looked in this direction to give 'norm' a sense, then he ought to recognize what has happened to the term 'norm', which he wanted to mean 'law — without bringing God in': it has ceased to mean 'law' at all; and *so* the expressions 'moral obligation', 'the moral ought', and 'duty' are best put on the Index, if he can manage it.

But meanwhile — is it not clear that there are several concepts that need investigating simply as part of the philosophy of psychology and — as I should recommend — *banishing ethics totally* from our minds? Namely — to begin with: 'action', 'intention', 'pleasure', 'wanting'. More will probably turn up if we start with these. Eventually it might be possible to advance to considering the concept of virtue; with which, I suppose, we should be beginning some sort of study of ethics.

I will end by describing the advantages of using the word 'ought' in a non-emphatic fashion, and not in a special 'moral' sense; of discarding the term 'wrong' in a 'moral' sense, and using such notions as 'unjust'.

It is possible, if one is allowed to proceed just by giving examples, to distinguish between the intrinsically unjust, and what is unjust given the circumstances. Seriously to get a man judicially punished for something which it can be clearly seen he has not done is intrinsically unjust. This might be done, of course, and often has been done, in all sorts of ways; by suborning false witnesses, by a rule of law by which something is 'deemed' to be the case which is admittedly not the case as a matter of fact, and by open insolence on the part of judges and powerful people when they more or less openly say: 'A fig for the fact that you did not do it; we mean to sentence you for it all the same'. What is unjust given, e.g., normal circumstances is to deprive people of their ostensible property without legal procedure, not to pay debts, not to keep contracts and a host of other things of the kind. Now, the circumstances can clearly make a great deal of difference in estimating the justice or injustice of such procedures as these; and these circumstances may *sometimes* include expected consequences; for example, a man's claim to a bit of property can become a nullity when its seizure and use can avert some obvious disaster: as, e.g., if you could use a machine of his to produce an explosion in which it would be destroyed, but by means of which you could divert a flood or make a gap which a fire could not jump. Now this certainly does not mean that what would ordinarily be an act of injustice, but is not intrinsically unjust, can always be rendered just by a reasonable calculation of better consequences; far from it; but the problems that would be raised in an attempt to draw a boundary line (or boundary area) here are obviously complicated. And while there are certainly some general remarks which ought to be made here, and some boundaries that can be drawn, the decision on particular cases would for the most part be determined κατὰ τὸν ὀρθὸν λόγον — 'according to what's reasonable' — e.g., that such-and-such a delay of payment of a *such-and-such* debt to a person *so* circumstanced, on the part of a person *so* circumstanced, would or would not be unjust, is really only to be decided 'according to what's reasonable'; and for this there can *in principle* be no canon other than giving a few examples. That is to say, while it is because of a big gap in philos-

ophy that we can give no general account of the concept of virtue
and the concept of justice, but have to proceed, using the concepts, only by giving examples; still there is an area where it is not
because of any gap, but is in principle the case, that there is no
account except by way of examples; and that is where the canon is
'what's reasonable': which of course is *not* a canon.

That is all I wish to say about what is just in some circumstances, unjust in others; and about the way in which expected
consequences can play a part in determining what is just. Returning to my example of the intrinsically unjust: if a procedure *is* one
of judicially punishing a man for what he is clearly understood
not to have done, there can be absolutely no argument about the
description of this as unjust. No circumstances, and no expected
consequences, which do *not* modify the description of the procedure as one of judicially punishing a man for what he is known
not to have done can modify the description of it as unjust.
Someone who attempted to dispute this would only be pretend-
ing not to know what 'unjust' means: for this is a paradigm case
of injustice.

And here we see the superiority of the term 'unjust' over the
terms 'morally right' and 'morally wrong'. For in the context of
English moral philosophy since Sidgwick it appears legitimate to
discuss whether it *might* be 'morally right' in some circumstances
to adopt that procedure; but it cannot be argued that the procedure would in any circumstances be just.

Now I am not able to do the philosophy involved — and I think
that no one in the present situation of English philosophy *can* do
the philosophy involved — but it is clear that a good man is a just
man; and a just man is a man who habitually refuses to commit or
participate in any unjust actions for fear of any consequences, or
to obtain any advantage, for himself or for anyone else. Perhaps
no one will disagree. But, it will be said, what *is* unjust is sometimes determined by expected consequences; and certainly that
is true. But there are cases where it is not: now if someone says, 'I

agree, but all this wants a lot of explaining', then he is right, and, what is more, the situation at present is that we can't do the explaining; we lack the philosophic equipment. But if someone really thinks, *in advance*,[6] that it is open to question whether such an action as procuring the judicial execution of the innocent should be quite excluded from consideration — I do not want to argue with him; he shows a corrupt mind.

In such cases our moral philosophers seek to impose a dilemma upon us. 'If we have a case where the term 'unjust' applies purely in virtue of a factual description, can't one raise the question whether one sometimes conceivably ought to do injustice? If 'what is unjust' is determined by considerations of whether it is *right* to do so-and-so in such-and-such circumstances, then the question whether it is 'right' to commit injustice can't arise, just because 'wrong' has been built into the definition of injustice. But if we have a case where the description 'unjust' applies purely in virtue of the facts, without bringing 'wrong' in, then the question can arise whether one 'ought' perhaps to commit an injustice, whether it might be 'right' to. And of course 'ought' and 'right' are being used in their *moral* senses here. Now either you must decide what is 'morally right' in the light of certain *other* 'principles', or you make a 'principle' about *this* and decide that an injustice is never 'right'; but even if you do the latter you are going beyond the facts; you are making a decision that you will not, or that it is wrong, to commit injustice. But in either

---

[6] If he thinks it in the concrete situation, he is of course merely a normally tempted human being. In discussion when this paper was read, as was perhaps to be expected, this case was produced: a government is required to have an innocent man tried, sentenced and executed under threat of a 'hydrogen bomb war'. It would seem strange to me to have much hope of so averting a war threatened by such men as made this demand. But the most important thing about the way in which cases like this are invented in discussions, is the assumption that only two courses are open: here, compliance or open defiance. No one can say in advance of such a situation what the possibilities are going to be — e.g. that there is none of stalling by a feigned willingness to comply, accompanied by a skilfully arranged 'escape' of the victim.

case, *if* the term 'unjust' is determined simply by the facts, it is not the term 'unjust' that determines that the term 'wrong' applies, but a decision that injustice is 'wrong', together with the diagnosis of the 'factual' description as entailing injustice. But the man who makes an absolute decision that injustice is 'wrong' has no footing on which to criticize someone who does *not* make that decision as 'judging falsely'.

In this argument 'wrong' of course is explained as meaning 'morally wrong', and all the atmosphere of the term is retained while its substance is guaranteed null. Now let us remember that 'morally wrong' is the term which is the heir of the notion 'illicit', or 'what there is an obligation *not* to do'; which belongs in a divine law theory of ethics. Here it really does add something to the description 'unjust' to say there is an obligation not to do it; for what obliges is the divine law — as rules oblige in a game. So if the divine law obliges not to commit injustice by forbidding injustice, it really does add something to the description 'unjust' to say there is an obligation not to do it. And it is because 'morally wrong' is the heir of this concept, but an heir that is cut off from the family of concepts from which it sprang, that 'morally wrong' *both* goes beyond the mere factual description 'unjust' *and* seems to have no discernible content except a certain compelling force, which I should call purely psychological. And such is the force of the term that philosophers actually suppose that the divine law notion can be dismissed as making no essential difference even if it is held — *because* they think that a 'practical principle' running 'I *ought* (i.e. am morally obliged) to obey divine laws' is required for the man who believes in divine laws. But actually this notion of obligation is a notion which only operates in the context of law. And I should be inclined to congratulate the present-day moral philosophers on depriving 'morally ought' of its now delusive appearance of content, if only they did not manifest a detestable desire to retain the atmosphere of the term.

It may be possible, if we are resolute, to discard the term 'morally ought', and simply return to the ordinary 'ought', which, we ought to notice, is such an extremely frequent term of human language that it is difficult to imagine getting on without it. Now if we do return to it, can't it reasonably be asked whether one might ever need to commit injustice, or whether it won't be the best thing to do? Of course it can. And the answers will be various. One man — a philosopher — may say that since justice is a virtue, and injustice a vice, and virtues and vices are built up by the performances of the action in which they are instanced, an act of injustice will tend to make a man bad; and essentially the flourishing of a man *qua* man consists in his being good (e.g. in virtues); but for any X to which such terms apply, X needs what makes it flourish, so a man needs, or ought to perform, only virtuous actions; and even if, as it must be admitted may happen, he flourishes less, or not at all, in inessentials, by avoiding injustice, his life is spoiled in essentials by not avoiding injustice — so he still needs to perform only just actions. That is roughly how Plato and Aristotle talk; but it can be seen that philosophically there is a huge gap, at present unfillable as far as we are concerned, which needs to be filled by an account of human nature, human action, the type of characteristic a virtue is, and above all of human 'flourishing'. And it is the last concept that appears the most doubtful. For it is a bit much to swallow that a man in pain and hunger and poor and friendless is flourishing, as Aristotle himself admitted. Further, someone might say that one at least needed to stay alive to flourish. Another man unimpressed by all that will say in a hard case 'What we need is such-and-such, which we won't get without doing this (which is unjust) — so this is what we ought to do'. Another man, who does not follow the rather elaborate reasoning of the philosophers, simply says 'I know it is in any case a disgraceful thing to say that one had better commit this unjust action'. The man who believes in divine laws will say perhaps 'It is forbidden, and however it looks, it cannot

be to anyone's profit to commit injustice'; he, like the Greek philosophers, can think in terms of flourishing. If he is a Stoic, he is
apt to have a decidedly strained notion of what flourishing consists in; if he is a Jew or a Christian, he need not have any very distinct notion: the way it will profit him to abstain from injustice is
something that he leaves it to God to determine, himself only saying 'It can't do me any good to go against his law'. (He also hopes
for a great reward in a new life later on, e.g. at the coming of Mes-
siah; but in this he is relying on special promises.)

It is left to modern moral philosophy — the moral philosophy
of all the well-known English ethicists since Sidgwick — to construct systems according to which the man who says 'We need
such-and-such, and will only get it this way' *may* be a virtuous
character: that is to say, it is left open to debate whether such a
procedure as the judicial punishment of the innocent may not in
some circumstances be the 'right' one to adopt; and though the
present Oxford moral philosophers would accord a man *permission* to 'make it his principle' not to do such a thing, they teach a
philosophy according to which the particular consequences of
such an action *could* 'morally' be taken into account by a man who
was debating what to do; and if they were such as to accord with
his ends, it might be a step in his moral education to frame a
moral principle under which he 'managed' (to use Mr Nowell-
Smith's phrase)[7] to bring the action; or it might be a new 'decision
of principle', making which was an advance in the formation of
his moral thinking (to adopt Mr Hare's conception), to decide: in
such-and-such circumstances one ought to procure the judicial
condemnation of the innocent. And that is my complaint.

---

[7]   *Ethics* (Harmondsworth: Penguin Books, 1954), p. 308.

14*

Good and Bad Human Action

The idea of the *morally* good, *morally* bad or *morally* neutral plays a great part at least in middle-class thinking and some philosophical thought in what I'll call the modern era. By 'the modern era' I choose to mean from the late eighteenth century onwards. For my thesis, I may be starting it a bit late; but let's not worry about that. Beginning it in the eighteenth century highlights the influence of Immanuel Kant and that is what I want to do. Kant's major influence has been that of emphasising the motive of duty. Duty is here not conceived as we conceive the duties of a job or office, or as in the expression 'on duty'. Nor is it connected directly with what things are for, as when Anselm asks what assertion is for and, getting the reply 'for saying that to be so which is so', infers 'That is what it ought to be doing then'. Rather what ought to be done or ought not to be done is somehow derivable from the categorical imperative 'Always act so that you can consistently universalise the maxim on which you act'. This connects up the idea of duty and the moral *ought* as a motive with *rational will*. (Kant himself doesn't think it applies to a holy will, that is it doesn't apply to the will of immaterial spirits or of God.) It leads to a contrast between doing something for the motive of duty and doing it with enjoyment — the more you like doing something, the less of a purely *moral* agent you are; and also

* From an undated manuscript of a lecture.

between doing something for the motive of duty and doing it because you are the sort of creature to whose form of life it belongs to do that in that sort of way — e.g. to engage in sexual intercourse only in marriage, that being, not necessarily the *usual*, but the good, wholesome and advantageous form to be the human form of life in respect of sexual activity. The Kantian system also leads — in its influence — to a contrast between duty and interest, and between *moral* and *prudential* motives. Prudential motives are *eo ipso* not moral or are morally bad.

Some of you may have had the thought that the idea of what is *morally* good, bad or neutral goes back at least to Aristotle — because 'moral' is a translation of his adjective ηθικη, though *etymologically* the English word deriving from ηθικη, is 'ethical'. Aristotle calls some virtues 'ethical' virtues — but that sounds odd in English and I dare say 'moral' virtues has a more comfortable because a more familiar ring. However, a great part of Aristotle's point is to distinguish between '*moral*' and '*intellectual*' virtues or excellences. The moral virtues are virtues of actions and feelings. The cardinal instances of virtue are justice, courage and temperance. Of these, justice is somewhat singular in that the Greek word [for] 'just', like our word 'just', is used in both a wider and a narrower sense. In the wider sense it covers the whole of 'uprightness'. In the narrower, it is to do with distribution, property, debts, desert and punishment and is equivalent to fairness in dealing with other people. *Intellectual* virtues are such as habitual soundness of practical judgment, skill in production (e.g. in making things, or singing, or drawing) and philosophic wisdom. Now it is *impossible* to have a moral virtue without *any* intellectual virtue, most generally without the first one mentioned. That was: habitual soundness of practical judgment. For it is part and parcel of a moral excellence in its exercise to use judgment; courage, for example, isn't just any boldness in face of any danger, but requires sound judgment about the danger and about its being worth facing out: that for which you choose to face a risk not being some triviality, in connexion with how great the risk is and how serious *what* you risk losing or causing. Similarly in the *narrower* sense of 'justice', to have that virtue you need judgment about fair division, or about the balance of different creditors' more or less urgent needs, also bringing in other things, such as size of a debt and time proposed to be spent in paying it. You need not *merely* to *make* judgments, but need *correctness* of judgment. So a fool can hardly be either just or brave.

In the way in which moderns use the word 'moral' it would be said in response to this: So there is a *moral* obligation to have good judgment, hence a *moral* obligation to have intellectual virtue. Thus, in spite of its origin, our modern use of the term 'moral' departs from the Aristotelian use of it.

On this I would comment that you can't even formulate those propositions about *moral* obligation to have good judgment or intellectual virtue in Aristotle's language. You can say that a human being *needs* to have the intellectual virtue of good sense in order to have any moral virtue; and the Greek for 'needs' would here be one also translateable as 'ought'. But if you did translate it as 'ought', saying: a human being ought to have the *intellectual* virtue of good sense in order to have *any* moral goodness, you aren't even using our word 'ought' in a way that raises or allows for the question 'do you mean *morally* ought?' — 'But may someone not be blameworthy for lacking intellectual virtue?' Yes, they may, if their lack of it is voluntary; in a brain-damaged spastic cripple who can neither speak nor move, the lack is not voluntary, but in someone not so incapacitated, the lack of good sense is voluntary and incurs blame rather than praise. 'But', it may be asked, 'isn't the blame *moral* blame? After all, you don't *praise* the state of the incapable spastic — you count it as highly defective; if, however, you *do* call *this* blame, you aren't using the term 'blame' in a *moral* sense.' Very well, let us say that every defect is something to blame just because it is a defect. 'But when the defect is *voluntary*, *then* we call the blame with which it is blamed *moral* blame; otherwise not.'

'Very well: you have now given a sense to 'moral' as an adjective attached to 'blame' and 'praise'. *Moral* blame is blame of some defect that is, or is supposed to be, voluntary; moral praise, likewise, praise of something good and advantageous that is or is supposed to be voluntary.' This leads to the question: voluntary *on whose part*? The part of the person who *is* defective, or *is* advantageously endued? Not necessarily; we may praise or blame a doctor for the state of a young child, a state which is not voluntary on its part, but is so on the part of the doctor.

In respect, then, of the objects of praise and blame, we can give a non-Aristotelian sense to the word 'moral': when defects and the opposite of defects receive blame and praise, the praise or blame is 'moral' when the defects or their opposites are or are thought to be voluntary.

This is not entirely satisfactory as defects in skill may be voluntary. 'You write rotten verses.' — 'I know I do, but I don't want to do any better.' 'Your spelling is bad.' — 'I don't care to spell properly.' 'I don't mind being a bad cook'; 'I don't mind dressing badly'; 'I don't mind running a messy shop'; 'I don't mind teaching badly'. Isn't it the case that some of us would respond to some of these with 'Oh well, that's all right then'? *I* don't have to settle anything about *this* except to say 'If it is ever not blameworthy to say "Oh well, that's all right then", then we have *not* reached a reasonable account of "moral" as an adjective of "praise" and "blame".' Further, to repeat: even if we had, we would only have said what we are going to *call* '*moral* praise' and '*moral* blame'.

There are those who think that an Aristotelian analogue to a sort of Kantian duty-for-duty's sake is to be seen in Aristotle's statement of a certain *condition* of virtuous action: namely, that virtuous acts must be chosen and chosen for themselves (*Nicomachean Ethics* 1105a33). The Aristotelian passage about virtuous acts being chosen *for themselves* means that to be an act of the virtue of justice an act has to be *chosen* precisely *qua* just. That is not the only condition given: there is a prior condition of knowledge — i.e. you have not only to *think* that what you propose doing is just, but your understanding has to be correct; and there is a subsequent condition, namely that you act out of a settled disposition to act justly. From other observations we gather that if you have the virtue, you will *like* acting justly — a remark which seems very unKantian in spirit. As indeed it is. Kant has a loftiness of thought on these subjects quite unlike Aristotle. In Raphael's picture *The Schools of Athens* the central figures are Plato, pointing upwards to heaven, and Aristotle, pointing downwards to earth. If we are to replace one of them by Kant, which will it be? Surely Plato! Is this not shown by the following passage.*

> And thus are categorical imperatives possible because the idea of freedom makes me a member of an intelligible world. Now if I were a member of only that world, all my actions *would* always accord with autonomy of the will. But since I intuit myself at the same time as a member of the world of sense, my actions *ought* so to accord. This categorical *ought* presents a synthetic a priori proposition, whereby in addition to my will as affected by sensuous desires there is added further the idea of the same will, but as belonging to the intelligible world, pure and practical of itself, and as containing the supreme condition of the former will insofar as reason is concerned ... The practical use of ordinary human reason bears out the correctness of this deduction. There is no one, not even the meanest villain, provided only that he is accustomed to the use of reason, who, when presented with examples of honesty of purpose, of steadfastness in following good maxims, and of sympathy and general benevolence (even when involved with great sacrifices of advantages and comfort) does not wish that he might also possess these qualities. Yet he cannot attain these in himself only because of his inclinations and

---

* At this point the manuscript of the lecture contains a page reference to an English translation of the final paragraph of the section of Kant's *Grundlegung* on 'How is a categorical imperative possible?' The relevant section is printed in the indented text.

impulses; but at the same time he wishes to be free from such inclinations which are a burden to him. He thereby proves that by having a will free of sensuous impulses he transfers himself in thought into an order of things entirely different from that of his desires in the field of sensibility. Since he cannot expect to obtain by the aforementioned wish any gratification of his desires or any condition that would satisfy any of his actual or even conceivable inclinations (inasmuch as through such an expectation the very idea that elicited the wish would be deprived of its preëminence) he can only expect a greater intrinsic worth of his own person. This better person he believes himself to be when he transfers himself to the standpoint of a member of the intellibible world, to which he is involuntarily forced by the idea of freedom, i.e. of being independent of determination by causes of the world of sense. From this standpoint he is conscious of having a good will, which by his own admission constitutes the law for the bad will belonging to him as a member of the world of sense — a law whose authority he acknowledges even while he transgresses it. The moral *ought* is, therefore, a necessary *would* insofar as he is a member of the intelligible world, and is thought by him as an *ought* only insofar as he regards himself as being at the same time a member of the world of sense. (Translation by James W. Ellington, from Immanuel Kant, *Ethical Philosophy* [Indianapolis/Cambridge: Hackett Publishing Company, 1983], p. 55.)

Reflecting on this we might think that Kant would claim to be both — he is Plato pointing upwards to the character of a good will, and Aristotle pointing downwards to the generation of the moral ought for the bad will which is that of a member of the world of sense. Part at least — and I would say a great part — of this is inspired or instigated by the picture of the deterministic physical world painted by natural science; the idea of freedom did not belong there at all; but it exists in the mind and 'makes me a member of an intelligible world', which is not, in Kant's conception, the world of natural science at all. Kant believes intensely in the moral ought: nevertheless for him it is a bastard progeny of the pure practical will, belonging to the intelligible world, and sensuous desires and inclinations.

Let us leave this hideous fantasy — for so it now seems — and return to the problem which we left behind. I mean the problem of *morally* good and bad action. This arose because I suggested that the morally praiseworthy and blameworthy were good and bad things which are voluntary. This forced us to notice that exercises of skill in making things, in writing, in singing, may be bad as exercises of skill. You may say they are then not exercises of *skill* but of ineptitude; but if they are voluntary they *will* be exercises of skill — you voluntarily spell wrong when you know how to spell right and use this knowledge to avoid doing so in writing something. Now this is blameworthy as a bit of spelling — blaming *is* saying 'that's spelt wrong'. But is it therefore blameworthy *as a human action*? Well, it may be, or may not be: so it isn't therefore *straightaway* blameworthy as a human action just because it is blameworthy as a bit of spelling. So its being a bit of spelling, though this does describe a human action, isn't a complete description of it as a human action, as subject to praise or blame *qua* human action.

Let us consider another example, that of teaching badly: I gave this example, meaning it to be a voluntary performance that we were to consider. Should we not say: that's bad action, bad behaviour? Well, why? If we rightly say it, won't it be because it is an *injustice* to the taught, to the pupil or pupils? But must it be? What makes it so? Is there even an implicit contract with the pupils? It is difficult to argue that there is or that there isn't. But suppose we take a case where there is *not* — forced teaching of some technique, deliberately done badly so that the pupil does not learn much. Here we'd not be able to appeal to contract. Without that, would the proceedings need a *justification*, in order not to be a case of bad human action? I put that to you as a question to think about.

Or again: doctoring is a skill. Suppose a doctor deliberately acts so as to keep his patients ill? And suppose he is being forced to practise his medicine upon them — so that *that* is not a matter of contract.

It would appear that if you are exercising upon people a skill which intrinsically relates to people and you voluntarily *mis*-exercise it, you need excuse — you need something that really *does* excuse you — if your proceedings are *not* to be a case of bad actions. This cannot be a matter of contract; it is still bad action if you are forced to engage in the exercise of your skill, though there is then no contract. Our question is 'Why? Why is this bad action unless there is some extraordinary excuse?' The answer would seem to be: 'Because you are harming human beings by your use of a skill *whose point is* to benefit human beings.' That of course means that the harm is direct: you are engaged in *directly* harming human beings, and *that* is unjust behaviour unless there is some solid excuse. To act unjustly is to act badly.

There is, however, an asymmetry between badness and goodness of action. I can bring this out by pointing to the fact that to act justly — in the narrow sense of 'justice' — is not necessarily to act well. Thus a doctor might on occasion truly say 'I did not act unjustly in my decision not to treat that patient; I did not owe it to him to treat him', but that would not shew that he was not acting *badly* in so deciding. If he *was* acting badly, there should be an answer to the question: What *kind* of badness of action was it? Spite towards someone? Licentiousness? Avarice? Refusal to treat a patient doesn't have to be formally something that makes it a bad action; *that* may reside in the circumstances and in what the doctor goes on to do. I mean that the act of refusing to treat a patient is not formally a spiteful act or an avaricious one or a licentious act, as it may be formally an unjust act because the man is *already* your patient and you are free and quite able to treat him. But we can imagine circumstances and aims on the part of the doctor (who perhaps is not committing any injustice against the patient) which shew his action to have been avaricious or spiteful. A *good* action, then, it is *not* — if such circumstances hold.

And we can say: a positive bad action is always an action which at least in *this* sense is an act of some vice; a good action one which is an exercise of some virtue and not of any vice. I say 'at least in this sense' because someone may perform a spiteful act, or an act whose motive is lust, without yet having the vice of spite or licentiousness: but his act is an act of spite, say, because it is such an act as a spiteful man — one habitually motivated by spite — is apt to do. (Omissions are an extension of the topic.)

What has become, now, of the notion of the *morally* good or *morally* bad as applied to human actions? They have become equivalent to 'good and bad' as applied to human actions as such. I mean 'That was a morally good action' is equivalent to '*Qua* human action, that was good' or 'That was a good human action', and 'That was a morally bad human action' is equivalent to '*Qua* human action, that was bad' or 'That was a bad human action'. I am so using 'human action' that nothing is a human action unless it is a voluntary action on the part of a human agent. Otherwise, like digesting your food and breathing and sweating, your acts are the acts of a human agent but are not what I call human actions. If, for example, you lie floating in water and you move your hands above and below you, and then repeat this the other way round, you turn over towards one side and the other in a way doubtless to be explained by Newtonian mechanics; but this motion of yours is not a human action, just the act of a body which happens to be a human being. So though it may well be a human act to *cause* it, and then you do voluntarily bring it about, it is not itself a human action. Of course you may deliberately kill someone by bringing about such an act of the human being that you are, as when you deliberately make yourself fall off a branch of a tree on to someone's neck; but that does not make the falling itself a human action any more than the falling of a log would be, which you deliberately brought about for the same purpose. The turn of your body is voluntary on your part; so is the falling of the log, if you voluntarily brought them about; but they are not themselves voluntary actions of yours; only the bringing about of them was that. Still, their happening can be called your doing, as when we say: 'Look at what resulted! That was your doing'.

Something can be a good human action, then, in spite of being a bad bit of spelling or a bit of bad cooking. And that is the distinction which provides the notion of the *morally* good with what content it has. 'They played that Rasumowsky Quartet very well — it was a good piece of playing; but it was bad on their part to play — or perhaps to play *it* in those circumstances' — i.e. there was good playing but it was bad behaviour. Here it will be redundant to say: 'You mean, it was *morally* bad'.

Now I can say something about the expression 'morally neutral'. Are all human actions either good or bad, or if mixed, then bad because a good action is one which has no aspect in which it is a bad action — none in which it is the act of some vice? This seems an extraordinary thing to say, for aren't there perfectly neutral actions? Like, for example, picking a dandelion flower as I walk along, or indeed, walking along from one point to another. To this I'd say: there are *neutral action-descriptions*, such as 'picking a dandelion flower', 'walking from point A to point B'. But that does not mean that a real action, so describable, will be neither a good action nor a bad one, but will be a neutral action. We haven't given it a description in respect of which there is any presumption that it is a good action, or yet a bad one. There are descriptions which do have such presumptions, such as 'cutting off a man's arm', 'preparing food', 'helping someone on to a bus', 'taking someone's children away', 'locking a man up in a cage'. Some of them sound bad, some good, and both impressions can be contradicted by citing further circumstances. If told that someone threw a pebble into a stream, we would not ask whether excuse existed for this nor whether it was a blameworthy thing to do in spite of first impressions. Such are the neutral action-descriptions. But to grant that there are vastly many neutral action-descriptions is not to grant that there are any actual human actions which are neither good actions nor bad actions.

Well, I said, not only that a bad action was one which is an act of some vice, at least in the sense that it is such an act as a vicious man of a certain sort is apt to do, but that a good action was one which is an exercise of some virtue and not of any vice. How does this fit in with there being vastly many neutral action-descriptions but no neutral human actions? Take the examples of plucking dandelion flowers or throwing a pebble into a stream. Are these human actions on the part of just any human agent we care to imagine? Well, not if our human agent is a baby, for example, or some other human incapable of human action. That is to say, voluntariness is again seen not to be enough to give us good or bad human action. The first case in which I pointed to this was that defects in the use of skill may be voluntary but the blame intended in pointing to such a defect may *not* be blame of what is done *qua* human action. We might now say that this shews that 'spelling wrong' or 'singing the wrong note' are neutral descriptions of action *qua* human actions, even if not neutral descriptions of actions *qua* exercises of skill. But in the cases I am now pointing to, there will be no human action being done by the human agents, because they have not yet reached the stage of deliberation and choice. Where humans have come to deliberation and choice, there will be a true answer to the question what they are up to in their lives. On occasion there will be a question of acting in accordance with or against some specialist virtue such as justice, or courage, or temperance, or truthfulness. At other times the question what they are up to will be answered by giving what they treat as final goals, and here their development or failure of good sense will shew itself in what can be discerned of their ranking of goals and their regard for the possible conflict of particular actions with greater and lesser goals. What is rightly thought of as not in conflict with worthwhile goals can be characterised as 'innocent', and it is as innocent that such actions, if they are chosen (that is truly are human actions), are reckoned as taking their place in the conduct of a virtuous life. They are chosen as inno-cent, and innocency of life, which would be destroyed by special vices, is itself a virtue of a more general kind than the specialist virtues we have so far mentioned. If you ask how such actions as nibbling a mushroom or walking round the block can be called 'chosen as innocent', then I will reply that there is sign of this (a) if they'd not be chosen if not innocent, and their innocency was mentioned if they were challenged, and (b) if the general tenor of the life in which they occur was the pursuit of good goals and the struggle to avoid vices.

In all this, desires and inclinations play a great part, many of them belonging to the world of sense, and others generated by imagination and intelligence: they are not the prostitute mother of a *'moral' ought* who seduces the pure intelligible will into begetting it.

15

Action, Intention and 'Double Effect'

It is customary in the dominant English and related schools of philosophy to restrict the terms 'action' or 'agency'. That is, when the topic is 'philosophy of action'. This is often done by an appeal to intuition about a few examples. If I fall over, you wouldn't usually call that an *action* on my part; it's not something that I *do*, it is rather something that happens to me. Donald Davidson has made a more serious attempt than this at explaining a restriction on the term 'action', or what he means by 'agency'. 'Intentional action' is an insufficient designation for him: it determines no class of events, because an action which is intentional under one description may not be intentional under another. And anyway there are unintentional actions, which he doesn't want to say are not actions in the restricted sense in which he wants to apply the term. So he suggests that we have an action (in the restricted sense) if what is done (no restriction on the ordinary sense here) is intentional under *some* description. This allows pouring out coffee when I meant to pour out tea to be an action, being intentional under the description 'pouring out liquid from this pot'. I fear, however, that it may allow tripping over the edge of the carpet to

* An address given on the occasion of receiving the Aquinas Medal of the American Catholic Philosophical Association on 17 April 1982, and subsequently published in the *Proceedings of the American Catholic Philosophical Association* Vol. 56 (1982): 12–25. Reprinted with the permission of the copyright holder, the American Catholic Philosophical Association.

be an action too, if every part of an intentional progress across the room is intentional under that description. But Davidson doesn't want to count tripping as an action. If this is right, then his account is wrong because it lets in what he wants to exclude. Furthermore, I don't think it comprises omissions, which are often actions.

I am inclined to think that the attempt, brave as it was, was misconceived anyway. There is a goal in view when people want to introduce a restricted sense of 'action', but I don't think it can be attained by trying to find a characterisation of a sub-class of events.

All the same, the point about there being many descriptions of any action, as indeed of any event or any object, is true. It has an importance which we shall see later.

What is being aimed at, I think, is the category called 'human action' by some scholastics: they made a contrast between 'human action' — *actus humanus* — and 'act of a human being' — *actus hominis*. Again, this is usually explained by examples. Idly stroking one's beard, or idly scratching one's head, may be an 'act of a human being' without being a 'human act'.[1] And I expect falling over or tripping up is so too; at any rate I lay it down that I will use the term 'act of a human being' in such a way that those things come under that heading. Also, that 'act of a human being' is a wider notion, which includes 'human action'.

The contrast is that human actions *are under the command of reason*: this does not mean just that reason *can* intervene to forbid — for that holds of idle actions too. What it does mean beyond that will, I hope, emerge.

We might say that human action = voluntary action. But that raises a question of meaning, like what we have just glanced at in the last paragraph. We are speaking of voluntary action *not* in a merely physiological sense; not in the sense in which idly strok-

---

[1]   I use the words 'act' and 'action' interchangeably without intending any difference of sense.

ing your beard *is* a voluntary action. Notice, too, that what is voluntary under one description may be non-voluntary or countervoluntary under another. We are not, like Davidson, attempting a classification which will divide all events into members and non-members of a class.

Nor are we using 'voluntary' as Aristotle uses ἑκούσιον, generally translated 'voluntary'. For Aristotle says that beasts and babies have the voluntary, but we would not say so in the sense of 'voluntary' that we are trying to introduce. Aristotle too introduces a restricted sense of 'action' — praxis, which beasts and babies don't have. But it is a bit too limited for us. It wouldn't include omissions unless calculated, or sudden impulsive actions.

Voluntariness does not require that there be any act of will, any formation of intention, any choice of what is voluntary; or even any positive voluntary act. What you were able to do and it was needful you should do, if you omit it in forgetfulness or sloth, falling asleep perhaps and sleeping through the time when you should have been doing it — your omission of it is voluntary. Unless indeed you fell asleep because you were drugged without the slightest consent on your part. Consent may reside in not taking care when you could have and, in the nature of the case as available to your understanding, you needed to.

I will now put forward a thesis, which I will later give reason for:

All human action is moral action. It is all either good or bad.
(It may be both).

This needs a lot of clarification. First, let me point to an implication. It means that 'moral' does not stand for an extra ingredient which some human actions have and some do not. The idea of the moral as an aspect that is to be seen in some human actions, or felt by the agent, and which may be lacking, perhaps is lacking if it is not felt by the agent — this idea is rejected by the equation 'Human action = moral action' or at least 'Human action = moral action of a human being'. For I am not concerned with angels, demons, fairies or Martians. I shall hope to shew that this equation is not a mere 'extensional equivalence' — two descriptions which happen to be true of the same things. The descriptions are equivalent in content.

All the same, not all human-action descriptions are moral action descriptions. E.g. 'walking', if a human being other than an infant is said to walk, is normally a human-action description, but it is not a moral action-description. (I say it is *normally* a human-action description to allow exclusion of sleep-walking (say), which would be the act of a human being, but not a human action). 'Chucking a pebble into the sea' is another such description, or 'Picking a flower'. Like 'walking', these are *indifferent* human-action descriptions.

This fact, that there are indifferent human-action descriptions, might lead someone to think that there are indifferent human actions. But that does not follow at all. It is the *particular* action that is always good or bad.

Note also that not all action-descriptions which can, and in the particular case often do, describe human actions, are such that whatever acts fall under them are good or bad human actions. For example the description, even when it does describe the action of a human being, still may *not* be describing a human action. As an instance, take 'Killing someone'. Suppose I am a parcel — I mean I've been made up into a parcel — and by sheer accident I get set rolling down a hill in such circumstances that I kill someone by knocking him over into the path of a rapid vehicle — that's not a human action on my part. It *is*, if I kill someone by an accident in driving my car — I reverse it by mistake, say, and kill a small child standing behind it.

As I said: 'Walking', though if it is applied to a non-infant human being it is normally a human-action description, is nevertheless not a moral action-description. By a moral action-description I mean one at least *suggesting* some *specific* goodness or badness about an act that falls under it. 'Walking', even when it is used to report a particular human action, does not suggest anything specific.

It is not even true that every *moral* action-description, as a description of a particular human action, entails that that particular action was good, or again, that it was bad. It may only entail that the action was, say, good, unless some aspect makes it bad. Or was bad, unless some excuse or justification either lets it have a certain goodness in as much as it is an action which is not wicked, or actually renders it specifically good.

This working of excuse may astonish. Someone has killed someone, let us say. We ask: Was it his *fault*? It turns out that it was not; although the action which as it turned out resulted in death *was* a human action. So: he has an excuse, he is perhaps exonerated; he is not *guilty of homicide*. But does that mean his action was *good*? If all actual human action that occurs is either good or bad, it seems as if his *excuse* renders his action *good*! But isn't that too paradoxical? Don't we want something between good and bad in actual particular occurrences of action?

Assume his action is not good *qua* killing, *qua* resulting in death. And we can suppose it was no particular species of good action; not the act of any specific virtue. But, just as anything that has positive being is good *qua* being (even if it is something that for some reason ought not to exist) so action is good as being action, i.e. *qua* belonging to the genus 'action'. (And it would be so, even if there were no specific goodness about it). Suppose, then, that all the things about it which make one want to say it was bad turn out to be not his fault: suppose they were just accidents for which he had no responsibility, except in the sense of (involuntarily) contributing some of the causation of a bad result. Then, there is not the *quicunque defectus* to make his action a bad human action.

Here I am invoking the principle 'Bonum ex integra causa; malum ex quocunque defectu'. This might be rendered: 'something is good by reason of being good in every respect, bad from being bad in any'. Here respects of good and bad have to belong to the thing under the description under which it is described as good or bad. Thus there might be a good human action — good *tout court*, not just good in this respect or that — which was by sheer accident an intervenient cause of some evil. Here some might say that that *act of a human being* had something bad about it, and so wasn't good *tout court*. That is, *if* I am right in the extensive application I give to the expression 'act of a human being'. But the *human act* has not got something wrong with it *qua* human act from being an involuntary cause of some evil. That respect of badness does not belong to it as a human act. For being the involuntary cause of something does not belong to it as a human act.

On the other hand, there might be nothing good about it *qua* human action, *except* that it was human action. I am still thinking of the same case, where the evil result is pure accident, not voluntarily caused by the agent. But he is presumably engaged in something or other in his being there or at least in his motion, if that is voluntary; and what he is up to may itself have been for a bad end, and hence bad on its own account.

Or it may have been subordinated to a bad end. But here I get into deep water. Is a wicked man, who keeps himself in good trim by physical exercise so as to pursue his life's purposes, acting badly or well in taking that exercise? I cannot answer this question, and to investigate it now would take too long.

It will be apparent why I said that an action — a human action — may be both good and bad. It may be good only in a certain respect, and bad in others; then it is not good *tout court*, but bad. And the respect *may* be: generically. In *this* respect all human actions are good, though many are bad *tout court*.

So far we've been speaking in a uniform way about the case of the bad upshot, whether there is excuse *or* exoneration. Alternatively, we may want to distinguish between these. With exoneration, an agent is in the clear; but if there is less than exoneration, we may say his action was bad as needing excuse and *therefore* pardon. In such a case we may say it was mixed. In *that* way, it was bad — if he had taken more care, he would have avoided the result; and yet the result was not one that, as we say, 'was to be expected in the nature of the case'. And in this way it was mixed; it had the goodness of being a human action and perhaps of being whatever sort of action he was engaged in intentionally; it lacks the defect of being a specifically wicked action, since it does not get this from the bad accidental result; and yet it has something of badness, that makes it seem to need pardon. For if we do distinguish between exoneration and excuse in this sort of case, this is where the distinction must be made. If it merits complete exoneration, then it has no badness from the bad upshot — e.g. the unfortunate result is 'utterly accidental, he couldn't have avoided it, it was sheer bad luck'.

From considering good and bad, we see that the extension of 'human action' is wider than that of 'intentional human action'. That is to say: something may be a human action under a description under which it is not an intentional action. Acts of carelessness, negligence and omission may be of this character. For though they can be intentional, they may not be so, but their not being intentional does not take the character of human action away from them. But a human action does not have something wrong with it *qua* human act — i.e. so as to be to that extent a bad human action — from being an involuntary cause of some evil. The involuntariness does mean that the badness is not in a respect belonging to it as a human action. By parity of consideration, voluntariness would mean that it was bad in such a respect.

To repeat: when I speak of moral action-descriptions, I mean ones which suggest, at least suggest, good or bad — unlike neutral or indifferent action-descriptions, which suggest nothing either way. However, one might object that *if* just being an action is good, then neutral action-descriptions must after all mention something good. (Even if in the particular case it also fails in goodness because of something bad about it then and there.) So how can I say that there are neutral action-descriptions? The answer is that the good or bad suggested by moral action-descriptions is *specific* goodness or badness. That in the particular case each human action is good or bad is a different point from the generic goodness of any action as being an action: it means that each human action is specifically good or specifically bad. It will be good, if good, for more than just being an action. Firstly, the particular thing that is done may itself be more than generically good. But also there are circumstances and ends to consider. For suppose the particular thing that is done is sufficiently specified by a neutral action-description, so that it — the particular thing that is done — might be called 'no more than generically good': then, if the agent's purpose or purposes in doing it are specifically good and circumstances import nothing bad about doing that thing for those purposes, the action will be specifically good. A neutral action-description reporting a human act may give 'the particular thing that was done' sufficiently for us to say: 'That was all right, unless the purpose or circumstances put a different complexion on it'. Or, it may be an inadequate description of the particular thing that was done: he didn't 'merely write his name on a bit of paper', he was signing such-and-such a contract.

To say that 'human action' and 'moral action (*sc.* of a human being)' are equivalent is to say that all human action *in concreto* is either good or bad *simpliciter*. There is no need to insert 'morally' and say 'morally good or bad'. The term 'moral' adds no sense to the phrase, because we are talking about human actions, and the 'moral' goodness of an action is nothing but its goodness as a human action. I mean: the goodness with which it is a good action. 'Moral' goodness is: goodness of actions, passions, and habits of action and feeling. The term is however a distinguishing one, restricted to specific goodness, goodness *simpliciter*, or to what comes closer to that than the generic good of being a human action or passion or disposition.

The idea that a human action could be called a 'pre-moral evil', or evil in a pre-moral sense, is extremely confused. Examples which are offered to prove it are killing and amputation.

Death is an evil, and a killing (of a human by a human) may not be a wicked action. For it may be blamelessly accidental and so, it is suggested, a 'pre-moral evil'. The amount of truth there is in this conclusion consists in this: the description 'killing someone' may be the description of an *act of a human being* (*actus hominis*) without describing a *human act* (*actus humanus*) — as when I was a parcel rolling down the hill. Note that when it *is* the description of an act of a human being, even though not of a human act, it is still a moral action-description. At least this is so if I am right in my application of these terms. For we ask whether it was the person's fault, was their excuse, and so on. If, as in the parcel case, it turns out that the act of knocking the victim over to his death wasn't a human act, that is sufficient to answer those questions: it wasn't his fault, it was in no way voluntary on his part. Only in the sense in which 'responsibility' means 'causality' was he responsible.

The fact that 'killing', even when applied to the interaction of two human beings, has this somewhat generic character, does not prove that a particular *human action* of killing someone is not established with a definite character of moral evil once it is clear that it was intentional and also was private — i.e. was not an action belonging to the exercise of civil authority. I would prefer to say 'a definite character of evil' because of my opinion that the term 'moral' there is strictly redundant; but I have to put it in as I am commenting on a conception of 'pre-moral' evil according to which an action of killing someone, fully deliberate, fully intentional, may only be evil in a 'pre-moral' sense. That is, as so far described or proposed it may be so.

Now this, if true, would not be true in the way in which the evil was pre-moral in the parcel case: namely, because, while death is an evil, it was not brought about by a human action. It would, rather, be true because of what is excluded by my word 'private'. Intentional killing in warfare, or by police in fighting violent criminals, or by execution of a death sentence — all these *can* be murderous, but they are not necessarily so, and that means that 'intentional killing of one human being by another' is a moral action-description whose applicability does not *eo ipso* prove the wickedness of the deed. The description is more determinate than is the bare word 'killing'; yet it is still somewhat indeterminate. But this indeterminateness of description does not signify an indeterminateness in the quality of the human act, given the sanity of the killer and the circumstances which make it 'private'.

If anyone thinks otherwise, he must have been misled by bad teaching. Or simply by a bad philosophic tradition, according to which the intentionalness of an action (a) can't be known to anyone but the agent and (b) is a matter of what the agent did it *for* — intention being often taken to mean purpose, or intention of the end. Now as to (a), 'intention can't be known, because it is something private', that is in general absurd. It is often, nay *usually* quite apparent that someone is doing such-and-such on purpose. It is no objection to this that error on the point is possible. Nor yet, that it is more difficult to know someone's further intentions, or the intentions with which he was doing what he was obviously doing on purpose, or what he was doing it all for.

Murder is a complex concept with many disparate elements in it. But you don't have to know what some private person killed his uncle for in order to know he committed murder, so long as he was awake, *compos mentis* and was doing the killing on purpose. (I say 'some private person' to exclude the cases of capital punishment, cops and robbers, and warfare all in a lump).

This means that although the mental element of *mens rea* is important in identifying a killing as a murder, the question whether someone has committed a murder can usually be answered as soon as the relevant facts are in, and having the facts in doesn't mean that all we have ascertained is the occurrence of a 'pre-moral evil'.

Amputation — of a limb, say — is a more pressing example for our immediate enquiry. This is because what someone is doing an amputation for is all-important. If it is needed for the life or health of the victim because of the physical condition or situation of his body, then it is all right as far as purpose goes, otherwise not. And this seems to lend real substance to the idea of a 'pre-moral evil' which is deliberately encompassed by a human action for the sake of a greater good. Someone cut off someone's hand, let us say. That sounds awful — could it be an indeterminate description of an action justified by circumstances: by who he was, and who his victim was? Suppose he was the public executioner and his victim a thief being punished according to law? If that would make it all right, then amputation as a moral problem would be rather like killing. But we don't have amputations as punishment 'in civilised countries'. I don't wish to raise the question whether such punishment is admissible at all: but the fact that we don't have it puts amputation into a special position: an evil inflicted, not as a punishment, but for the sake of a greater good in some other way. The evil is all in the particular thing that is purposely done, but the evil of it and the intentionalness do not determine the quality of the act. That is principally determined by what it was done for. So you have a pre-moral evil, and the goodness or badness of the action of *doing* it is principally a matter of the intention of the end. This gives us a pattern which, it might be said, we can surely apply elsewhere! 'If deliberately cutting off a hand is so far forth only pre-moral evil, then can't the same be said of killing your uncle, or aborting your baby or ...? What will give it its *moral* character (and maybe a lovely one) is what you do it for'.

'Cutting off a limb' is a moral action-description by my criteria. It is also indeterminate, suggesting evil, raising the question of excuse or justification. Who did it to whom, in what circumstances, and what for? When we know the answer to these questions we should be able to tell the quality of the act. The thing that makes it of importance for our discussion is the dominant role of the question 'What for?' If this role is described by reference to 'a greater good', then the road is thrown open to a generalisation which threatens to destroy many absolute prohibitions of kinds of act.

The important thing about a justified amputation — as we 'in civilised countries' understand it — is that it is for the life, health or capacity-to-function of the individual human being who suffers it. The lesser evil for that human being's physical condition or integrity is chosen for the sake of the greater good of that human being's life or condition or capacity. So there really is here a case in which *an* intrinsic evil is inflicted for the sake of a more valuable good. But the evil and the good concern the bodily condition of the single human individual. He occupies a pre-eminent position in questions about good and bad action.

Once this is clear, it should also be clear that in this case too we have an indeterminate description whose kind of indeterminateness is exploited to argue for a characterisation of many bad actions as so far 'pre-moral evils'. Because in *this* case the principal determinant is the 'what for', it is suggested that this is quite generally so. Old authorities are invoked, who wrote of all the factors that go to determine the specific goodness or badness of actions. These factors certainly include intention. Against the background of certain modern traditions in philosophy — especially the Cartesian — it is hardly noticed that intention may relate to the intentionalness of the particular act that is done, as well as to the purpose for which it is done. Now there are several kinds of action which, if they are done intentionally, are evidently evil actions, no matter what they are done for. The good end only sanctifies such means as either are good considered in themselves, or would naturally fall merely under a neutral action-description. (Amputation, when justified, is an exception to this 'only'.)*

My phrase 'if they are done intentionally' signifies a sufficient condition, not a necessary one. This will become clear if we return to our earlier topic of murder.

For here there can be borderline cases arising because murder is not committed only where there was an intention to kill. The arsonist who burns down a house, not caring that there are people there, is as much a murderer if they are burned to death by his action, as if he had aimed to kill them. This action falls squarely within a penumbra surrounding the hard-core part of the concept of murder, which contains only intentional killing. The penumbra is fuzzy at the outer edges — that is, there are borderline cases. But that fact does not mean that an absolute prohibition on murder makes no sense.

And similarly for other intrinsically evil deeds. The descriptions might be simple and easy to apply, like 'sodomy', or have cases in which the application was somewhat obscure or disputable, like 'lying'; but none of that creates a conceptual difficulty about the notion of absolute wrongness — whether great wrongness, or small as in many instances of lying.

The fact that there is murder where death foreseeably results from one's action, without the actual intention of killing, naturally leads to a problem. One cannot say that *no* action may be done which foreseeably or probably leads to some death, or that all such actions are murderous. Why, the very begetting of a child would be murder at that rate — for the child will surely die. Or if that seems too zany an example: you can't build roads and fast vehicles, you can't have various sports and races, you can't have ships voyaging over the seas, without its being predictable that there will be deaths resulting. And much that is done in medicine

* This parenthetical sentence, which does not appear in the printed version of the paper, was inserted in Professor Anscombe's handwriting in the typescript of the paper.

and surgery is done knowing it involves the risk of death — pain-killing drugs which may kill the patient before his disease does, and high-risk surgery.

Therefore some distinction needs to be made, or some distinctions.

This is a problem for those who hold that deliberately killing is absolutely out in the sort of case we may have to consider. If you don't hold that, it seems you don't get into a bind. For the whole thing begins by saying

(a)   You must not kill either as an end or as a means to some end.

(b)   Not all action that leads to someone's, or people's death, though this is not intended, is murderous and so forbidden.

(c)   Often such action *is* murderous, and so is forbidden.

It is here that we have the famous 'doctrine of double effect'. 'Double effect' is an unfortunate Latinism. What we are talking about is death as a side-effect which is brought about as well as the effect being aimed at.

I will call it the 'principle of side-effects' that the prohibition on murder does not cover *all* bringing about of deaths which are not intended. Not that such deaths aren't often murder. But the quite clear and certain prohibition on intentional killing (with the relevant 'public' exceptions) does not catch you when your action brings about an unintended death.

So much seems clear. But notice that the principle is modest: it says 'where you must not aim at someone's death, causing it does not *necessarily* incur guilt'.

The principle is unexceptionably illustrated by some examples of dangerous surgery, by some closings of doors to contain fire or water; or by having ships and airlines. In these we are helped by thinking of the deaths as either remote or uncertain. But an unintended death which is a foreseeable consequence of one's action may be neither. *Then* we are confronted with cases where it strikes people that there is little difference between direct and indirect killing. Imagine a pot-holer[2] stuck with people behind him and water rising to drown them. And imagine two cases: in one, he can be blown up; in the other, a rock *can* be moved to open another escape route, but it will crush his head. He will be killed by it.

Someone who will equally choose either course clearly prefers saving these lives to the avoidance of any intentional killing. Such cases are discussed with a note of absolute necessity about saving lives — a presupposition that is paramount.

The example of the stuck pot-holer was invented (without the choice of ways of escape) to illustrate the iniquity of abortion: you wouldn't say you could kill the pot-holer to get out — it was argued. But people did say just that — at least if the posture of the pot-holer was so described that he was going to get drowned too!

Yet situations must often have occurred where people were in a tight corner, could have saved themselves by killing one of their number, and that has not occurred to them as an option at all.

If that were the attitude of the people in the cave, they wouldn't do either thing.

Indeed someone might say of moving the rock and crushing his head: 'Isn't that direct killing too?' The point of not calling it direct was that it isn't his being crushed that gives the escape route — and so his being crushed can be something you don't *intend*.

'Direct' and 'indirect' are dodgy terms; sometimes they relate to off-shoots, as it were, from a given sequence of causes, and sometimes to immediacy or remoteness, and sometimes to what is intended or not. I note with curiosity that McCormick uses the concepts of direct and indirect intention, saying that they are centuries old tools of moral theology. If that is so, I'd like to know the

---

[2]   A cave explorer.

sources. I myself know of 'direct' and 'indirect' intention only as terms introduced by Jeremy Bentham. He called it 'indirectly intended' if you took a shot at something and hit something else, if you knew that was a possibility. Fr. McCormick's sense seems to be the same. 'Indirectly intended' thus means 'Unintended, but the possibility was foreseen'. While I am speaking of Fr. McCormick, I will also remark on his curious use of 'intention in a psychological sense'.[3] With respect, there is no other relevant sense.

Returning to the pot-holer, I note that the 'doctrine of double effect' is supposed to say that the people could move the rock, though they must *not*, not on any account, blow up the pot-holer. And this is what is found intolerably artificial and unnatural. But we may ask: Is that because of what is allowed, or what is forbidden? What I've called 'the principle of side effects' is related to an absolute prohibition on seeking someone's death, either as end or as means. I've spoken of that. Now, if the objection is to what is here *allowed*, note that the principle of side effects does not state or imply that they can move the rock. It does not say *when* you may foreseeably cause death.

And why should we have a package deal here, as in what is called the 'doctrine of double effect'?

Now — perhaps because of this teaching — there might be people among those in the cave who, even seeing the undesired consequence, would move the rock, though they would refuse to blow the man up because that would mean choosing his death as means of escape. This is not a meaningless stance. They'd be shewing themselves as people who will reject any policy making the death of innocent people a means or an end.

But, to repeat: you cannot deduce the permissibility of moving the rock from the principle of side-effects. It determines nothing about that, except perhaps that it is not excluded on the score of

[3]   My references are to his *Ambiguity in Moral Choice*. [The Père Marquette Lecture in Theology 1973. Milwaukee: Marquette University Press 1973]

being intentional killing. We have to say 'perhaps' because of the possible closeness of the result. As I have described the case, we are only given that moving the rock will crush the pot-holer's head. This might be a result so immediate that the action could not be called 'taking the risk that that would happen'. If so, then it is at best a dubious business to say 'We don't intend that result'. At most, it is no part of the aim, in securing the opening, that the man's head should be crushed.

At this point the Doctrine of Double Effect helps itself to an absurd device, of choosing a description under which the action is intentional, and giving the action under that description as *the* intentional act. 'I am moving what blocks that egress', or 'I am removing a rock which is in the way'. The suggestion is that that is *all* I am doing as a means to my end. This is as if one could say: 'I am merely moving a knife through such-and-such a region of space', regardless of the fact that that space is manifestly occupied by a human neck, or by a rope supporting a climber. 'Nonsense', we want to say, 'doing that is doing this, and so closely that you can't pretend only the first gives you a description under which the act is intentional'. For an act does not merely have many descriptions, under some of which it is indeed not intentional: it has several under which it is intentional. So you cannot choose just one of these, and claim to have excluded others by that. Nor can you simply bring it about that you intend *this* and not *that* by an inner act of 'directing your intention'. Circumstances, and the immediate facts about the means you are choosing to your ends, dictate what descriptions of your intention you must admit. *Nota bene* that here 'intention' relates to the intentionalness of the action you are performing as means.

Suppose for example that you want to train people in habits of supporting the Church with money. If you exact money from them as a condition of baptism you cannot say you are not making them pay for it.

All this is relevant to our pot-holer only where the crushing of his head is an immediate effect of moving the rock. Here a ground for saying you can intend to move the rock and not intend to crush the head is that you might not know that in moving the rock you would crush his head. That is true, we may suppose; which does differentiate this case from the simoniacal one. But if you *do* know, then where the crushing is immediate you cannot pretend not to intend it if you are willing to move the rock.

Let us now consider the case where the result is not so immediate — the rock you are moving has to take a path after your immediate moving of it, and in the path that it will take it will crush his head. Here there is indeed room for saying that you did not intend that result, even though you could foresee it. And that is the sort of case we have to consider. The Doctrine of Double Effect is supposed to allow you to move the rock, if the balance of good over bad results is favourable. The Principle of Side Effects says no more than that moving the rock is not excluded by the prohibition on intentional killing. For, as I have explained it, that principle is not a package deal and it does not say what circumstances or needs excuse unintended causing of death.

Some principle or principles are needed, and if we adopt that one principle, of the balance of good over evil in the expected upshot, then it becomes obscure why we could not do this where the causation of death was perfectly intentional. And that seems to be the principal ground on which some thinkers throw the whole package out of the window, and talk about a deliberate killing, for example, as *so far* a 'pre-moral evil'. They may help themselves by the confused considerations I discussed earlier, but the nerve of the rejection of former doctrine is here.

I formerly understood the Doctrine of Double Effect, *not* as a package deal, but rather as what I have called the 'principle of side-effects', and I thought I was only doing a work of clarification in formulating it and remarking that it does not tell us what to allow and what to forbid when we have left the area of intentional killing.[4] I have come to realise that the Doctrine of Double Effect comprises several things, merely *including* this 'principle of side effects', and that we should split it up.

Having accepted the principle of side effects, we need some further principle or principles on which to judge the unintended causing of death. There is one which both seems obvious and covers a good many cases. The intrinsic certainty of the death of the victim, or its great likelihood from the nature of the case, would exclude moving the rock. Here is a reasonable principle. Surgery would be thought murderous, even though it was not done in order to kill, but, say, to get an organ for someone else, if the death of the subject were expected as a near consequence, pretty certain from the nature of the operation.

It will be apparent that this principle tells you rather what you can't do than what you can. Also, it is particularly devised for the causing of death; causing of other harm is not covered by it. I think that these are not faults.

I will end by protesting at the ascription of the Doctrine of Double Effect to Aquinas: the phrase '*duplex effectus*' occurs in his discussion of killing in self-defence. (*Summa Theologica* IIa IIae, Q. 64 art. 7) 'Ex actu ergo alicuius se defendentis duplex effectus sequi potest: unus quidem, conservatio propriae vitae; alius autem, occisio invadentis'. His doctrine is severe: he holds that one may not aim at the death of one's assailant, but one is guiltless if it occurs unintended as a result of one's use of means proportionate to the end of repelling him. One must moderate the force one uses, to suit the end; if one uses more than is required ('si utatur maiori violentia quam opporteat') one's act is rendered illicit. Those who wished to see in this text the package Doctrine of Double Effect claimed that in speaking of proportionate means St. Thomas was introducing their doctrine of a proportion of good over evil in the upshot. I am not concerned to discuss St.

---

[4]   See 'Murder and the Morality of Euthanasia' below, esp. pp. 274–277.

Thomas' view on self-defence, only to note the false interpretation.

If we want to know St. Thomas' general opinion on responsibility for evil consequences of actions, this is not the place to look, but rather at what he says about the relation of an *eventus sequens* to the goodness or badness of an action (Ia IIae, Q.20 art. 5):

> Si est praecogitatus, manifestum est quod addit ad bonitatem vel malitiam. Cum enim aliquis cogitans quod ex opere suo multa mala possunt sequi nec propter hoc dimittit: ex hoc apparet voluntas eius esse magis inordinata.
>
> Si autem eventus sequens non sit praecogitatus, tunc distinguendum est. Quia si per se sequitur ex tali actu, et ut in pluribus, secundum hoc eventus sequens addit ad bonitatem vel malitiam actus: manifestum est enim meliorem actum esse ex suo genere, ex quo possunt plura bona sequi; et peiorem ex quo nata sunt plura mala sequi. Si vero per accidens, et ut in paucioribus, tunc eventus sequens non addit ad bonitatem vel ad malitiam actus: non enim datur iudicium de re aliqua secundum illud quod est per accidens, sed solum secundum quod est per se.[5]

---

[5] **Translation:** If it (the consequent event) is pre-conceived [foreseen], it manifestly adds to the goodness or badness of the action. For when someone considers that much that is bad can follow from what he does, and does not give it up on that account, this shews that his will is the more inordinate.

But if the consequent event is not preconceived [foreseen], then it is necessary to distinguish. For if it follows from that kind of action *per se* and in most cases, then the consequent event does accordingly add to the goodness or badness of the action; for it is clear that that action is better in kind, from which more goods can follow, and worse, from which more evils are liable to follow. But if it is *per accidens*, and in rather few cases, then the consequent event does not add to the goodness or to the badness of an action: for there isn't judgment on any matter according to what is *per accidens*, but only what is *per se*.

16

The Controversy over a New Morality

'In view of the way it all worked out, I regret having made that decision.' Sometimes one has such a thought. 'When I see what it all led to, I wish I had decided *not* to take that line.'

Ought I to have been able to see it would turn out so? Perhaps: at least as a likelihood. But perhaps not; for events are much at the mercy of chance, and by chance also coincide to produce unexpected results.

Whether what I do now will result in a greater sum of good than anything else I might do, is unknowable. This is so, whether I mean a greater sum of good for the universe or for mankind or (except in my last hour) for myself. We have to admit this unless we rely on some doctrine, itself uncertain, about the workings of divine providence.

This is certain, however: the whole future of the universe is in God's care and not ours. If deity does not exist, it cannot be in anyone's care. For such beings as Plato's demiurge are mere fictions, and if they did exist, the whole future of the universe would not be in their power to determine.

---

* Text of an untitled and undated manuscript in English for which a German translation in typescript exists ('Der Streit um eine neue Moral') that is evidently the text of a paper given by Professor Anscombe to a German-speaking audience (probably at some time in the mid-1980s). The reference in the text to German moral theology is almost certainly to the consequentialist writings of the German moral theologian Bruno Schüller SJ.

You ask 'How so?' — A demiurge, if he made the world, did not make it out of nothing. Whatever he made it from had possibilities and impossibilities independently of his will. Both he and it were subject to necessity, chance and fate. 'But', you may say, 'one can have the care of something without having total power over it'. That is so, within the limits of the possibilities left open. Even within those limits one cannot have the care of something unless one has some power to determine what possibilities shall be actualised. And even such limited power is itself subject to chance impediment. Now, if the whole future of the universe is in someone's care, the totality of whatever comes to be and whatever happens is wholly in his care. That totality would include all interferences in the development of things and processes. Such a being is therefore not subject to ἀνάγκη, that necessity which ruled even what the Greeks called gods, nor yet to chance. Nor to fate: for fate was what happened under the rule of necessity and chance.

'But one can have *some* care for the whole future of the universe, because one can determine what among some few limited possibilities shall be actualised.' I did not say one couldn't. But I do say it now. Being able to determine that this or that possibility be actualised is *necessary* for being able to care for something, but is not *enough* to guarantee that one can do so. If one is just a caretaker (as we speak of the caretaker of a house), one has got to know what is good or bad for what one is to take care of, so far as one is to do so. For example, Alfred the Great didn't take care of the cakes, he let them burn. If he had been taking care, he would not have let them burn. This is not just because he could determine whether they were left to burn or not but also because he knew it is not good for cakes to be burnt. With my 'if he had been taking care' I meant: if he had been taking care *of the cakes*. He was taking care of something else: at any rate he was worrying about the rescue of his Kingdom from the Vikings. *That* he took care of with success. So his neglect of the cakes *perhaps* resulted in a greater sum of good for England than taking care of them would have. Who can say? It is unknowable. And I was saying: it is unknowable whether 'what I do now' will result in a greater sum of good altogether than anything else I might do instead.

What *is* knowable is e.g. that not letting cakes burn is better for them than letting them burn. This is a true general observation. In a particular case in which the house is catching fire and one puts that fire out, 'not letting the cakes burn', as ordinarily understood, might however be *no* better for them because they will burn with the house if one attends to them and not to it. Anyway they don't matter in comparison with the house. In another case, not letting them burn will indeed be better for them but in the circumstances worse for some human being who staggers in choking on a bone and needs, say, to be stood on his head and shaken if he is not to choke to death. Meanwhile, the cakes burn. But they don't matter in comparison with the life of a human being.

Let me return to my opening. 'When I see what it led to, I wish I hadn't made that decision.' This is a familiar thought, even if not a frequent one. Now suppose one asks 'Why?' and gets the answer 'Well, what it led to would not have happened, if I had not done such-and-such'. In some cases this at least *seems* to be a reasonable remark, probably true. 'If I had not decided to keep the paraquat, Tom would not have mixed *it* with water and left *it* in the refrigerator in a Coca Cola bottle, and then John would not have been poisoned by drinking *it*.' So far, so good. 'And John would still be alive.' Even for uncritical thinking, that is at best a probable sort of conclusion. And even on the way, a small alteration makes a difference. 'If I had not decided to keep the paraquat, Tom would not have mixed paraquat with water etc.' At best, perhaps probable. Why probable? 'Well, I am assuming that everything *except* my keeping the paraquat would have been the same.' No you aren't. You are assuming indeed that Tom would not have formed a plan of getting some paraquat with the same upshot — on hearing you had thrown yours away. 'But I am assuming all his relevant actions would have been the same.' Are you?

The regretful reflexions about one's decision concern what it actually played a part in producing. '*That* would not have happened if I had not ...' is sometimes certain, depending on one's specification of '*that*' ('John would not have drunk *it* if I had thrown *it* down the drain'); sometimes seems highly likely because one just doesn't consider alternative unexpected happenings which might have led to the same upshot described in general terms; and is sometimes doubtful even to uncritical commonsense consideration. 'I wish I had not decided to oppose that marriage. They wouldn't have got married but for my opposition, and so they would have been happily married to more suitable partners.'

I will not pause to dwell on the actual difficulty of formulating what one means by 'all the relevant things being the same' — except of course the relevant things that are actually excluded by assuming the truth of a false supposition running e.g. 'I threw that paraquat away', which you turn into the antecedent of a subjunctive conditional 'If I had thrown that paraquat away, John would not have been poisoned'. That difficulty, along with doubts about the justification of the assumption, if you can formulate it, and about the justification of assumptions you *can* formulate, like 'If we had given her dialysis on Wednesday, she wouldn't have been dead by Friday'. (Even here there is a hidden assumption: 'if everything else had been normal'.) All these things have led some philosophers to think that there is no such thing in any particular case as: what would have happened if what was done had not been done or what was not done had been done.

I will only note that some philosophers *per contra* are moved by a sort of determinism to think that there always are the exact things that would have happened if ... R.M. Hare, for example, thinks that one can speak identifyingly of the child that would have been conceived if *N.* and *M.* had had intercourse at … o'clock on …, when they had no intercourse then.

About this, I will remark that the determinism which would have to be true in order for *that* to be true would imply that the past history of things could have been different from the first. Given the starting point, all that does happen happens necessarily. Or is conception an especially determined event?

Some such determinism seems to be implicit in the belief that, knowable or not, there *is* a sum of value and disvalue resulting from what I do now and that what I ought to do is what gives a greater sum of good, or lesser sum of evil, than anything I might do instead. This doctrine is curiously called 'teleological' in some current German moral theology, and the same name is given to any system of moral philosophy that regards desirable consequences as the sole criterion for what one ought or ought not to do. Of course, one may not speak like G.E. Moore of the total value and disvalue in the universe; e.g. one may restrict one's field to mankind; also the doctrine does not go so far [as to] say what *are* desirable consequences. Whatever is decided on these questions, the teaching is that one ought to aim at the best consequences and that there are no other true 'ought' propositions. A teaching in which lying and (for a Christian) denying Christ, sodomy, and procuring someone's execution by false witness against him are said to be things on no account to do for the sake of bringing about any good or preventing any evil, is equally curiously called 'deontological'.

These designations are curious because they are said to be frequent in English philosophy. I am an English philosopher and can assure you they are not. 'Teleological' among us suggests some sort of Aristotelianism or something like it. 'Deontological' suggests Kant: duty for duty's sake is the only ethical motive.

The division of systems of moral philosophy into 'teleological' — ethics only to do with consequences — and 'deontological' — i.e. containing statements that various kinds of action are bad (or good), wrong (or right) regardless of consequences — is made by C.D. Broad. He quickly says that the terms are 'ideal abstractions' and do not designate any actual philosophies. Here he might concede that Kant at least *tried* to be what Broad called a 'monistic deontologist'. All actual moral philosophers are mixed; I would say this includes Kant in his arguments in practice.

Broad is no very distinguished ethicist, and in introducing this division he did not remark that 'It is always and only right to act in the way that will produce the best consequences' or 'Actions for the sake of the best consequences are always good actions and no others' seem to fall under both definitions. The first one may not seem to say that actions of a certain kind are right *regardless of consequences*, but if it can be used as a guide at all, since total consequences if I do such-and-such are unknowable, it is necessary to go by tendency to produce the best calculable consequences. Indeed Broad speaks of the tendencies of kinds of action. Now why is it right to adopt this guide about what is right? Because it *will* produce the best consequences? That is far from clear; it is indeed disprovable. But even if it were true, why is it right to aim at the best consequences? Is the answer 'It just *is* so and you ought to be able to see it'? This is supposed to be an answer characteristic of that non-existent beast, the 'deontologist'.

The first non-existent beast, the 'teleologist', is rather more existent than the other. The idea that it is right to act 'for the best' is a very common one; and if acting for the best involves committing one of those sins which I mentioned, then in *this* case they won't be sins. I fear that this is something people — some people — actually want to hear.

Let us consider the problems that beset doctors, some of whom in the United States have now begun to be seriously interested in medical ethics. Think of the doctor prescribing and arranging dialysis for a patient long nearly comatose, moving about a bit, grimacing, opening her eyes sometimes, but without any communication with the people who look after her or her relations and friends who come to see her. The doctor has convinced himself that the human being, the human mind, isn't there any more. She is effectively dead. *She*, the person, died more than six months ago. This is based on the lack of any human communication. The family have discussed the matter with him. The daughters who visited her often thought the dialysis should be stopped. The sons demurred, but then visited her and thought so too. The obstacle was the husband, who had beaten his wife and treated her cruelly and never did visit her. 'If you do that', he said, 'I'll take you to court.' So the dialysis goes on. If it weren't for the husband, the doctor would stop it. He is in a deeply confused state. He tells himself and others that she *is* dead. The 'person' is no longer there. (I must tell you that in English and American the word 'person' is a very dangerous one: it is only 'persons' who have rights, and you can be a human being without being a person; human beings *become* persons at some stage of development.) Well, let's say this doctor thinks the *human being* is no longer there; he is not confusing himself like that with the word 'person'. So stopping dialysis isn't deciding for the death of a human being. So he might be easy in *this* case; it would be deciding for the death of something, but not killing a human being. But what about other cases?

Here he is caught in a net. He believes that he ought not to kill his patients. At least, he says he never has, and is obviously worried at the idea. But at the same time he thinks — and this is a *very* common view — that a doctor ought to do what is best for the patient. So suppose he thinks what is best for the patient is: *not* to go on having the treatment; and suppose the decision to stop the treatment is a decision which, if carried out, means death within a day or two, as with the dialysis patient? The decision *against* the treatment is then a decision *for* death. So if he thinks of stopping the treatment, he has got to think it best for the patient to die. This opens the door to thinking it best for the patient to be killed. He has difficulty in distinguishing between killing and letting die when the letting die is refusing a treatment without which the patient certainly will die very soon.

I believe that what is getting this good man — for as you may have realised I am describing something I was directly acquainted with — what is getting him into a real dangerous bind is the conviction that he has got to do what is best for his patient, which means that he has got to think best what he feels impelled to do.

In general, thinking you should do your best for your patients is obviously the right attitude for a doctor. But here? The question what a doctor's duties are to his patient is insufficiently discussed. In particular, I have never seen the following discussed.

May not a doctor with a dying patient say: 'I don't want to go on with this treatment of him, and I do not have to. I am not saying I would condemn someone who did want to go on, or that there is a disagreement between us about what is best for the patient. The only disagreement there is [is] that I do not know and perhaps the other would think he knew. But I do no wrong to this dying man in discontinuing this treatment; and, given that, I do it because I do not want to go on giving him this or any other life-prolonging treatment.'

The idea that a doctor *must*, even here, in such a case, conceive himself as doing what is best for the patient proves harmful and dangerous. He won't be able to help thinking of his discontinuation as (a) doing what is best and (b) killing.

In general it is false moral philosophy to say that one must always do what it is best to do. Or that if there is something better to do than one is doing, and one knows this, one is acting wrongly. Again, a false ethic: 'Wisdom is justified in all her children'.

Good and bad are not equal and opposite characteristics. A thing is good, and so is an action, if and only if there is *nothing* bad about it, as that kind of thing, or as a human action. It is bad if there is *something* wrong with it.

Moral goodness or badness is not some new, higher order ingredient which gets injected into a fully human action from what is called the agent's *Gesinnung*. If you take *that* view, you will call fully human, fully intentional particular actions not yet as such 'morally' good or bad. If such action is, for example, one of robbing a poor man or killing a child, you will say that the characterisation so far only mentions 'pre-moral evil', the 'pre-moral' evil that the man has not the means he had of buying food, and the child loses its life.

This is awful nonsense. Of course we consider the kind of thing that is done, or omitted, the circumstances and the consequences, in many, many cases of deciding what to do or whether we were to blame. So I did in discussing the famous story of Alfred and the cakes. But that does not mean that there are not certain descriptions of actions such that *if* an action, fully human, satisfies one of these descriptions, that is enough to characterise it as a wicked act.

'Good' is not in the same position as 'bad'. For calling an action specifically good, the act of a virtue, we do indeed need to know, not merely that it was not a wicked kind of act, and not merely that it was for a good or innocent end, but also the spirit (*Gesinnung*) which inspired it. A good spirit, however, cannot inspire an action of a wicked kind: that is, an action which satisfies one of those descriptions which provide us with a cut-off point. Every action has many descriptions: e.g. 'depositing ink on paper with a pen', 'signing a document', 'subscribing a false statement', 'warranting the truth of a false statement incriminating someone in a capital charge'. The last but one is perhaps already at a cut-off point, but we might need to know more about the case: was it a joke, for example? With the last, we have reached a decisive cut-off point. If that was what it was, it was a wicked act, a great violation of justice.

17

Must One Obey One's Conscience?

If you do what you are convinced is wrong, though it is in truth *not* wrong, are you doing wrong? Or if you decide *not* to do something which you believe is no obligation for you to do — though in fact it *is* what you ought to do — are you acting wrongly?

Perhaps it is clearer to ask: is your *will* wrong in these cases?

Aristotle reports someone as saying that bad principles plus weakness of will in acting according to them would mean your actions were all right. But he clearly doesn't believe this and it may have been a joke. At any rate he certainly thought that wrongness about principles was a cause of wickedness, if it was easy to be right.

Let's say that in the cases imagined, what you have is a false conscience. We can then ask our question in the form: is a false conscience *binding*?

'I know *what* he did was wrong, but since he thought it was right to do that sort of thing, *he* wasn't doing wrong — at least subjectively he wasn't doing wrong.' Someone might say: Isn't subjectivity the important thing here? If it is correct to say that, then that would give an answer to the question as we first raised it, which was: you do what you are convinced is wrong, though it isn't. Well then, subjectively you are doing wrong in that case.

---

* Text of an unpublished and undated manuscript of notes for a lecture; description of the examples to be referred to in the lecture was left unscripted.

The question whether a false conscience is *binding* arises only where it says — falsely — that you *must*, or again must *not*, do something. A conscience that says you *may* do something or not do it, you have a right to do it but you need not do it, obviously would not *bind* you to do or not do the thing, whatever it was. That is the case — the sort of case — considered in the argument 'What he did was wrong *but* he thought it was right, i.e. all right, so *he* wasn't doing wrong subjectively speaking'. However, there is something the argument is being *used* for and that is to *excuse*. So there are two different questions: 'Does a false conscience *bind*?' — where it falsely commands or forbids; and: 'Does a false conscience *excuse*?' — when it *lets* you do something wrong. We can of course ask whether it excuses *also* in the cases where it commands or forbids wrongly. Here it might be said to *excuse* wrong action because the man with the false conscience obeys it *believing* that that action is obligatory; and to excuse wrong *failure* to do something where the man with the false conscience consults it and believes that the thing he does not do would be wrong to do though there's nothing wrong with it. (Gambling, betting)

However in connexion with *excusing* there is also false conscience believing that something is permissible which is in fact not permissible. This makes an extra possibility about false conscience *excusing*, which doesn't apply to the question whether a false conscience *binds*.

'Does a false conscience *bind* one?' is equivalent to the question: 'Suppose a will that *does not conform* to a *false* conscience forbidding what is in fact obligatory or commanding what is in fact *im*permissible — is that a bad will?'

And 'Does a false conscience *excuse*?' is equivalent to the question 'Suppose a will that *conforms* to a false conscience wrongly forbidding or commanding or *allowing* something — is that a good will?'

What I mean by a will conforming to a conscience is the voluntary action or voluntary omission being according to what the conscience says. Conscience is judgment about what is all right, or wrong, or obligatory to do, so when I speak of conscience commanding something I mean its judging that that thing is obligatory, that one *must* do it on pain of doing wrong if one doesn't. Similarly when I speak of conscience forbidding something, I mean its judging that one *must not* do that thing on pain of doing wrong if one does it. And when I speak of conscience allowing something I mean its judging that one may do it, but need not; one won't be doing wrong if one does it, nor yet if one doesn't.

So I hope it is clear what the question 'Is a will conforming to a false conscience which wrongly forbids or commands or allows something a good will?' means. Similarly for the question about a will *not* conforming to a conscience.

Some people might object that a will is only a *good* will if it means the will in a voluntary action which is a good action, and that it isn't a good will if one merely does what one may do but need not. Or that it has got to be an action with a specially good purpose. So writing a story to earn some money which one does not seriously need would not be either a good or a bad action as far as my description goes, and so the will in it would not be a *good* will though perhaps not a bad one either. Well, here and now I will only say I don't agree, but I won't go into the matter which is quite complicated.

Now reverting to the questions about false conscience binding or excusing a will that conforms to it, I will remind you that some people will say: There's no such thing as false conscience. Conscience is conscience and infallibly tells you what is right and what is wrong. So conscience *always* binds, or else legitimately leaves you morally free to do or not do, and the answer to the question of my title 'Must one obey one's conscience?' is simply 'Of course one must'.

Well, in comment on that, consider Huckleberry Finn.

Or as Mark Twain is really being highly satirical in all that bit of the story, consider the German politician and member of Hitler's government, Himmler.

In face of these examples, particularly the second, one might say: Clearly a false conscience does not bind, nor does it excuse. And so one might want to say: the will that is *in conformity with* a false conscience is *simply* bad and can't be good.

This is, however, a very severe sort of case to consider — I consider it only to upset the suggestion that conscience is infallible. But this observation does carry in it the suggestion that a will *in conformity* with a false conscience is good just because it is in conformity with a conscience, *if* the error in the conscience is not a very serious error leading to what are *obviously* enormously wicked actions. Apart from such frightfulness in what one thinks one ought to do, it is always bad to go against one's conscience. And that would carry with it the suggestion that apart from frightful cases, conscience, even if it is in error, does excuse and the will that conforms to it is a good will. For, given not too unreasonable mistakes making one's conscience a 'false' conscience, conscience simply does bind and one must be doing wrong in going against it even if it consists of mistaken judgment about what things are right and wrong in the situation one is in.

As the frightful cases have to be treated as *exceptional* for what one thinks along these lines, it is perhaps clearest to stick to the question 'Is a will that does *not* conform to a false judgment, a false conscience, a bad will?' — and to amplify this by saying 'Is it always a bad will?' For *that* was the equivalent of the question whether a false conscience *binds*.

The question whether it is — at least sometimes — a *good* will is then firmly fixed as equivalent to whether a false conscience *excuses*.

Here I will point to the opinion, clearly maintained by some, that a false conscience always *binds*. That is, that the will in someone *not* conforming to a *false* conscience, at least in doing what in fact he ought not, or failing to do what he ought, is always a *bad* will. But also that it does not excuse — i.e. that *conforming* to a false conscience is not something containing goodness of will.

In short, it is wrong to act contrary to your false conscience but not right to act according to it.

I think we might modify this by saying that if your false judgment about what you ought to do is based on a *blameless* mistake about the particular facts of the case, then your false judgment about what you ought to do *is* itself blameless and your action in conformity with it *is* excused by the fact that you *are* acting in conformity with a conscience which is mistaken.

But otherwise, there seems to be no way out, no way of acting rightly. If you act *against* your conscience you are doing wrong because you are doing what you *think* wrong, i.e. you are willing to do wrong. And if you act in accordance with your conscience you are doing whatever *is* the wrong that your conscience allows, or failing to carry out the obligation that your conscience says is none.

There is a way out, but you have to know that you need one and it may well take time. The way out is to *find out* that your conscience is a wrong one.

18

Glanville Williams' The Sanctity of Life and the Criminal Law: A Review

This is not a work of academic interest: indeed it is mysterious how an academic lawyer came to write it. A woman beat her two year old child to death: 'her husband, who had presented the overburdened woman with six children, was exonerated from complicity!' (40) Inmates of mental institutions who are allowed parole on condition of sterilisation are sterilised 'voluntarily', since in any other sense of the word 'few if any choices in life are voluntary, for every choice involves the acceptance of a course that is more preferred in place of one that is less preferred'. (88) The Biblical commandment against adultery is void of content because it 'leaves numberless problems unresolved'. (127) The author is not, however, ignorant — as one might infer — that that commandment is part of a code of law; the explanation lies elsewhere. He has written a book of polemical propaganda, aimed at persuading what may be called people of roughly *New Statesman* mentality. By this is meant both a certain set of opinions and a

---

* This review was commissioned at the time of the publication of Williams' book but the law journal which commissioned it then declined to publish it. Numbers in brackets in the text are page references to the English edition of *The Sanctity of Life and the Criminal Law* (London: Faber & Faber, 1958).

frame of mind inhibiting the critical faculty in face of arguments in favour of what one approves or against what one disapproves. This frame of mind is found among people of many opinions; it is the belief of your reviewer that this particular set of opinions cannot exist apart from it.

Dr Williams' propaganda is for the following views and proposals:

(1) 'Liberty should prevail' for the 'eugenic killing' of physically and mentally defective babies by their mothers; his practical legal proposal — devised in a search for something 'acceptable' — is that courts should discharge without punishment when this has been done. (31)

(2) It is crazy to introduce modern medicine and sanitation to the backward populations of poor and densely peopled places without seeing to it that the birth rate is kept down in these places, while in this country it is irrational policy to operate 'a family allowance scheme which gives an incentive to produce children only to the poorest orders of society'. People should be given an incentive to be parents 'commensurate with their social status'; but there are no definite proposals made here, and there would surely be grave difficulties: it is not mere democratic prejudice, as is suggested in this passage, that would make a legislator shrink from the task of socially grading, say, such men as Dr Williams, with a view to determining whether to make it worth their while to beget children. (68–9, 71)

(3) Defectives and people believed likely to transmit defect should be sterilised; with the aid of intensive labour on the part of social workers this need not be compulsory; sterilisation should also be widely adopted as a contraceptive measure. (Chapter 3)

(4) A statute should be passed declaring that AID babies are 'deemed to be the natural children of the husband and wife'. (137)

(5)   Abortion cannot morally be considered murder at all, at
      any time in the life of the unborn child (unless, possibly, he
      would give that name to destruction after viability for any
      other reason than the life or health of the mother); it should
      be within the discretion of doctors to perform abortion for
      any reason they think fit up to the time of viability.

(6)   Suicide is not wrong: it should be provided by law that it
      shall be no offence for a doctor to kill his patient on pur-
      pose, so long as it is done in good faith with the consent of
      the patient to save him from severe pain in an illness
      believed to be of an incurable and fatal character. (305) (By
      this measure, it would clearly be in order for a doctor to
      persuade the patient, so long as he did it out of conviction
      that the patient ought to cease to endure pain.) Capital
      punishment is not one of the topics of the book, nor is the
      author's moral and political thought described sufficiently
      for us to guess what he would think about this.

A familiar course of argument is very prominent: certain
things may be done, first, to save life; then, to save health; then, to
save mental health; this is widely interpreted to cover strain or
inconvenience. (See 222–3)

A great deal of the book is devoted to argument concerning the
morality of infanticide, contraception, abortion, sterilisation,
artificial insemination and suicide; Dr Glanville Williams' arguments will hardly impress those who object to these things, and
ought not to impress those who do not, since the treatment is
superficial. An extraordinary amount of space is given up to
attacks on the Catholic Church; this is not well done and would
have been better omitted, and the space used for more solid discussion of the author's moral position (which is vaguely
explained as 'utilitarian') or more explanation of the consequences of his proposals.

Dr Glanville Williams has two systematic errors concerning
the Catholic Church: he thinks that its doctrines have to be justi-

fied by strict derivation from Biblical proof texts, and hence does a great deal of queer Bible-punching; and he thinks that what any Catholic moral theologian writes can safely be taken as Catholic teaching if it has not been explicitly condemned. His level of acquaintance with Catholicism is indicated by the fact that he thinks that the Immaculate Conception means a conception without copulation (132); his level of scholarship, by the fact that he supposes 'animus' to be the scholastic Latin for 'soul' (143). Other errors are: that insistence on baptising infants before death is a concession to uneducated Catholic opinion (180); that there is nothing against castration in the Old Testament (cf. *Deuteronomy* 23: 1; in this context, he remarks that the Bible 'often mentions eunuchs', which he supposes would embarrass 'fundamentalists': 100); that there is nothing 'to justify worldly punishment for any sin whatever' in the New Testament (232; cf. *Romans* 13: 1–7); that St. Augustine taught that Adam's sin was sexual lust (179; cf. *Retractations* Bk.I, c.15); that St. Augustine objected to any use of the safe period (whereas in fact the Augustine text he cites, *De Moribus Manichaeorum* c.65, is directed against the Manichean teaching that allowed second grade Manichees to 'marry' so long as they aimed at avoiding procreation *altogether* by this method); that St. Thomas Aquinas never discussed whether celibacy was a sin (cf. *Summa theologiae* IIa IIae, q.152, art.2); that the objection of the Catholic Church to artificial insemination confounds it with adultery; that the Church has no account of theft but what coincides with the state's law; that the practice of *coitus reservatus* is permissible. Not to extend the list of detailed errors to the point of tedium, we may note his general sniping: there are frequent references to 'true Christianity', 'the simple philosophy of the Gospels', to Christianity as the religion of love, which is identified as nothing but sparing people pain or hardship; this is no doubt *ad captandum*. He designates the Mosaic Code as barbaric; here he makes much play with 'Thou shalt not suffer a witch to live', since like Lecky he seems to think it an old wives' tale that witchcraft was ever practised. We should remember that colonial administrators still need to restrain the activities of witch doctors. The Christian concern for chastity he regards as morbid; one would suppose from his remarks that the detail into which a theologian enters when he thinks out his subject was confined to sexual matters and occasioned by neurosis.

There is one matter of substance here: Dr Glanville Williams attacks the doctrine of 'double effect'. Now, to make an epigram, the corruption of non-Catholic moral thought has consisted in the denial of this doctrine, and the corruption of Catholic thought in the abuse of it. The doctrine states that in considering an intentional action we must distinguish between what is intended and what can be foreseen but is not intended. What is intentional will be the end (supposing it to be achieved) and the means chosen for it; and in order for an action to be sound, both end and chosen means must be legitimate. Things which can be foreseen as side effects of what is done, which would not themselves be permissible either as ends or as means, will not vitiate the action if it is itself necessary; and may not vitiate it if it is good and the side effects not disproportionately evil; a standard illustration would be that a woman could take quinine (if it were the only remedy) to cure malaria, though it might also cause abortion, but could not take a remedy with that sort of effect to relieve a headache. Now only if we make this distinction between the intentional and the foreseen is it possible to avoid a course of reasoning which will justify anything at all, however atrocious. And we all do make such a distinction: for example, a man who goes to prison rather than do something disgraceful may thereby knowingly deprive his family of support, but is not held to be therefore guilty of this as if he had aimed at it or chosen it as a means to some end of his. But ever since the seventeenth century a false and absurd conception of intention has prevailed, which derives from Cartesian psychology; according to this conception an intention is a secret mental act which is producible at will. In the event, theologians often treated the 'direction of intention' as something that could be accomplished by telling oneself at the time of action 'What I really mean to be doing is …'. This tendency of thought has led to repeated condemnations by the Holy See from the seventeenth century to the present day: then, a typical suggestion was that a servant could go and hold the ladder for a burglarious master, so long as he 'directed his intention' purely to the earning of his pay; and at the present day the conception produced the doctrine of *coitus reservatus*, which is equivalent to the practice of withdrawal accompanied by an 'intention' not to ejaculate; the ejaculation that then took place would be 'accidental' and *praeter intentionem*. Such doctrines have had to be condemned as they came up. Dr Williams thus has some justification in speaking of a subtle and sophistical doctrine; as he says, if you justify the destruction of an ectopic fetus in that way, you can equally use it to justify the killing of the child in the womb. But this accidental perversion of the doctrine of double effect is nothing against its essential soundness. He himself knows very well that it is one thing to give a man drugs to ease his pain, knowing that their cumulative effect may kill him before the disease does, and another to poison him intentionally; he denies the moral importance of the distinction in order to push people over from accepting the one into accepting the other (288) but his knowledge that there is a distinction comes out in his quite correct use of the word 'intention(al)' when he speaks of what he wants (e.g. 283). He knows the difference between the lack of obligation (recently declared by the Pope) to prolong life by such extraordinary measures as were hideously employed upon Dylan Thomas, and the 'involuntary euthanasia' of the senile to which he looks forward (with bated breath) on page 310; but if challenged he professes to have meant no more than the first, which certainly involves no 'traumatic' change in our conception of the sanctity of life.

Dr Williams says (165n) that there is no such thing as dishonest belief.

19

Who is Wronged? Philippa Foot on Double Effect: One Point

She says:

> We are about to give to a patient who needs it to save his life, a massive dose of a certain drug in short supply. There arrive, however, five other patients each of whom could be saved by one fifth of that dose. We say with regret that we cannot spare our whole supply of the drug for a single patient, just as we should say that we could not spare the whole resources of a ward for one dangerously ill individual when ambulances arrive bringing in the victims of a multiple crash. We feel bound to let one man die rather than many if that is our only choice.

I feel a curious disagreement about this. There seems to me nothing wrong with giving the single patient the massive dose and letting the others die, or with refusing to deprive the single patient of care necessary to keep him alive because the hands needed for that care could help in saving the many victims of an accident. The latter case is vaguely sketched, and one pictures resources being lavishly used beyond necessity on one. But let it

* First published in *The Oxford Review* 5 (1967): 16–17, in response to Philippa Foot's paper 'The Problem of Abortion and the Doctrine of Double Effect', which appeared in the same number, pp. 5–15.

be made exact; let there be a machine which it takes three people to operate — it just will not work unless there are three on the job; and these three could be summoned away to help more than one person. It seems to me justifiable to say one can't spare those three people because of the job they are doing, if their work seems roughly as likely to save that one person as to save several to whose aid they could be called. Not that it seems (absolutely) *necessary* to keep them on the job they are doing; but either course, to leave the one to die or to keep them working his machine, seems OK. Yet Mrs Foot regards it as obvious that one must save the greater number.

Why is this, and how could the disagreement be resolved? Suppose I am the doctor, and I don't use the drug at all. Whom do I wrong? None of them can say: 'you owed it to *me*'. For there might be nine, and if *one* can say that, all can; but if I used it, I let one at least go without and he can't say I owed it to *him*. Yet all can reproach me if I gave it to none. It was there, ready to supply human need, and human need was not supplied. So any one of them can say: you ought to have used it to help us who needed it; and so all are wronged. But if it was used for someone, as much as he needed it to keep him alive, no one has any ground for accusing me of having wronged *himself*. Why, just because he was one of the five who could have been saved, is he wronged in not being saved, if someone is supplied with it who needed it? What is *his* claim, except the claim that what was needed go to him rather than be wasted? But it was not wasted. So he was not wronged. So who was wronged? And if no one was wronged, what injury did I do?

Similarly if there are a lot of people stranded on a rock, and one person on another, and someone goes with a boat to rescue the single one, what cause, so far, have any of the others for complaint? They are not injured unless help that was owing to them was withheld. There was the boat that could have helped them; but it was not left idle; no, it went to save that other one. What is the accusation that each of them can make? What wrong can he claim has been done him? None whatever: unless the preference signalizes some ignoble contempt.

I do not mean that 'because they are more' isn't a good reason for helping these and not that one, or these rather than those. It is a perfectly intelligible reason. But it doesn't follow from that that a man acts badly if he doesn't make it his reason. He acts badly if human need for what is in his power to give doesn't work in him as a reason. He acts badly if he chooses to rescue rich people rather than poor ones, having ill regard for the poor ones because they are poor. But he doesn't act badly if he uses his resources to save X, or X, Y and Z, *for no bad reason*, and is not affected by the consideration that he could save a larger number of people. For, once more: who can say he is wronged? And if no one is wronged, how does the rescuer commit any wrong?

In this connexion, the following observation is of some importance, as the contrary may be taken for granted by some: when I do action A for reasons R, it is not necessary or even usual for me to have any special reason for doing-action-A-rather-than-action-B, which may also be possible.

20

Prolegomenon to a Pursuit of the Definition of Murder

The Illegal and the Unlawful

Preamble on equality

Remember the bed of Procrustes. Strangers were made equal to it. Some were extended, others lopped. Did they receive equal treatment? Well, they were equally treated inasmuch as they all were equalised with the bed, unequally in that different procedures were adopted.

It means nothing to speak of equality unless you know the respect in which things are said to be unequal, or in which we may seek to make people equal. Nor should we regard with anything but contempt the dodge of saying 'That's not an inequality, it's rather a difference' about an inequality which we regard as not mattering. Whenever qualities admit of more or less, or there is occasion to have more or fewer of anything, then there is a clear sense for inequality.

As I have maintained during this conference, inequality in respect of possessions or social status or prestige is not of itself something that needs justification. The idea of generally justifying it on grounds of merit is merely laughable. It is a matter of

* First published in *Dialectics and Humanism* 4 (1979): 73–7.

luck. Its existence neither has nor stands in need of justification, either in itself or *prima facie*. Thus where there is an objection to an inequality of advantage of some kind, we want to know what the objection is — it has not been given already in calling the inequality inequality.

I reject the suggestion that retributive justice is any sub-species of distributive justice. Where there is something to be newly divided among people, some principle of equal division — no doubt to be differently formulated in different cases — seems fair and reasonable; and this is distributive justice. So here justice has to do with equal shares of some goods. But the justice of the criminal law in dealing with offences is not a justice that has to do with fair shares of anything. Here we are dealing with a far more important sense of 'justice'. And equality does come into it. I may say: everybody has or ought to have a right not to be murdered. In a just system of law, there will not be some class of people, identified by their origins or social status, who can murder or be murdered with impunity.

Murder is therefore a topic which has to do with equality in a deeper way than any equality of shares in material advantages. And that is why it is my topic in a conference on justice and equality.

Two errors in defining 'murder'

Some recent German visitors to New Zealand were discussing human rights. The right to life was mentioned. An old Maori professor in the university suddenly spoke: 'What nonsense! It is a man's business to kill'. His meaning was: 'It is part of the business of being a man to do some killing'. They were horrified, but did not know what to say to him. They had in their cultural inheritance, as he had not, the commandment 'Thou shalt do no murder'. What the restrictions on killing in his ethic were, I do not know; naturally there will have been such. But against the background of this story that commandment is seen as rebuking an intelligible ideal of manliness. It would be a kind of conversion seriously to give it up.

The *concept* of murder could be explained to such a man; the prohibition of the *thing* was not part of his ethic. Thus it is possible to grasp the concept without accepting the prohibition. This shows that it is wrong to define murder as 'wrong killing' ('killing that is wrong') as people sometimes do; or as 'wrong deliberate killing'. There are several reasons for making the mistake. The most significant of them is that a decision that some *kind* of killing is wrong (capital punishment or warfare or 'mercy-killing') equates or assimilates it to murder; or even straightway counts it as such. And justifying a kind of killing removes it from that heading.

Another error is to think that murder is a purely juridical notion. (As it is when one says, 'In England, it is no longer murder for a mother to kill her young baby'). The most serious consideration which may lead to this opinion is the following: killings which are done with the authority of the state are not generally reckoned to be murder. Now this, if correct, means that there is such a thing as killing that is an exercise of legitimate authority. The right conclusion to draw would be that we cannot define murder quite without reference to the state, to government and laws, where these exist. And this does not prove that murder is only or even essentially a juridical notion.

But that consideration might make someone think that murder could be only what the state disallows in the way of deliberate killing, while it itself can have its licensees do whatever it pleases. We might justly object to this with St. Augustine's 'Remota justitia, quid sunt regna nisi magna latrocinia'? ('Take away justice, and what are States but big Mafias'?) But the dictum is less simple to apply than may appear. For the justice of what is done cannot always be determined independently of whether it is done by authority. Tolstoy and Camus indeed write as if this were not so, calling capital punishment just the same as murder, or worse for its pretensions. Camus is abusive about the mere suggestion of any reason to the contrary. But the reason they offer is the absurdity of doing to a man by way of punishment what *he* should not have done to another. Equally, then, it would be wicked and absurd for a court to lock him up for unlawful imprisonment of someone else, or to fine him for extorting money. Someone who argues like this is either confused or does not really believe in civil authority at all.

The opinion that *murder* is a purely juridical notion is wrong, because it is clear that there is a moral notion of murder. The idea of citing murder as typical of what a wicked man is ready to do does not depend on the existence of a legal system providing for the punishment of murders. The Anglo-Saxons, for example, might well have spoken so; but we are told that they did not have a legal system of that kind. Again, people sometimes speak of 'legalised murder'. 'You killed him quite legally, but it was murder just the same' someone might say; nor need he be objecting to the law under which the other sheltered to exercise a liberty of killing. It might be said, for example, to an armed policeman who had killed some private enemy, having got him into a situation in which the police of that country are allowed to shoot to kill. The one who makes the comment need not be objecting to that code of practice. He is referring to something in the heart. The wicked heart has seen the opportunity of a legal disguise of an action.

The definition of murder as 'unlawful killing'

Just as some people explain 'murder' as 'killing that is wrong', so others explain it as 'unlawful killing'. This *may* express the opinion we are combating. If so, the question arises how the difference between being lawful and unlawful, legal and illegal, could possibly confer such a character on an act as is indicated by calling it 'murder'. Contrast the lawful and unlawful sale of some commodity, say salt. A special term for the unlawful sale of salt could not *eo ipso* be invested with any awfulness. Nor is it just that death and killing are in any case awful. A peculiar gravity atta-ches to the idea 'murder', as opposed to that of causing a purely accidental death. It is not to be accounted for by the existence of a law against killing.

The explanation 'unlawful killing', however, may not express that opinion. It may be connected with a notion of natural law, or the moral law, of what is conceived as a law which is prior to the setting up of positive human law. For those who do not wish to speak of a *law* here, the equivalent would be to say that there is a moral notion of murder which positive law attempts to capture.

So understood, the suggestions of the phrase 'unlawful killing' are not quite the same as of 'killing that is wrong'. If murder is *defined* as wrong, the question whether it might be right to com-mit a murder cannot arise. The judgment that it would be wrong has gone into the decision to *call* it murder. Whereas the question 'Would it be right here, or ever, to commit an act answering to the moral concept "murder"?' is plainly a real question. And so may be 'Would it be right here, or ever, to violate the moral law'? The suggestion of the definition 'wrong killing' is that moral intuition judges the situation, determining the application of the terms 'right' and 'wrong' to the proposed act, without the aid of an intervening term like 'murder'. The suggestion of 'unlawful' is that of *objectivity*, i.e. of a standard, not modifiable by the one who is seeking an answer, by which the act has the character of being murder. (Or, as we shall have to add, manslaughter; 'unlawful' by itself is not discriminating enough.)

It may seem, then, that the terms 'lawful' and 'unlawful' are ambiguous. In one sense, they are synonymous with 'legal' and 'illegal'; to ascertain whether these apply, you only have to look it up, in the statute book perhaps. The other sense is more obscure; but it makes some reference to morality.

I mean to argue that this second sense of 'lawful' and 'unlaw-ful' is not one in which it has no close relation to actual law and administration of justice. It would indeed be strange if the explanation 'unlawful killing' were altogether wrong; strange if 'unlawfulness' here were quite divorced from any connexion with human law; but strange again if just any — no matter what — killing that was *legal* in any society were thereby straightway determined not to be murder. We hear of a legal doctrine in England, for example, that 'the King can do no wrong'. This will hardly prevent the term 'murderer' from coming into the discussion, when it is debated whether a king of England privily did away with some of his relations.

The thing is, that the concept of the 'unlawful' to which we are pointing actually often figures in actual laws. If a law refers to an 'unlawful' act, that does not necessarily mean that we can find out what is intended by looking up a statute or the earlier practice of the courts. It *would* mean that, if the act in question were the sale of salt or the possession of a still. It does not have to, if what is in question is acts which are wrongs or wrong doings independently of any legal system.

Not wishing to be entangled in the historical facts concerning particular practice in legislation and law courts, I will invent a suppositious case. Though suppositious, it is perfectly possible, and it illustrates the fact about the idea of the *lawful* and *unlawful* which I have just spoken of.

Let a criminal charge have the form 'that — did wilfully and unlawfully —'. And now let us suppose that a new statute prescribes penalties for 'unlawful detention'. *Must* there be prior statute or regulation prohibiting certain forms of detention of one person by another, or allowing it *only* under certain conditions? We are not obliged to suppose so. We need not even suppose that there is a body of non-statute law (which could be set forth in law-books) derivable from the practice of the courts, it being a known possible complaint there that one had been locked up without sufficient excuse, whether by officials or private persons.

The statute that I am imagining — it would belong to a rather earlier state of society than ours — would thus create a *new* possibility of complaint. Part of this possibility would be, to complain of being locked up without there being law or license for it; and the consequent practice of the courts would help to detemine what *counted* as law or license for locking someone up. But that would not be the whole story. The Courts will indeed (we may suppose) treat as unlawful any detention in which officials have engaged, relying on insufficient legal title. But there will be a further area to be developed, that of lack of legitimate excuse. For example, if the person detained counted as a child and was in some way subject to the authority of the detainer. But also there may be excuses which are reckoned as exculpating by the court's estimate of the situation. Such estimates will no doubt soon acquire constraints by various principles which get crystallised in rules of law. But at bottom there will (we may suppose) be estimates governed by a conception of what a reasonable man would consider reasonable.

None of this supposition I have made is over-fanciful. And now let us ask: 'What does "unlawful" mean here?' If, when the practice of the courts is highly developed, I say 'Surely this is unlawful detention', that means 'It's a wrong of a kind the law is prepared to punish'. But the word was used, as I imagined it, in a statute *before* the courts' practice was developed. *Then*, and in the early stages of that development, what does the plaintiff's complaint of 'unlawful detention' mean? The answer is clear. It means: 'I am wronged by having been locked up, and it is for you to punish the one who wronged me'.

I supposed a statute creating an offence that the law had not dealt with as such before. I did so to make the point that such a statute could intelligibly contain the word 'unlawful' without reference to prior law forbidding certain acts. (And in this I was not being inventive). But, statute or no statute, it is the acceptance by the courts of the task of convicting that provides the extra beyond something's being *a wrong*, when it is called 'unlawful'. My suppositious statute therefore *looks forward* to the practice of the courts. It itself provides implicitly both that some detentions will need justification by legal entitlement, *and* that other detentions which are wrongs against the detained will now become possible matter for complaint; and it also implicitly invites the courts to develop what will count as incurring the penalty, by their practice.

This fiction brings out how 'unlawful' can be an adjective attaching to wrongs which are wrongs independently of the law, and how it then has a moral and normative ring to it and does not sound equivalent to 'illegal'. Nevertheless, in this use, it still has a connexion with actual human law.

If all this is right, then we shall not want to stop with a definition of murder as 'unlawful killing' or 'deliberate unlawful killing' even though we do not positively object to it. We shall want to find that objective concept, i.e. that standard not modifiable by those seeking an answer, by which an act has the character of being a murder. That it is a standard which has partly been formulated precisely by attempts to capture it in laws will not surprise us either.

'Murder' is a complex and high-level action description. A sufficient consideration of it would comprehend 'the whole man': the agency peculiar to man, his social being and possession of laws, his moral subjectivity and mystical value.

21

Murder and the Morality of Euthanasia

Murder is a complex of disparate elements, not merely the killing of one human being by another. There is also the mental element of intent. Yet 'murder' cannot be explained just as intentional killing: for civil authority introduces the possibility that there may be killing which is legitimate even though intentional — in struggle with violent law-breakers or, it may be, in capital punishment. The right account is one whereby murder is killing which involves a special degree and kind of responsibility for death, a responsibility which is guilt.

Responsibility has three levels. (1) The primary level is that at which a mere cause (for example, a stroke of lightning) or contributory condition (such as the temperature of the atmosphere)

* Between 1978 and 1981 Professor Anscombe was a member of a multi-disciplinary working party convened by the Linacre Centre for Healthcare Ethics to consider trends towards euthanasia in contemporary healthcare practice. The Centre published the working party's Report in 1982, *Euthanasia and Clinical Practice: Trends, Principles and Alternatives* (since reprinted in Luke Gormally [ed] *Euthanasia, Clinical Practice and the Law*. London: The Linacre Centre, 1994; pp. 1–107). Professor Anscombe was the principal author of Chapter 3 of the Report, 'Murder and the Morality of Euthanasia: Some Philosophical Considerations'. But she did not write all parts of that chapter, as has sometimes been assumed. The present text reproduces the final draft of the paper that she contributed to the composition of that chapter.

is said to be responsible for something happening. (2) At a higher level, where a rational agent is involved, responsibility also includes callability to account. Someone responsible in this sense may have to answer the question of guilt. (3) The third level is that of guilt itself.

When hi-jackers say that 'they will not be responsible' for deaths if they blow up a plane because their demands are not met, they mean that they will not be guilty; they are not denying level (2) responsibility, but claiming to have an exonerating answer. One who is callable to account may not be guilty, even though he did cause death, because there is an exonerating answer. The range of such answers is very wide: 'He was sleep-walking'; 'He stumbled'; 'He did not know he was administering poison'; 'He did not intend death but something else which was quite legitimate'; 'He was acting with legitimate authority'; 'He had no duty to act to prevent death'. In default of an exonerating answer, the gravest sort of responsibility for a death entails that one has committed murder. It is determined by the knowledge and will with which one acts.

It should be noticed that advantage to be got by deliberately killing someone is not counted as exonerating. If someone maintains that it can justify, then what is thereby justified will be murder itself.

Unsurprisingly, then, we cannot offer a sharp and simple definition of murder. But there is a central part of its extension which can be reasonably well-defined, namely *the intentional killing of the innocent*. Whenever this is done by rulers, soldiers, terrorists or other violent men, reference is made, in reporting it, to the murder of innocent victims. This gives us one of our paradigms of the murderer, and constitutes the hard core of the concept of murder. We shall see it is surrounded by a relatively fuzzy penumbra.

There are, however, other intentional killings which are murder, though not all philosophers agree that this is so in 'the state of nature', i.e. where there is no government. These are: vengeful killing where the victim has wronged the killer, and planned killing by a private person in self-defence.

But murder is not done only where the killing is quite intentional. The victim may be attacked in order to hurt him badly, or to expose him to serious danger. Or the target may have been someone else. Or the killer may not be focusing on any victim — for example, he blows up a plane or burns down a house to get insurance money, not caring whether or even that there are people inside. Such killing may be more callous and heinous than some that is intentional.

English lawyers have often used an artificial sense of 'intention' in these contexts, together with technical senses of 'malice' to help it out. For in these contexts no weight is given to the distinction between intending death and foreseeing that there is a serious risk of death as a result of one's act. Yet this distinction is well understood and treated as significant when doctors give pain-killing drugs or surgeons do dangerous operations. Thus the idea that foresight entails intention is applied only in connexion with serious wrongdoing of the sort that used to be called felony. It may have arisen from the obvious murderousness of such killers as our arsonist. Guilt requires in law guilty intent, and this was perhaps assumed to be the intent of committing the very crime charged. On this assumption, the intention to kill the victim would have to be somehow attributable; this in turn made it necessary to think foresight sufficient for the requisite intention, and so 'intention' acquired a special sense in writings of jurisprudents.

In addition there used to be the assumption that the accused understood what any rational agent in his situation would understand. This would give the rationale of counting it murder when someone dies of being savagely beaten up. But since the enactment of the Criminal Justice Act 1967, #5.8, foreseeability by a reasonable person is not to be taken as legal proof of either foresight or intention. And after 1967 the law fell into confusion: the abolition of 'felony murder' ('constructive malice') in 1957 and the enactment of 1967 together left a gap: it seemed that the equation of intention and actual foresight had to provide for the whole doctrine of murder where the killing is not intended (in the ordinary sense), and it became a moot point whether, and how, to justify a verdict of murder where death results from serious bodily harm.

What we ought to say is (1) that intention and foresight are distinct and (2) the intention (i.e. the purpose) of harm or danger to the victim is not a necessary part of the mental element in murder. Even without such intent unlawful acts can be murderous. 'Unlawful' is closer in sense to 'wrongful' than to 'illegal', and the unlawfulness of an act may reside in its endangering someone's life without excuse. (We will not go into the distinction between murder and manslaughter here: it will be drawn according to the malice involved.)

So long as the equation of intention and foresight is made only in connexion with gravely unlawful acts, it may seem harmless. But so to restrict it is highly illogical. Of course this equation is never actually made in such cases as high-risk surgery. But if intention and foresight of the probability of death can be equated at all, it may well be asked why not there. If the equation were made, it would certainly not be inferred that the surgeon is a murderer if his patient dies. But the alternative inference would be that the 'intention' to kill is acceptable for good purposes.

There are two conceptions competing for our acceptance. One, that there is an absolute prohibition on murder: this has up to now (forgetting about abortion, which has never been legally classified with murder) been the stance of English law, as well as being the teaching of the Judaeo-Christian tradition. The other, which appears in the Model Penal Code, and makes progress in many minds, would allow necessity as an exculpating plea in some cases of perfectly intentional killing. 'Necessity' can be understood in a very restricted or a widely extended way according to what we insist on trying to get or avoid.

There is sometimes good excuse for endangering people's lives or for doing what will certainly lead to deaths; e.g. having a system of rail or air transport; or again, opening flood-gates or closing fire-doors in certain emergencies. If there is no significant difference allowed between intending and foreseeing death, it will follow that one may also plan the death of innocent people as means to an end.

Here the Judaeo-Christian teaching enters its interdict, forbidding all killing of the innocent as end or as means. We might rely on religious authority for this; but it has also generally been held that the moral law is accessible to reason.

Some think it would be within the competence of the State to authorise such killing as seems necessary for the common good. But the right of the State to use violence has such a foundation as to put that idea right out of court. For the foundation is the human need of protection against unjust attack. The fact that the attack is unjust secures the justice of supplying the need by the use and threat of violence. The need creates the first task of government, which cannot be supplied in a large society without laws and an administration of justice. Only when we have these have we civil authority. But if the civil authority itself attacks innocent people, it nullifies the basis on which its use of violence is different from that of a gangster band. This remains true even if it pleads the common good as an excuse for exterminating innocent people. Its role in promoting the common good enables it to make pertinent laws for violating which people may be punished. But that does not mean that an attack on people's lives when they are not lawbreakers but just as part of a scheme for future advantage, is within the competence of government. In acting so, the civil authority would be nullifying the basis of its own right to command violence.

Civil authority cannot make it policy to decide on or license the killing of innocent people without losing the character of civil authority. And, whatever the appearances, the decision to take part in such killing is necessarily a private one. People rightly suppose that public authority can be invoked, and that this makes all the difference, if what is in question is e.g. police action against violent law-breakers; but whatever may be enacted by wicked legislation, the case is quite otherwise for killing innocent people and it is merely error and confusion to think the responsibility can be referred to the civil authority.

With this confusion cleared away, we have to consider the essentially private decision: to kill an innocent person because it seems a good idea that he should die. What is the basis of the prohibition?

First, someone who is murdered suffers a great wrong. Utilitarian types of morality are here compelled to talk only of the disturbing effect of murder on the living. But clearly the victim is the primary one to be wronged, and this is enough objection to murder in most cases.

If someone is wronged, he has a right which is violated. But the wrongfulness of murder seems to be the basis of the right, rather than *vice versa*, because (a) there is not a simple right to life, but rather a right not to be murdered, and (b) if there were a certain right to life upon which the wrongfulness of murder is based, it would be difficult to see why it should not be waivable.

The prohibition on murder is indeed a great charter of right to all of us, but it is the prohibition that comes first and not the right.

The prohibition is so basic that it is difficult to answer the question as to why murder is intrinsically wrongful. Some think they can get an answer out of more general principles. Here we shall rather point to the character of rational argument to shew that it is wrong to steal, or commit adultery, or that we ought to keep a rule of the road where there is traffic, or a close season for game or fish where stocks must be replenished. The arguments are of the form 'Obedience to this law is needed for human good'. The unit whose good the argument seeks is the human individual, considered generally. To kill him, then, is to destroy that being which is the point of those considerations.

Why then are there exceptions? Why may some men be made targets in war, fought in civil struggle, killed in putting them down as violent law-breakers, perhaps assassinated if they are tyrants, and executed if found guilty of some crimes? The answer is that where this is so, what they receive is justice, they themselves being unjust assailants. We could not replace 'innocent' by 'healthy' and 'unjust attackers' by 'lepers' in the argument for the State's right to use violence, and come up with a sound argument for exterminating lepers. The harmfulness of lepers not being their own will, they cannot be justly attacked.

The meaningfulness of these considerations brings us face to face with the truth that man is spirit. He moves in the categories of innocence and answerability and desert — one of the many signs of a leap to another kind of existence from the life of the other animals. The very question 'Why may we not kill innocent people?' asks whether it may not be *justified* to do so, and this is itself a manifestation of this different life.

Here some present day philosophers produce arguments based on the concept of a person in support of killing young infants and the senile. They say that mere biologically human life does not constitute 'personhood', and it is only a person who has what we call human dignity and the right not to be killed. A person is defined by certain qualities and capacities. Since these are lacking in the newborn and the senile, they fall outside the ban on murder.

Such thinkers trade on the weight of the word 'person', although they define it wrongly in terms of characteristics which may come and go and which are a matter of degree.

For a person is a substantial individual being with his own identity, which he has as an individual of a particular species. In our case the species is 'human being'. Having named an individual human being we use the name with the same reference so long as it is the *same human being* we are talking about. A human being is a person because the kind to which he belongs is characterised by rational nature. Thus we have the same individual, and hence the same person, when we have the same human being. One is a person just by being of this kind, and that does indeed import a tremendous dignity. It is a mere trick to draw on the weight that this word 'person' has because of this sense — thrashed out long ago — if you then go on to explain the word so that it is rather like the word 'magnet'. A piece of iron gets magnetised and so *becomes* a magnet; later it may get demagnetised and *stops* being a magnet though it is still the same piece of iron. If indeed you explain the word 'person' as meaning someone e.g. who can talk (has self-consciousness) and lead a social life (have inter-personal relations) you may say that someone can be the same human being but no longer a person. It does not come so easy to say 'Since he can no longer do such-and-such, he no longer has rights, and it is in order to kill him'.

You cannot be killing a human being and not be killing a person.

The one kind of killing innocent people which seems to escape the argument that it is unjust, i.e. that someone is wronged, is voluntary euthanasia. So far, most propaganda for euthanasia assumes it should be voluntary. Like the first justifications for induced abortion, this is only a way-station. But it impresses, because it strikes people as not wronging someone to kill him if he wills it. However, it needs pointing out that they would still think it was wronging him, but for the accompanying judgment that his condition is so irremediably wretched that it is fortunate for him 'to die'. This judgment is paramount, and that is why the stress on voluntariness tends to be spurious. Though some people are serious about it, upon the whole it is merely getting the foot in the door. The drive is in the direction of killing people when their lives are judged useless or burdensome to themselves or the world. This judgment is readily made of people whose mental capacity is gone or much diminished.

The drive to get doctors killing people and to have this accepted in medical ethics ought to be regarded as sinister even by those who regard suicide in face of terminal suffering as justified and worthy of a human being. If the ground for this opinion is the dignity of human freedom and self-determination, it is inconsonant with this to ask someone else to do so grave a thing. At this point it is often said that people who would kill themselves if they could are rendered unable to do it by physical incapacity. This is less often true than may be supposed, as it is usually possible to stop eating; though the point is not of interest to Christians, who would not be recommending suicide in any form. But with the plea 'Kill me: I need death but cannot kill myself' it becomes clear that it is not the dignity of human self-determination that is in question. What is demanded is that such suffering people be treated as we treat the other animals. The impulse 'to put an animal out of its misery' is an impulse of sympathy with a creature that resembles us. The attitude is mistakenly called mercy or care: you cannot take care of something by destroying it. But you can judge it not worth preserving, and sympathy makes it feel indecent to put up with its gross suffering, and may even incline one to terminate a reduced and pathetic existence.

But men, being spirit as well as flesh, are not the same as the other animals. Whatever blasphemes the spirit in man is evil, discouraging, at best trivialising, at worst doing dirt on life. Such is the considered recommendation of suicide and killing in face of suffering. We should not confuse this with the personal desperation which may lead to suicide. That may excite our pity; but — propaganda in favour of death as a remedy is different. It is irreligious, in a sense in which the contrasting religious attitude — one of respect before the mystery of human life — is not necessarily connected only with some one particular religious system. Propaganda puts in the mouth of the potential suicide: 'I belong to myself, and I can set conditions on which I will consent to go on living'. Life is regarded as a good or bad hotel, which must not be too bad to be worth staying in.[1] To the man of religious feeling, the claim lacks reverence and insight. A religious attitude may be merely incipient, prompting a certain fear before the idea of ever destroying a human life, and refusing to make a 'quality of life' judgment to terminate a human being. Or it may be more developed, perceiving that men are made by God in God's likeness, to know and love God. The love of God is the direction of the will to its true end. The human heart and will are set on amenity; they may also be set on what is just[2]: that is (when it comes to dying) set in acceptance of life — which is God's gift — and of death, as it comes from him. This goes even for the most incompetently alive in whom the will is manifested mainly in the vital operations. Here there is unlikely to be any possibility of a contrast between the two orientations. But where there is intellectual consciousness there can be contrast: the human being then operates under one or the other of these conceptions of what counts ultimately for him: either amenity only, or acceptance, which is obedience in spirit, which is justice. Acceptance of life and death is what justice is in circumstances of unavoidable dying: it is accord with God's will.

Such perception of what a human being is makes one perceive human death as awesome, human life as always to be treated with a respect which is a sign and acknowledgement of what it is for.

To fight a human being to the death, to try him, condemn him to death and execute him, are grave and tragic actions. But they may be compatible with this awe and respect. To kill him

---

[1]　See Hume's *Dialogues Concerning Natural Religion*, Part XI.

[2]　See St. Anselm, *De Casu Diaboli*, c. 12.

(whether he is oneself or someone else) because one judges his life is wretched or not worth living, is not.

These are the valuations which lie behind justice and the canons of right dealing which preserve us generally where they are observed. Those who do not know how to value human life in this way do badly to fight this valuation. Possibly doctors sometimes kill their patients in what they conceive to be a spirit of mercy. If so, they do better to keep quiet about it than to try to change the hitherto accepted ethic, which is based upon these values. It is not necessary or good, for those who do not have a religious attitude to life, to seek to destroy it where its principles inspire our treatment of people.

To complete our account of murder, we need to consider omissions. It is certainly possible to commit murder (morally speaking) by omission, as when, in order that the patient should die, a medical attendant omits e.g. to turn on an apparatus; or when people deliberately neglect to feed their child. Thus the fact that one 'did nothing' is not itself proof that there is not the gravest responsibility for death.

In the utilitarian type of morality labelled 'consequentialism' it is supposed (a) that we always ought to act so as to produce the best possible future state of things, and hence (b) that in not doing something that one could do one is always just as responsible for the consequences as with positive action. It is even maintained that (a) expresses what anyone has to mean who has a moral view at all.[3] This last can be quickly disproved: the Socratic view that one ought to suffer wrong rather than inflict it cannot even be formulated in consequentialist terms.[4] Furthermore, the consequentialist doctrine strikes at an enormously important part of traditional morality; for since it entails that one cannot know

[3]   See G.E. Moore, *Principia Ethica* (Cambridge: Cambridge University Press, 1903), pp. 24-5.

[4]   I owe this observation to Dr A Müller. [See A Müller, 'Radical Subjectivity: Morality versus Utilitarianism', *Ratio* 19 (1977): 115-32.]

one's duty, it gets modified into the doctrine that one must always act for the best according to one's beliefs about consequences, and thus it leads to the characteristic view that there can be no such thing as the guilt of doing evil that good may come.

Although no sane person will even try to make the constant calculations required by consequentialist theory, it is influential where it maintains that it is all one *not* to do something that would preserve or prolong a life, and to do something positive to terminate it. The examples we have given shew that this is sometimes true. But it is generally false.

First, omission is not mere not-doing. Something not done is omitted if it ought to have been done, or was needed for some enterprise in hand, or was expected etc. It is the cook who spoils the potatoes by not putting salt in the water; it is *his* omission and not that of someone else, say the gardener.

Second, omission contrasts with positive action in two important ways. (1) A positive action carries the presumption that the agent incurs the responsibility of intentionally doing it; omission does not. (2) Blame for a positive act seldom depends on how difficult not acting would have been. Blame for an omission must take account of the difficulty, inconvenience, etc., of the omitted act.

When something is omitted intentionally and this results in harm, the omission may have been for the sake of the harm or for some other reason. If the former is the whole story, the harm is to be laid at the door of the non-acting agent as much as if he had done something positive for the same purpose. In law, this character of his omission will probably not be considered, as it is seldom detectable. When, though intentional, the omission is not for the sake of harm, the moral question will be what the reason was and whether it exculpates. In the absence of an exculpating explanation the harm of the result, even though it is not intended, still lies at the door of the person whose omission is responsible for it. For the harm is voluntary. And, since negligence too is voluntary, so also may be the harm produced by an *un*intended omission, if it constitutes negligence. For behaviour can be voluntary though it is not deliberate or thought about.

The principle by which such harm is voluntary was stated succinctly by St. Thomas: it was both possible and necessary for the will (or: the agent) to act, and it (he) did not.[5]

'Possible' and 'necessary' have many applications. Something may be not-possible in various ways. These may even include excessive difficulty: this of course would be serious or not according to circumstances. If it is somehow — seriously — impossible, an act cannot be called ethically necessary, although it may be physically possible and necessary for a certain result. If harm can be avoided only by a wicked, i.e. ethically impossible act, then there arises no guilt (in respect of the unaverted harm) for not doing the thing. E.g. a surgeon who will not kill one person, *A*, to save another, *B*, 'lets *B* die' but cannot be called guilty of his death. This is not because he 'only let him die': for, if what he omitted had been ethically possible we may suppose the case to be one in which it would have been necessary.

We must now consider a doctor who omits saving remedies, not for the sake of having the patient die, and not because they are in any way impossible. There can be various justifications. It might be that resources are needed elsewhere too. Or the consideration may be solely about the patient himself. Here all will agree that only what benefits him has a rightful place. And it is possible for someone with the greatest respect for life to think it does not seem a misfortune for the patient to die soon. This however is a deep matter which he cannot know; and so the consideration justifying non-adoption of means of prolonging life can only be that such means are an affliction to the patient, which he can reasonably be spared. It will be relevant that he is dying anyway, if that is the case.

---

[5]   St. Thomas Aquinas, *Summa Theologiae* Ia IIae q. 6, art. 3.

It follows from our considerations that wrongfulness in 'letting die' will always be a consequence of a particular moral necessity of saving life. That there are such necessities is clear; but it is a mistake to think that the mere circumstance that if one did nothing some life would be lost that might have been saved imposes a necessity to do that thing. Indeed the interests served by those who argue that such non-action is equivalent to murder are not those of promoting an impossible moral concern but rather those of breaking down the objection to murder as this is commonly understood.[6]

So much for omission. It remains to say a little more of murder where the death of the victim is a side-effect. These cases constitute the penumbra or fuzzy area surrounding the central areas of murder, intentional killing. An absolute prohibition on murder, which we have in our inherited moral law, cannot be confined to intentional killing. But not all deliberate action involving risk can be prohibited. So it must be possible to have sufficient excuse for risking or accepting death as a side-effect. This is readily grasped in the case of doctors giving pain-killing drugs. The statement that this is possible is known from Catholic moral theology as the 'principle of double effect'. The phrase is needlessly mystifying: 'double effect' only means 'side effect'.

A side effect is one not intended by the agent. The principle is of course not that, so long as death is not what you intend, you can cause it with a clear conscience. Nor does it imply that burning a house down to get insurance money without regard to people in it getting killed, is *less* heinous than intentionally killing the people (for the same purpose, we may suppose). The principle of the side-effect merely states a possibility: where you may not aim at someone's death, causing it does not necessarily incur guilt; it can be that there are necessities which in the circumstances are

---

[6]　See in particular J. Rachels, 'Active and Passive Euthanasia', *New England Journal of Medicine* 292 (1975): 78–80; J Glover, *Causing Death and Saving Lives* (Harmondsworth: Penguin, 1977), pp. 91–112.

great enough, or that there are legitimate purposes in hand of such a kind, to provide a valid excuse for risking or accepting that you cause death. Without such excuse, foreseeable killing is either murder or manslaughter.

The principle seems unexceptionably instanced in examples such as we have already mentioned — dangerous surgery, closing doors to contain fire or water, having ships and aeroplanes and races. In them, we are helped by thinking of the deaths as remote or uncertain. But of course an unintended death which is a foreseeable consequence of one's action may be neither. Then we are confronted with cases where it strikes people that there is little difference between direct and indirect killing. Imagine a pot-holer stuck with people behind him, and water rising to drown them all. And suppose two cases: in one, he can be blown up; in the other, a rock can be moved to open another escape route, but it will crush him to death.

Someone who will choose either course clearly prefers saving these lives to the avoidance of any intentional killing of innocent people. Such cases are often discussed with a note of absolute necessity about saving lives: a presupposition that this is unconditionally paramount. The stuck pot-holer (without the choice of methods of escape) was invented to illustrate the iniquity of abortion: you would not say you could kill the pot-holer to get out — it was argued. But people did say just that, at least if the case was described so that the pot-holer himself was going to drown too.

But situations must often have occurred where people were in a tight corner together, and could have saved themselves by killing one of their number, and that has not struck them as a serious option at all. If that were the attitude of the people in the cave, they would likely be equally unwilling either to destroy their companion directly, or to move the rock and crush him. Indeed someone might ask: 'Isn't that direct killing too?' But the point of not calling it direct was that it isn't his being crushed that gives the escape route: that is only an unavoidable consequence of moving the rock. They might adopt this means without realising the consequence, and that possibility indicates some difference.

Here the 'doctrine of double effect' is supposed to say that they can move the rock, though they cannot blow the man up. And this is what people find intolerably artificial and unnatural. But we must ask: is this because of what is here allowed, or what is forbidden? The principle of the side effect alludes to an absolute prohibition on seeking someone's death, as end or as means. We have expounded that prohibition. But if the objection is to what is here allowed, we ought to notice that the principle does not state or imply that they can move the rock. For it does not say what necessities excuse foreseeably causing death.

There might be people among them who, seeing the consequence, would move the rock, though they would not blow the man up because that would be choosing his death as the means of escape. They thus shew themselves as people who will absolutely reject any policy making the death of innocent people a means or end. This is a far from meaningless stance.

But, to repeat, you cannot deduce the permissibility of moving the rock from the principle of double effect. It determines nothing about that, except that it is not excluded on the score of being intentional killing. The claim that the necessity of saving the trapped people is a sufficient excuse for moving the rock may be controverted: it may be said that the immediacy and intrinsic certainty of the death of the victim excludes moving the rock. To say this is to introduce a new principle to use in judging killings which are not intended as end or as means. It is a reasonable principle. Surgery, for example, would be thought murderous, though not done in order to kill but, say, to get an organ for someone else, if the death of the patient was expected as a pretty immediate consequence, certain from the nature of the operation.

It will be clear why the area of murder which we have called the penumbra is not sharply defined. Necessity is a highly relative term: we invoke the necessity of relieving pain when we accept the risk of giving pain-killing drugs, but where the risk is considerable we shall allow it only in cases of terminal illness. There are gradations and shadings when there is a balance of importance between ends being sought and risks to life, as also in the weight of the circumstances which affect the balance, and there are also gradations of uncertainty and remoteness. Where agents are anyway 'up to no good' (like the arsonist) the killings they do without purposing to kill will usually fall squarely within the penumbra. Other cases will also fall there, like the hypothetical surgery above. And there are cases also which fall clearly outside it. But there will of necessity be borderline cases. Nor need the borderline be between murder and manslaughter; it may be between murder and innocence.

22

Commentary on John Harris's

'Ethical problems in the management of some severely handicapped children'

It is a pretty scene: a doctor deciding that it is in a child's best interests to die. Similarly is Dr Harris making the same decision, though in a more abstract and generic kind of way. The way you make the decision is: see what you'd think of a proposal that you should swap your life for this (sort of) life. If the idea is horrid, if you'd rather die, then to die is in the best interests of the being you're considering — not a medical decision of course; it is just done by imagining a proposition. What a lot of creatures you have reason to kill under that method of reckoning! They have only to be incapable of consent, and you'd have a *sufficient* reason.

'But no!' it may be replied, 'It's got to be your business, and it *is* the doctor's business for these are his patients'. To repeat, this is not a medical decision, even if in making it the doctor refers to some medical facts. In the case in hand, it is a reversion to the

* From the *Journal of Medical Ethics* 7 (1981): 122–3. John Harris's article, on which the present text is a commentary, appears on pages 117–20 of the same number. Reprinted with the permission of the BMJ Publishing Group.

ancient human tendency to kill unwanted children. This is cloaked in the language of moral concern. But it is a decision about the worthwhileness or value of a life, and medicine tells us nothing about that. Doctor Lorber happened to be in a position of *power* because of his profession. But essentially he was no more justified in deciding to kill babies by neglect and starvation than I would be entitled to kill some incompetent who fell into my hands, and who I thought would be better off dead.

As Dr Harris reports the matter, Dr Lorber *aimed* at the death of the children; it was to be accomplished by non-treatment and sometimes by starvation. As Dr Harris indicates, if you are aiming at someone's death it hardly makes a difference whether you bring it about by omission of treatment and failure to feed, or if you do it more actively. The infamous thing is to aim at the patient's death.

Clearly it isn't enough for Dr Harris to have people killing (on purpose) by omission; he wants to get them doing it by commission. Now while there isn't much difference in the wicked intent (the only one I can see is that in adopting the method of neglect you leave it longer open to change your mind), yet there is *some* difference about what you do.

For wilful starvation there can be no excuse. The same can't be said without qualification about failing to operate or to adopt some course of treatment. There is a question here which needs discussion: whether, when and why a doctor has an obligation to do anything for someone? I mean: to do anything in the way of medical treatment. Has he such an obligation simply because of (say) the existence of a National Health Service, and because he belongs to it? Can't a doctor sometimes say: 'I do not want to treat this patient, I actually don't want him as a patient of mine'? Can he sometimes, or can he never, say the following?: 'I do not want to prolong this person's life by taking medical measures to do so. I am not saying it is *better* not to; I would say nothing against another practitioner who might want to. But I don't want to. And I don't have to.'

This is a deep and important question of medical ethics, which has perhaps been discussed. I have not seen discussion of it.

I think I perceive in the writing of Dr Harris a blindness to *such* a possibility of non-treatment. This may be because of an assumption that the doctor into whose hands such people have somehow come, is ethically obliged *either* to aim at their cure *or* one way or another to seek for them not to be cured. Perhaps the assumption (which I am attributing to Dr Harris) should be limited to people who will die of their sickness if medical measures are not taken. Either way such an assumption seems absurd.

Suppose we consider a different assumption: a doctor into whose hands sick people come *is ethically obliged (if he can) to treat them with a view to curing them*. This Dr Harris does not believe; but I think he believes it is true *except* in the case where the doctor would justifiably aim at his patient's death. But, forgetting about *that* exception, I am still disposed to think the assumption is *not* universally true, though setting limits to it is not easy. Of course, a doctor might not allow people to 'come into his hands', and it is another question when he is entitled, or not entitled, to refuse to let this happen. But if they somehow *have* come into his hands — by being born to patients, for example — that is where there is need to examine the particular assumption I have mentioned.

Another presumption I seem to detect in Dr Harris's writing, is the presumption that action and omission are everywhere equivalent. Philosophers, I fear, often seem to think that *either* omission is never equivalent to positive action that has the same result, *or* it always is. Glover[1], at least, thinks that he has demonstrated the latter by disproving the former. Now if you have an obligation to do something positive, the intentional omission of it for the sake of some result (such as death) may very well deserve the same

---

[1]   J. Glover, *Causing Death and Saving Lives* (Harmondsworth: Penguin Books, 1977), chapter 7.

blame as positive action to produce the same result. But it by no means follows that we ought always to be calculating the expectable consequences of every non-doing of something we could do, along with those of every possible positive action, and that we are responsible for every upshot that is less than the best possible by such a comprehensive calculation. Indeed, such a proposition is obviously absurd. (Which does not mean that, within certain limits of practicable policy, with cut-and-dried possibilities, such a calculation may not be required. This must sometimes be the case in medicine.)

If Dr Harris has reported Lorber correctly, Lorber claimed to be aiming at the death of the children by non-treatment. This was sometimes, though not always, supplemented by starvation. We have heard of this elsewhere since 1975.[2] It looks as if Dr Lorber may have been a bit confused between a policy of not trying to cure — not operating, for example — and a policy of aiming at death, by omission. In the former case it makes sense, even though a rather vague sense, to speak of 'letting nature take its course'. It is a question, as I have said, whether, and when, *such* an omission of treatment is admissible. It is not the same thing as aiming at death, if the children receive ordinary care — are fed and kept clean and warm, saved from choking brought on by accident, etc. The distinction between ordinary care and surgical or medical measures to cure their condition is not at all meaningless. I am disposed to think that good practice would demand that the best available means be adopted to cure them; but as I have said, it is debatable; it may only *usually* be so, and a contrary decision is not yet the same as a decision to aim at their death.

It is possible that Dr Lorber was indeed aiming to kill by omission, and if so his action is only to be discriminated from 'positive euthanasia' by unclarity about his actions. Such unclarity is more difficult when positive action is taken to kill. And I should judge

---

[2]   R.B. Zachary, 'Give every baby a chance'. *The Nursing Mirror*, September 14, 1978.

that the contempt for human lives is therefore greater with positive action.

Dr Harris is misinformed about the Nazis. Positive euthanasia began as a privilege which was accorded to Aryans.

23

Sins of Omission?
The Non-Treatment
of Controls in
Clinical Trials

Thou shalt have one God only: who
Would be at the expense of two? ...

Do not adultery commit;
Advantage rarely comes of it.

Certainly Clough's commandments are satirical. No need, then,
to seek a respectable sense of 'officiously to keep alive' for him to
have had in mind. Sure, there is such a sense. Clough might have
circled round it with:

Strive to maintain your patients' breath
For doctor's profits cease with death.

As Michael Lockwood observes, doctors are newly fond of the
distinction between killing and allowing to die. But we mustn't
forget what their bigwigs *call* 'allowing to die': poisoning and
starving. So

---

* This is the text of Professor Anscombe's response to Michael Lockwood's paper
on the topic of the title in an Aristotelian Society Symposium; published in
Proceedings of the Aristotelian Society: Supplementary Volume 57 (1983): 223–7.
Reprinted by courtesy of the Editor of the Aristotelian Society: © 1983.

> The medical profession's rather fussed
> If it can't count on privacy and trust.

This medical line needs to be considered by philosophy with its sights set otherwise than Dr Lockwood's are. So let us turn to his concerns: omission and positive action. He tells us his topic is omission of treatment of groups of patients chosen to be controls. Yet one of his examples concerns the omission of treatment of premature babies with high concentrations of oxygen. The point of this was not to show that high concentrations did good, but on the contrary to prove that they tended to do harm. For this there was already evidence — for example, premature babies in Russia were not put into oxygen tents and did not tend to go blind. (Personal conversation at the time with the Reader in Ophthalmology at Oxford.)

The medical profession has convinced itself that German measles in early pregnancy is apt to cause various handicaps. This conviction has arisen (has it not?) without giving a lot of pregnant women German measles and abstaining from doing so with a 'control group'.

The first thing we have to note is that in these matters of testing with control groups we have one of Bacon's 'idols of the theatre'.[1] The established church of this idol is so strong that doctors are willing to forget the principle *primum non nocere* in its cult.

> Think not that much of finding out
> For proof's the thing to give you clout.

Dr Lockwood does momentarily note the difference between trying to find out and trying to prove. But it needed more dwelling on.

The outline of his paper seems to be this: where a doctor is trying to prove something which he already believes, he may aim at this by using a control group to which he does not give a treatment. The ethics of such omission is announced as the question.

---

[1]   *Novum Organum* Bk. 1

But in the case of the premature babies, the question is rather the ethics of giving a high concentration of oxygen, not of omitting it. Lockwood loses sight of this fact by sliding weakly away from the omission-commission difference; apparently because it is 'difficult' to make out its 'moral significance'. So after all the topic is *not* what it was announced to be, the ethics of omission. It is simply that of treating your patients as experimental subjects. Hence the difference between trying to prove harm and trying to prove benefit turned out not so important as Dr Lockwood did obviously feel it was. That is, judging by his sentences. Meanwhile the original question seems to have got lost.

The topic is a tangled one. Our first observation must be that doctors should not sacrifice their patients to that idol. For each patient they should do what they can that they believe is good or at least gives him a better chance. ('Can' here could be lengthily discussed, but that would be a distraction.)

The general dictum doesn't cover the whole ground. For there is the possibility of not so much *believing* that some treatment *would* be good, as *suspecting* that it *might* be. In such a case, one might not have any *very* positive conviction that it would at least do no harm. With or without this, and according to circumstances, one might reasonably try the treatment. First, perhaps, on one patient, then on more than one. The ones it wasn't tried on would then be controls, without need to abstain from the prior preferred treatment and without ritually making them so. This would be a form of trying to find out. If the treatment seemed rather successful, it would be just to give it to all cases not counter-indicated. Further success would be or approach proof. Whether one was inwardly 'trying to prove', or 'trying to do one's best for each patient', or both, might very well be a matter of cast of mind, coming out in whatever showed one's interest.

Here is room for the consideration: 'I've no right to a confident judgment yet and [perhaps] it's not an ailment justifying desperate measures; so I must just go on trying this on some patients until the results are indicative one way or the other.'

This sounds to have been the situation in the example of burns sustained by undernourished Indians. That is, at the first stage. Once the vaccine had been found to reduce the number of deaths greatly, we have a case of sinful omission at the second stage. It might not be wrong to try something further. It is the control group left without treatment either by the vaccine or by the other things that seems to need excuse. But

> Of crowds of very poor you may make use
> 'Twould be redundant to require excuse.*

The idol demands its sacrifices. But what of the possibility of no supplies, *unless* the idol is served? Here surely Dr Lockwood is somewhat credulous. People can't know that there won't ever again be supplies of such-and-such a drug, but make it rather come true by their acceptance of such bland assurances. The short term is another matter: a matter which will be just one form of shortage of supplies. In such shortage, and in the absence of any other treatment, you might well make an experiment, having a number of untreated people effectively as control group. In the long term, if supplies seemed to depend on the service of the idol — well, there are questions like: 'How long is this long term?' 'To what extent will you be compromising, fostering rotten attitudes?' 'What about a campaign, making the devil of a shindy, keeping on at it as Plimsoll kept on about the Plimsoll line?'

The variety of possibilities one can imagine (both for what the case is and for what might be done) brings out how impossible it is to lay down a principle beyond that of *primum non nocere*. Once we have said that, we have not said everything; but the matter is subject to Aristotle's leaden rule — the ruler that bends in and out of the many corners, holes and bulges of all sorts of shapes.

---

* The original printed version has 'superfluous' instead of 'redundant'. The change to 'redundant' was made by Professor Anscombe on a copy of the printed paper.

Dr Lockwood has a sort of goodhearted attitude which he cannot turn into a firm statement even where there seems to be room for it, because of his feeble acceptance that there isn't a 'significant' difference between act and omission. If he seriously thinks that, it is puzzling why he felt a special problem about the control groups purposely left without a treatment for the sake of proving its value.

It is easy to construct a case in which a deliberate omission of what was easy to do is (at least on first inspection) quite equivalent to a commission with the same result and for the same motive. A medical attendant, for example, sets up an apparatus necessary for the saving of someone's life, and deliberately omits to turn a certain tap that must be turned, because he wants the person to die. He actually deliberates about it, and decides not to turn on the tap. Or — the case of commission — he set it all up correctly with the tap on, and then, with similar deliberation and for the same end, he turns the tap off.

It is awfully usual, in discussing the difference between positive act and omission, to think it sufficient to show that there *can* be examples where the moral quality of the deed is the same in the two cases: where, namely, the result is the same, the intention is the same, and the kind of particular responsibility for what happens is the same. I fear that showing this is thought enough to establish that the difference between act and omission is never 'morally significant'. Or is never 'morally significant' where the motive is the same and so is the upshot.

Need I do more than point out that the conclusion doesn't follow? The person who is refuted by the argument is one who holds that 'I didn't actually *do* anything to bring about the (evil) result, I merely omitted to do what would have prevented it' is necessarily always an exonerating plea if it is true. Or at least necessarily prevents guilt from being just the same as if he had done something positive to bring about the evil result.

It is perhaps worthwhile to observe the use that is made of the belief that the difference between positive act and omission is never 'morally significant'. First, it seems to be thought that to omit something is merely not to do it; or not to do it when one could do it. Second, the difference between act and omission *not* being 'morally significant', we are responsible for anything that happens which wouldn't have happened if we had done something which we did not do, though we could have done it. (The qualifications which might be added to this rather crude statement to make it faintly more plausible do not include anything about the matter's being one's business or the like.)

Startling deductions are made from these starting points. If I spend some money on amusement (e.g.) which I might have given to some charitable concern, and if, *if* I had, some life would have been saved, then I have killed someone just as much as if I had cut someone's throat.

The purpose of such arguments seems to be not to arouse an impossible conscientiousness in our conduct, but to loosen our consciences in respect of what would normally be counted as murder.

Dr Lockwood does not sound as if he favoured any form of consequentialism all that much. But his willingness to simply say 'It's difficult to show that the difference between act and omission is morally significant, at least where the motive is the same' seems to have led him into a swift slide — first, *away* from considering the problem he said he was interested in at the beginning, and second, into a disregard (after all) of a doctor's obligation not to harm his patients.

Non-treatment can amount to willingness to harm: this is a truth which means that if someone is a doctor's patient, the doctor may need special excuse for some non-treatment of that person. It is not the same truth as that which lays it on the doctor *primum non nocere,* for this latter, I take it, refers exclusively to positive action. But the proposition about non-treatment is one

that deserves more investigation than either Dr Lockwood or I
have given it. My complaint about him is that he has let himself
be deflected from this interesting and difficult task by some easy
and spurious reasoning about acts and omissions.

Index

abortion, xvi, xix, 45, 54, 65–6, 68, 70, 72, 73, 245, 264, 275.

action, causation of, 89–108; Chisholm on, 77–87. *See also*: voluntary movement, explanation of.

action descriptions, 96, 149–50, 172, 223, 235, 260; moral, 210–15; neutral/indifferent, 204–5, 210.

action, explanation of: by causal efficacy, 110–11; by intention, 95ff, 106–7.

acts/omissions, 281–3, 289–90. *See also*: omissions.

adultery, 181.

agent causality, 80–3.

allowing to die, 285–91 *passim*; when wrongful, 274.

amenity, orientation of will to, 270.

amputation, 217–9.

angels, 17–25 *passim*.

Anscombe, G E M, xiii–xxi, 114.

Aquinas, St Thomas, 54, 60, 80, 156, 225–6, 246, 273.

Aristotle, xx, 3, 24, 54, 61–2, 64, 91, 169–70, 175, 180, 182, 193, 197; leaden rule of, 288; on conditions of virtuous action, 198–9; on *euboulia* (good counsel), 145, 155; on *eupraxia* (doing well), 153–8; on pleasure, 171; on practical inference, 114–20, 132, 142–7; on practical truth, 151–8; on wrongness about principles, 237.

artificial insemination, 70, 245, 246; by donor, 244.

Augustine, St, 246, 255.

authority: civil/State, 215, 255, 265; foundation of civil, 265–6; religious, 265.

Averroes: on intellect, 24.

Bacon, 286.

behaviourism, 6, 7.

belief: and action, xv, 95ff; and inference, 130–1, 135–9.

Bentham, J, 222; on pleasure, 171.

Bohm, D, 104.

Broad, C D, 232.

brute facts, 172–3.

Butler, Bishop: on conscience, 170, 172.

Camus, A, 255–6.

capital punishment, 69, 255–6, 261.

care, 269; God's, 227–30; limits of human, 227–30.

casuistry, method of, 185.

Catholic Church, 245–8.

causal chains, 83, 92–3.

causal explanation, varieties of, 91ff, 95ff.

causation of action, *see*: action, causation of.

cause, final, 55–8.
  See also: teleology.

cause, formal, 57.

children, upbringing of, 166–7.
  See also: handicapped children.

Chisholm, R M, xiv; on action, 77–87.

coitus reservatus, 246, 248.

common good, 265.

conscience: definition of, 239; false as binding, xx, 238–41, and as excusing, 238–41; loosening of, 290; not infallible, 239–40.
  See also: Butler, Bishop.

consequentialism, xvii, 180–6, 271–2, 290; and virtue ethics, xvii–xviii, xxi.

contraception, 70, 166, 245.

contract: and obligation, 187–8.

controls in clinical trials, ethics of non-treatment of, 286–91.

corruption, of Catholic and non-Catholic moral thought, 247; of youth, *see* Oxford Moral Philosophy.

courage, virtue of, 196–7.

Cretney, Stephen, xvi.

Davidson, D: on explanation of action, 110–11.

death, 215, 233; aimed at by omission, 281–2; as deserved, 67–8 (*see also*: capital punishment); as side effect, 274–6 (*see also*: double effect, doctrine of).

definition, 28–31.

democracy, 67.

deontological (ethics), 231–2.

Descartes, 5–6, 15.

determinism, 103–6, 200, 230–1.

dignity: of human being as impregnable, 67–73, and violation of, 67–73; of human nature (knowledge of), 59–66 *passim*; of self–determination, 269.

divine legislator, 186.
  See also: law, divine.

doctors: duties of, 234, 280–81, 287; involved in killing, 269, 279–83 *passim*.

'doing what is best', 232–5.

double effect, doctrine of, 220–26, 247–8, 274–7.

dualism, Cartesian, 6.

ectopic pregnancy, xvi, 248.

embryo, early human, xviii–xx; experiments with, 70.
  See also: zygote.

ends in practical reasoning and action, 114–20, 141–7; general, specific, particular, 141f; generic, 141–7; ultimate/architectonic, xx–xxi, 147.

equality, 253–4; of all human beings, 67–73 *passim*.

essence, concept of, 28; expressed in grammar, 28–38.

eugenic killing, 244.
  See also: Williams, Glanville.

euthanasia, 70, 261–77 *passim*; and Nazis, 283; and quality of life judgment, 270; justification for, 269; non–voluntary, 68; propaganda for, 268–9, 270; voluntary, 268.

evolution, 36.

examples in moral philosophy, 163.

excuse, 211–13, 215, 217, 265.

exoneration/exculpation, 212–3, 262, 272–3, 289; for harmful omissions, 272–3.

false witness, 231.

fatherhood, 70–1.

finding out/proving, distinction between, 286.

Foot, Philippa, xvii, 249–51.

foresight and intention, xviii, 183–5, 219–25, 247–8, 263–5.

form, 17–21.

forms, Platonic, 3–4, 17.

Frege, 29–31, 34; on concepts, 29; on numbers, 3–4; on numerical functions, 29–31.

gametes (sperm and ovum), 42–4.

Geach, Peter, xi.

God, love of, 270.

Goethe, 6.

good sense, virtue of, 63–6, 196–7, 205–6.

goodness/badness of human action, 195–206, 211–20, 234–5.

goods of fortune, 61–3.

grammar, *see*: essence.

handicapped children, treatment of, 279–83; neglect and starvation of, 280ff.

Hare, R M, 161, 181, 194, 230–1; on imperative inference, 121–3.

Harris, John, 279–83.

Hebrew–Christian ethic, 181, 182. *See also*: Judaeo–Christian teaching/tradition; law conception of ethics.

human action: as subject to praise or blame, 201–3; goodness and badness of, 195–206, 211–20; intentional, 213, 216, 218–25; nature of, 203–4.

human being, rational nature of, 268. *See also*: person, concept of.

human dignity, 67–73, 267; as metaphysically determined, 6–7; of rational nature, 268.

human flourishing, 193–4; and Christianity, 194; and Judaism, 194; and Stoicism, 194.

human generation, character of, 70–2.

human life, valuation of, x, 6–7, 271. *See also*: spirit, man as.

human need: and human good, 267; as reason for action, 250–1; for protection against unjust attack, 265.

human rights, 254. *See also*: right.

human soul, intellectual nature of, 17, 21–5.

Hume, David, xv, 59; on is–ought transition, 171, 172–3, 176–80.

idolatry, 181.

identity of living body, 50–8.

ignorance, 'politic', 65–6.

imagination, 21–2.

immediate animation, 46, 54.

imperative inference, 121ff.

in vitro fertilisation, 70.

indeterminism, 104–6.

inequality, 253–4.

infanticide, 245.

injustice: intrinsic, 188–190; 'in the circumstances', 188–190.

innocency of life, 206.

innocent, the: killing, 181 prohibited by Judaeo–Christian teaching, 264, 265 (*see also*: murder); punishing, 189.

intellect, nature of, 17, 22–5.

intellectual virtue, 170, 196–7; blameworthiness for lack of, 197–8.

intended/foreseen distinction: *see* foresight and intention.

intention, 95ff, 106–7, 183–5, 261–5; artificial sense in English law, 263.
See also: action, explanation of.

intentionalness of an act, 216, 218.

involuntariness, 213.

involuntary euthanasia, 248.

James, William, 78.

Jews. *See*: law conception of ethics; Judaeo–Christian teaching; Torah.

Judaeo–Christian teaching/tradition, 264, 265.

justice, 163–4; distributive, 254; retributive, 254; valuations underlying, 271; virtue of, 63–4, 196–7, 199, 202–3.
See also: injustice.

Kant, 172, 195–200; on categorical imperative, 195; on idea of freedom, 200; influence on modern understanding of morality, 195ff; on motive of duty, 195ff; on universalizable maxims, 171.

Kenny, Anthony: on logic of satisfactoriness, 121–3.

killing, intentional: by civil authority, 215–6, 261; by commission, 280; in warfare, 216; judicial execution, 216 (*see also*: capital punishment); just, 267; of the innocent (*see*: innocent, the; murder); of unwanted children, 280; private, 215–6; prohibition on, 220, 224.

knowledge: connatural, 59–66; indifferent/non–indifferent, 59–66.

language as created, 36–8.

Law Commission, xvi.

law conception of ethics, 175–6; influences on: Christianity, Stoics, Torah, 175–6.

law, divine, xx, 175, 176, 185, 186, 192, 193.

lawful: *see* unlawful.

legislation, concept of, 171.

Lejeune, Jérome, 39, 40, 45–50, 52–3, 55, 57.

lies, 166, 219, 231; Kant on, 171.

'life not worth living': doctors incompetent to judge, 280; judging (as justification for suicide/euthanasia), 271.

Locke, 28, 32, 171.

Lockwood, M, 285–91,

logic of satisfactoriness, 121ff.

logical behaviourism, 7.

Lorber, John, 280, 282.

McCormick, Richard, 221–2.

Makin, Stephen, 55–6.

matter/mind distinction: ancients and medievals on, 5–6; Descartes on, 5–6.

matter, proximate, 58.

mechanism, philosophy of, 104–6.
medical decision, 279–80.
  See also: doctors, duties of.
medical ethics, 281.
Mill, J S, 172, 180, 182; on pleasure, 171.
mind/brain identity, 6.
Moore, G E, xv, 180, 182, 231.
moral earnestness, 161–2.
moral law, 257, 265.
  See also: law conception of ethics.
'moral', meaning of term, 146,
  169–70, 195–206 *passim*, 209–10.
'moral ought', xx, 147, 169–94 *passim*; Kant on, 195–200.
moral virtue, 170, 196–7.
motherhood, 70–1.
Müller, A, 115, 271n.
murder, xix, 67, 68, 182, 216–7,
  219ff, 261–77 *passim*, 290; absolute prohibition of, 264, 266,
  274; and 'necessity' as exculpating plea, 264–5; by omission,
  271–4; commandment prohibiting, 254–5; concept/definition
  of, 253–60; core of concept of
  (*i.e.* intentional killing of innocent), 262–3; mental element in,
  263–4; not purely juridical
  notion, 255–6; penumbra of
  concept of, 276–7; understood
  as 'killing that is wrong', 254–7
  (*see also*: pre–moral evil); understood as 'unlawful killing',
  256–60, 262.
mystical value of man, 260.
  See also: spirit, man as.

naturalistic fallacy, 171.
Nazis, 283.

negligence, 272–3.
  See also: omissions.
non–treatment: of controls in clinical trials, 285–91; of handicapped children, 279–83.
norms, societal, 186–7.
Nowell–Smith, P, 194.

obligation, concept of, xx,
  169–194 *passim*.
omissions, 271–4, 281–3, 289–90;
  of treatment (justifications for),
  273–4; wrongful, 274, 288.
  See also: non–treatment.
Oxford moral philosophy, xiii–xv,
  161–7, 194.
Oxford objectivists, 180 and n.4.

parental authority, 166–7.
person, concept of, 233, 267–8;
  used in justifying killing innocent human beings, 267–8.
Plato, 3, 17, 33, 35, 60, 157, 163–4,
  193.
pleasure, concept of, 171–2; Aristotle on, 171; Bentham on, 171;
  Locke on, 171; Mill on, 171;
  Ryle on, 171.
poisoning by doctors, 285.
pot–holer (example), 221, 275–6.
practical falsehood, 157–9.
practical inference, xv, 109–147;
  form of, 133–40.
practical judgment, sound, *see*:
  good sense, virtue of.
practical truth, 144 and n.14,
  149–58.
practical wisdom, virtue of, 63–6,
  196.
pre–moral evil, 215–20, 235.
procreation, *see*: human generation.

profession of faith, false, 181.

prohibitions, absolute, 218, 264, 276.

propaganda, *see*: euthanasia.

prudence, *see*: good sense, virtue of.

psychology, philosophy of: need for, 169, 174, 188.

Quine, W van O, 21.

quality of life judgment and euthanasia, 270.

realism vs. idealism, 36.

religious attitude before mystery of human life, 269–70, 271. *See also*: spirit, man as.

respect for human dignity: and respect for human life, 67–73 *passim*, 270–1; and respect for human sexuality, 70–2.

responsibility: and guilt, 262; conceptions of, 164–5, 215, 261; for evil consequences of actions (Aquinas on), 226.

right: not to be murdered, 254, 266–7; to life, 254, 266.

Ross, A, 122.

Ross, W D, 180n.

Ryle, Gilbert, 13, 171.

saving lives, the relevance of numbers to, 249–51.

sensation, 5–6.

sexual intercourse and marriage, 196.

side effects, 274ff; principle of, 220ff, 274ff. *See also*: double effect, doctrine of.

Sidgwick, H, 169, 180–5, 190, 194; on responsibility for foreseen consequences of one's action, 183–5.

simony, 223–4.

skill, defects in exercise of, 198, 201–5.

slavery, 67.

Socrates, 33, 157.

sodomy, 181, 231.

soul: animal, 18–22; as primary principle of life, 18–20; as principle of unity of living thing, 51–58; human/rational, xix, 3, 5–6, – and immateriality of, 15; vegetative, 18–22.

spirit, man as, 3–16 *passim*, 267, 269. *See also*: mystical value of man.

starvation: of handicapped children, 280–3, 285; wilful, 280.

statistical laws, 105–6.

sterilisation, 245.

Stoics, *see*: law conception of ethics.

substance, immaterial, 3–16 *passim*.

suffering, 165–6.

suicide, 245, 269.

supervenient descriptions, 104–6.

surgery, 225; dangerous, 220, 'gender reassignment', 70.

teleological (ethics), 231–2.

teleology: of conscious action, 96ff. *See also*: causes, final.

Temple, Archbishop William, 161–2.

Tolstoy, 255.

Torah, 177n. *See also*: law conception of ethics.

thinking, immateriality of, 9–16.
treachery, 181.
Truman, President Harry, xiv, xvii.
twins, identical/monozygotic, 39–44, 45–7, 50, 53–4.

unity of multicellular organism, 49–58.
  See also: soul.
unlawful, concept of, 175, 257–60.
utilitarianism: on intentional killing, 266.
  See also: consequentialism.

validity: of practical inference, 110, 112–147 *passim*; of theoretical inference, 112–147 *passim*.
value/disvalue (total) of choices, impossibility of calculating, 227–31.
vicarious punishment, 181.
vice, 202–6.
virtue, 60, 170, 174; and mistaken conscience, xx; and norms, 188; ethics, xx–xxi; intellectual, 170, 196–7; moral, 170, 196–7.
voluntary euthanasia, *see*: euthanasia, voluntary.
voluntary movement, explanation of: by physiological causes, 77–87 *passim*, 89–108 *passim*; Chisholm's, 77–87.
von Mises, Richard, 105.
von Wright, G H, xv; on backwards causation, 78–9; on practical inference, 110–47.

war, 166.
will, good/bad, 238–41; Kant on, 199–200.

Williams, Glanville, xvi–xvii, 243–8.
Wittgenstein, Ludwig, 7–12, 16, 28, 31, 34–5, 80, 109, 171.

zygote, 39–44, 45–58 *passim*.